African Arguments

African Arguments is a series of short books about Africa today. Aimed at the growing number of students and general readers who want to know more about the African continent, these books highlight many of the longer-term strategic as well as immediate political issues. They will get to the heart of why Africa is the way it is and how it is changing. The books are scholarly but engaged, substantive as well as topical.

Series editors

Titles already published

Forthcoming

Published by Zed Books and the IAI with the support of the following organizations:

International African Institute The International African Institute's principal aim is to promote scholarly understanding of Africa, notably its changing societies, cultures and languages. Founded in 1926 and based in London, it supports a range of seminars and publications including the journal *Africa*.

www.internationalafricaninostitute.org

Royal African Society Now more than a hundred years old, the Royal African Society today is Britain's leading organization promoting Africa's cause. Through its journal, *African Affairs*, and by organizing meetings, discussions and other activities, the society strengthens links between Africa and Britain and encourages understanding of Africa and its relations with the rest of the world.

www.royalafricansociety.org

The World Peace Foundation, founded in 1910, is located at the Fletcher School, Tufts University. The Foundation's mission is to promote innovative research and teaching, believing that these are critical to the challenges of making peace around the world, and should go hand in hand with advocacy and practical engagement with the toughest issues. Its central theme is 'reinventing peace' for the twenty-first century.

www.worldpeacefoundation.org

About the authors

Adam Branch is associate professor of political science at San Diego State University. From 2011 to 2014 he was research fellow at the Makerere Institute of Social Research, Kampala. He is the author of *Displacing Human Rights: War and Intervention in Northern Uganda* as well as articles and book chapters on political violence, humanitarian intervention, and international law, largely focused on East Africa.

Zachariah Mampilly is director of the programme in Africana studies and associate professor of political science and international studies at Vassar College. From 2012 to 2013 he was a Fulbright visiting professor at the Department of Political Science, University of Dar es Salaam. He is the author of *Rebel Rulers: Insurgent Governance and Civilian Life during War* as well as articles and essays on the history and politics of Africa and South Asia.

ADAM BRANCH AND
ZACHARIAH MAMPILLY

Africa uprising

Popular protest and political change

Zed Books
LONDON

in association with

International African Institute
Royal African Society
World Peace Foundation

Africa Uprising: Popular Protest and Political Change was first published in association with the International African Institute, the Royal African Society and the World Peace Foundation in 2015 by Zed Books Ltd, 7 Cynthia Street, London N1 9JF, UK

www.zedbooks.co.uk
www.internationalafricaninstitute.org
www.royalafricansociety.org
www.worldpeacefoundation.org

Set in OurType Arnhem and Futura Bold by Ewan Smith, London
Printed and bound in the United States of America by Edwards Brothers Malloy
Index: <ed.emery@thefreeuniversity.net>
Cover image © Akintunde Akinleye/Reuters/Corbis
Cover designed by www.roguefour.co.uk

A catalogue record for this book is available from the British Library

ISBN 978-1-78032-998-7 hb
ISBN 978-1-78032-997-0 pb
ISBN 978-1-78360-000-7 pdf
ISBN 978-1-78032-999-4 epub
ISBN 978-1-78360-001-4 mobi

Contents

Abbreviations and acronyms

A4C	Activists for Change (Uganda)
AWU	Abeokuta Women's Union (Nigeria)
CEO	chief executive officer
CPA	comprehensive peace agreement (Sudan)
CPP	Convention People's Party (Ghana)
CUD	Coalition for Unity and Democracy (Ethiopia)
EPRDF	Ethiopian People's Revolutionary Democratic Front
FAO	Food and Agriculture Organization (UN)
FDC	Forum for Democratic Change (Uganda)
FIWON	Federation of Informal Workers' Organizations of Nigeria
GDP	gross domestic product
IMF	International Monetary Fund
JAF	Joint Action Front (Nigeria)
KACITA	Kampala City Traders' Association (Uganda)
KUSU	Khartoum University Student Union (Sudan)
NANS	National Association of Nigerian Students/National Alliance for the Salvation of the Homeland (Sudan)
NATO	North Atlantic Treaty Organization
NCP	National Congress Party (Sudan)
NGO	non-governmental organization
NLC	Nigerian Labour Congress
NRA	National Resistance Army (Uganda)
NRM	National Resistance Movement (Uganda)
NUP	National United Party (Sudan)
PT	Partido dos Trabalhadores (Brazil – Workers' Party)
SAP	structural adjustment programme
SMS	short message service
SNG	Save Nigeria Group

SPLM/A Sudan People's Liberation Movement/Army
TPLF   Tigrayan People's Revolutionary Front (Ethiopia)
UDPS   Union pour la démocratie et le progrès social (Zaire)
UNF   United National Front (Sudan)

Acknowledgements

Any book on popular protest today cannot help but be an intervention into a terrain of collective hope but also of significant state violence. For this reason, many people who contributed in fundamental ways to the research and writing of this book cannot be named. We have thanked them in person, and they know how extensively we have relied on them in our work.

Of those whose names can appear in print, we would first like to thank all those involved in the ongoing protest wave in Africa who were willing to be interviewed for this book. Their names are found throughout the chapters that follow.

We would next like to thank all those who read, commented on, or discussed the book with us, guiding us through what we realized early on was an impossibly vast topic for which we were quite unprepared. Among these friends and colleagues are Omolade Adunbi, Miriam Auma, Rotimi Babatunde, Balghis Badri, Josephine Nyakubia Baker, Gerald Bareebe, Nafisa Bedri, George Bob-Milliar, Sheriden Booker, Jordan Branch, Florence Brisset-Foucault, Kwami Coleman, Kimberlé Crenshaw, Kim Yi Dionne, Nisrin El-Amin, Alvaro Enrigue, Gacheke Gachihi, Nimmi Gowrinathan, Dalia Haj Omar, Rehab Hamed, Luke Harris, Anneeth Hundle, Ogaga Ifowodo, Joseph Kasule, George Lipsitz, Valeria Luiselli, Giuliano Martiniello, Hafiz Mohamed, Richard Mutumba, Ham Namakajjo, Arthur Owor, Sandrine Perrot, Joschka Philipps, Melina Platas Izama, Andrew Elias State, Jason Stearns, Jon Temin, Antonio Tomás, and Adrian Yen.

Samuel Rosenberg provided excellent research assistance. Eren and Watson Branch were, as always, the ideal critical readers and editors of the entire manuscript.

We were privileged to present various stages of our work to a number of engaged audiences. We thank Samar Al-Bulushi and Scott Ross for organizing a roundtable through Yale's Macmillan Center, during which we received excellent feedback from Yousuf Al-Bulushi, Corinna Jentzch, Daniel Magaziner, and Samson Opondo. We also thank Chris Day for inviting us to present our work at the Southeastern Regional Seminar in African Studies (SERSAS) conference at the College of Charleston, as well as the organizers and participants in panels at which we presented our work at the 2014 African Studies Association meeting.

The book also benefited from the counsel of the series editors, Alex de Waal and Alcinda Honwana, and was guided from its inception by the steady and patient hands of Ken Barlow and Stephanie Kitchen. We are grateful for their support.

Finally, Zachariah would like to thank his students at the University of Dar es Salaam for the illuminating conversations about many of the themes explored in this book. He also acknowledges generous financial support from Vassar College that funded research trips to Sudan and southern Tanzania.

Adam would like to thank his colleagues and students at the Makerere Institute of Social Research, Kampala. There, for several years, he was fortunate enough to be involved in a collective project somewhat different from those described in this book but equally committed to creating new political imaginations.

1 | Protests and possibilities

'Africa Rising!' shout the magazine covers, books, movies, and advertising campaigns – all breathlessly proclaiming the dawn of a new era across Africa. No longer part of a 'hopeless continent', Africa's growing economies and burgeoning middle class, it is declared, represent a true break from the past. GDP growth rates reach unprecedented heights, and foreign capital pours into oil and gas investment in East Africa. Vast new private housing colonies rise from the sea in Lagos, Nigeria, while Angola's Isabel Dos Santos displaces Oprah Winfrey as the richest black woman in the world. Elite 'Afropolitans' are the continent's new global face, and networked Kenyans work to solve everything from election violence to health care delivery with SMS messaging.

The African middle class is celebrated as both the driver and the beneficiary of today's transformation. The African Development Bank (2011) announced that the middle class had grown to 350 million people by 2010 – but only by including all those with daily consumption expenditures of more than $2, barely enough to survive in many urban areas. A realistically defined middle class would comprise only a narrow sliver of Africa's population, set against a backdrop in which nearly half of all Africans live in extreme poverty, with their numbers growing (UN 2014).

Yesterday's 'Afro-pessimism' and today's 'Afro-optimism' equally misrepresent the actual political transformations unfolding across the continent. Both leave out the vast majority of Africans, dismissing them as helpless victims or ignoring them in favour of the new African elite. This oversight is indefensible. For almost a decade now, huge numbers of people from across Africa's urban populations have been taking to their cities' streets to demand change. Popular protest has been sweeping the continent, erupting in dozens of countries from Egypt to South Africa, Ethiopia to Senegal, Sudan to Angola. These protesters are seeking to fundamentally transform Africa's political and economic inequities. Yet there has been little effort to understand how they see their continent today or what their visions might be for Africa's future. Perhaps we need to abandon the simplistic narrative of Africa Rising and instead focus on Africa's *Up*risings.

Africa is not alone in experiencing an upsurge in popular protest, as protest now occupies the centre of the global political stage.[1] Worldwide, people are taking to the streets, giving new life to a form of political action often thought of as a historical relic in today's era of expanding security states and the apparent triumph of global elites. The Arab Awakening, the anti-austerity protests of Europe's *indignados*, the Occupy movement in the US and beyond, the anti-corruption protests across both rural and urban Asia, the students, middle class, poor, and indigenous in streets and squares across Latin America – all these are providing new inspiration for many who had lost faith in the potential for transformative popular struggles.

In the debate over today's global protest, various positions have been staked out. The protests are cast as the ultimate challenge to capitalism, a rejection of liberal democracy, an uprising by the 'multitude', the work of social-media-savvy youth, or an outburst by frustrated middle classes. The most hyperbolic accounts lack awareness of national and regional histories outside of the West, and none is immediately helpful in comprehending the recent wave of popular protest in Africa, which has arisen in response to a distinct conjuncture of economic, political, and social developments.

Indeed, Africa has been largely ignored within the conversation over today's global protest wave. This silence derives in part from long-standing Western images of Africa as too rural, too traditional, and too bound by ethnicity for modern political protest to arise. Such prejudices also mean that those few African protests that do make it into the international press tend to be dismissed as riots or looting. Violence is often seen as the sole driver of political change in Africa by media fixated on warlords, child soldiers, and humanitarian intervention. Even when popular protest on the African continent is deemed politically momentous, as it was in Tunisia and Egypt in 2011, it is turned into an *Arab* Spring, divorced from its geographical location, with analysts asking whether Africa might 'follow' with an awakening of its own (Ford 2012; Juma 2011).

Given Africa's long exclusion from Western narratives of world history, the continent's current absence from this debate should not surprise us. However, it is entirely unjustified. The wave of popular protests in African countries, north and south, east and west, demands to be taken seriously and not discounted as merely an echo of protest elsewhere. In this book we emphasize the need to look inward to Africa's own past and its own history of protest before looking outward to events in the rest of the world in order to explain today's continental protest wave. Today's uprisings build on a history of African protest that stretches back to the anti-colonial struggle, a legacy that has survived despite overwhelming odds. This book seeks to place protest in Africa within the broader debate about today's outbreak of protest around the world – but it does so by discerning what makes that protest specifically African.

Neither analysts nor activists can afford to ignore this current upsurge of protest. The two previous major protest waves – those of the late colonial period and of the late 1980s to early 1990s – preceded the most important continent-wide political transformations of the last hundred years. The first culminated in the end of colonial rule, and the second marked the end of many single-party and military states and the establishment of multiparty democracies throughout Africa. Likewise, today's wave of protest should encourage us to ask what political transformations it may foretell.

Just as it is indefensible to dismiss or ignore popular protest in Africa, we cannot afford to romanticize protest either. Protest should not be seen as part of a perennial struggle of 'the people' against colonial, post-colonial, or neo-colonial political oppression. Protest occurs in a convoluted and tension-ridden social reality and is comprised of forces whose politics are themselves complex, fraught with antagonisms and limited by contradictions. Protest takes many forms and can have different meanings depending on who is involved, what their demands are, and how they relate to other social and political groups. Even as protest challenges state power, it is structured by that power and so reveals both political possibilities and political limitations. Protest can usher in new orders or founder on the old ones, give birth to unifying demands for justice and democracy or entrench political divisions and dilemmas.

From this perspective, the North African protests of 2011 do not reveal some supposed contrast between the north and the rest of the continent. Instead, they speak to the continued vitality of long histories of protest throughout Africa – just as the turmoil in Libya and Egypt at the time of this writing is a reminder of the grave challenges, internal and external, that popular demands for political change face everywhere.[2] While in the West it may be conventional to imagine the Sahara as an impenetrable barrier dividing the Arab North from the rest of Africa, or even to exclude parts of Southern Africa from the 'real' Africa,[3] we take a different approach. We maintain that what has occurred across North Africa involves important similarities to and continuities with events unfolding elsewhere throughout the continent. In the pages ahead we avoid these geographic divisions and instead speak of all of Africa.

This continental approach allows us to better understand how political phenomena can spread across national borders and regions, even leaping across vast distances from Egypt to Uganda, Senegal to Malawi, South Africa to Nigeria. This book explores some of these continental histories of protest. Our focus is on the most recent wave – emerging slowly in the middle of the 2000s, cresting in 2011, and rippling widely into the present – a period within which we place the North African uprisings. In order to contextualize this ongoing third wave of protest, we first look back to the two previous waves, discovering what they tell us about

4

the politics of African protest and what they suggest about the possibilities for future political transformation.

Protest and political imagination

In 1996, at the age of 57, the eminent Nigerian political scholar, Claude Ake, died in a highly suspicious plane crash that killed all on board. Sani Abacha, the Nigerian dictator, was rumoured to have orchestrated the crash in revenge for Ake's scathing critiques of his regime and for supporting pro-democracy movements. A keen first-hand observer of Nigeria's unsuccessful struggle for democracy in 1993, Ake remained, until his death, optimistic about Africa's future, writing that 'the pressures for democratization are so strong that for most of Africa it is no longer a question of whether there will be a democratic transition but when' (1995: 135).

Ake's optimism in the face of repeated disappointment not only provides a relevant political lesson but also suggests an important analytical approach that can provide a corrective to the present dominant framework for understanding protest. This framework tends to focus only on the failures of protest movements, especially the disparity between their lofty promise and their modest achievements in bringing about political change. In this view, the anti-colonial struggle brought independence but set the stage for the depredations of post-colonial dictatorships, while the second wave of protest brought an end to single-party states and ushered in political and economic liberalization but did little to effect substantive change in the lives of most Africans.

Today's wave of protest, from this vantage point, has even less to show for itself, for it has largely failed to bring about even formal political changes. In North Africa the narrative of a 'winter' following the 'spring' has gained currency. Tunisia remains polarized by political assassination and governmental infighting; Libya finds militias controlling large parts of the country; and Egypt's optimism has been displaced by a brutal military takeover. Looking ahead to our cases, we have seen Nigeria's protests petering out amid factional squabbles between organizers, Uganda's movement crushed by President Yoweri Museveni,

Ethiopian protesters facing a newly repressive state, and Sudan's movements unable to generate sufficient support to pose a threat to the government. Although we must note exceptions, such as the political transitions brought about by the protests in Senegal, Guinea, Niger, Madagascar, and, most recently, Burkina Faso,[4] for most of the continent the protest wave seems to have had little impact on state politics.

It is indisputable that, again and again, protests across Africa seem unable to effect substantive reforms in national politics despite their success in bringing tens of thousands of people into the streets. However, the commonly drawn conclusion – that protests are meaningful only if they are able to realize concrete reforms in national politics as demanded by the protesters – is not accurate. In this view, most of Africa's protests, in which demands are often multiple, unclear, and rarely entirely realized, would be consigned to the dustbin of history.

Ake can help point us towards an alternative to this restrictive understanding and its tendency to dismiss African protest because of what it fails to accomplish instead of taking seriously what it *does* achieve. Ake remained sceptical of the relevance of formal democratization to the lives of most Africans, a scepticism vindicated by the repeated upsurge of protest despite reform. For him, formal democratization was too often a subterfuge undertaken by African autocrats to curry favour with international audiences and co-opt popular energies through superficial institutional remedies. Ake instead emphasized the importance of popular democratic movements regardless of any specific liberal reforms they might introduce. He refused to measure Africa's progress according to formal indices of democracy and suggested instead that the real value of protest movements was in their effect on the political consciousness and imagination of African societies (ibid.). Popular protests, in his conception, are a mechanism through which Africa's peoples can achieve 'self-realization' by inventing new visions of democracy and development in which popular interests come first.

With Ake's advice in mind, we do not spend our time in this

book lamenting the failure of protest to effect formal political change. Instead, we focus on the often dramatic developments that accompany protest in popular organization, political consciousness, and political imagination. As diverse social groups seek to understand and challenge their own oppression, they reveal new political possibilities whose resonance can reach far beyond their place of origin, transforming people's understandings of politics nationally, regionally, and even globally.

This approach requires nuanced understanding of the social forces involved in protest so as to grasp the diverse transformations that collective action can bring about. It demands that those taking to the streets be contextualized within African political history and not be taken merely as representatives of universal economic or political identities. The politics of protest in Africa cannot be read from models imported from other historical experiences of what 'proper' protest is supposed to look like. The political relevance of large numbers of people taking to the streets to effect change in their lives must be discerned from those people's specific political context, from their particular historical experiences and present conditions. Many of the analytical distinctions that are used to understand protest elsewhere – the division between political and economic protest, between demonstrations and rioting, between violence and non-violence, between direct and indirect action – may not be productive in analysing protest in Africa.[5]

This book thus seeks out what is specific to African protest. This allows us to avoid preconceptions of what protest should look like, preconceptions that are often a hindrance to understanding the true extent and relevance of Africa's uprisings. For instance, many analysts – including the influential theorist of non-violent action, Gene Sharp (2005) – tend to privilege protests that conform to a 'civil society' model. According to this model, primarily derived from the Western experience, protests are organized, disciplined, and non-violent and should work symbolically within civil society to pressure the state into reform based on clear political demands.[6] Forms of protest that diverge from this model – as the ongoing protest wave in Africa seems to do – tend to be ignored as irrelevant. Likewise, the full extent of protest's political repercussions may be missed when those repercussions fall outside the expectations of the civil society model.[7] Instead of this limiting approach, analysis should start from political reality in Africa and locate protest within that reality rather than presuming that protest is a universal phenomenon with a fixed politics. Protest should be historicized, and theory should be built upon the actual experience of protest across the continent.

Dilemmas of protest

A principal argument of this book is that there exists a historical continuity to popular protest in Africa, one based in the persistence of the social and political structures shaping the urban milieu from which protest arises. These structures have their origin in colonial rule and the stark divides it enforced. Under colonialism, urban areas were violently separated from rural areas, and then each was fragmented further. The urban was divided into a small, relatively privileged, elite and working class on one side, opposed to a large underclass subject to constant state coercion on the other. The rural was divided through the institutionalization and enforcement of tribalism, leading to deep ethnic fragmentation. Frantz Fanon put it most succinctly: 'the colonial world is a world divided into compartments' (1963: 37). This led those living in the different compartments to have fundamentally different political and economic concerns, expectations, identities, and forms of politics. These structural divides remained the foundation of colonial and then post-colonial rule, and even now any effort to reform the state has to deal with them or run the risk of reinforcing these divides and the inequalities they support (Mamdani 1996).

The history of protest, therefore, represents the history of collective political efforts that are shaped by this legacy of fragmentation and that attempt to understand and overcome it, with greater or lesser success. It is a history in which the main actors – urban political and economic elites, the working class, the underclass, and rural populations – recur in each of the three waves of protest, even as the specific details of their identities, political imaginations, and relations may shift over time. Throughout this history, popular protests have run up against two constant national political dilemmas: how to overcome political divides within the urban, and how to overcome the political divide between the urban and the rural. Our focus within this history of protest is on the urban underclass, a group often marginal to accounts of popular protest despite their centrality to all three waves and their key importance for future political change. By working towards a theorization of the politics of this urban 'political society', as we term it, insight can be gained into the broader possibilities and limitations of protest and politics in Africa today.

Additional dilemmas obstruct the path protest must follow to bring about political change. Since the colonial era, the urban underclass has faced dramatic state violence, especially in response to any effort on its part at political mobilization. This prevalence of violence can make non-violent protest on the part of urban political society a near-suicidal strategy, as Fanon relates. Overcoming state violence, while not letting its own violence eviscerate protest of its inclusive and transformative potential, has thus been a dilemma for political society mobilization from the beginning. It also means the line between violent and non-violent collective action will have to be rethought in the case of political society uprisings.

Finally, the dilemmas facing African protest are, of course, not all internal. The international political and economic order also deeply influences, and often constrains, popular protest, as it does African politics generally. Since the inception of colonialism, democratic struggles in Africa have had to contend with international forces that systematically subvert the conditions for democracy and violently undermine the terrain on which democratic movements can work. Destructive international interference, whether in the form of colonialism, Cold War clientelism, structural adjustment, 'humanitarian' interventions, or the war on terror, presents a dilemma for all African political struggles

9

including popular protest. Indeed, it is often unclear how much substantive change can even be realized on the national level without corresponding changes on the international level.

What makes protest particularly challenging – and exciting – to study is that it represents a moment in which national political questions are suddenly raised and thrown into the midst of public attention. Protest represents a time when the unpredictable, unknown, and unforeseen suddenly take centre stage (Arendt 1990). It is a realm of contingency even as it takes place within fixed structures and conditions. Narrow protests turn popular, visionary leaders emerge to give voice to what everyone knew but no one would say, and novel possibilities arise as new answers to old dilemmas are put forth in practice. Protest can also be a time when existing inequalities and divisions are further entrenched, with urban ethnic riots standing as a stark example.

Protest, therefore, should not be judged according to whether it achieves its explicit demands, for those demands often change in the course of the protest or may never have been directly stated. Instead, protest should be understood according to how it attempts to transform the national political questions that structure state power and how that protest answers, avoids, or is torn apart by the deep political dilemmas that may require resolution for democratic change to take hold. Our study is therefore concerned with the evolving political imaginations forged by the divergent forces involved in African protests and with the efforts made to transcend the structural dilemmas out of which protest is born.

What lies ahead

This book is in two parts. The first, comprising Chapters 2 through 4, proposes a history of the three major waves of protest in Africa: the anti-colonial protests in the late 1940s and 1950s, the anti-austerity protests in the late 1980s and early 1990s, and the ongoing wave stretching from Tunisia to South Africa. As noted, the two earlier waves helped usher in the two most important periods of widespread political change on the continent over the last century. By examining each wave individually, we expose the debates and questions that resonate through time.

Although focusing on three waves, we recognize that significant protests can be found outside of these periods. Prior to the nationalist mobilizations of the 1940s, for example, as early as 1915 the Reverend John Chilembwe led a popular uprising in contemporary Malawi against British colonial rule challenging its land policies and forced conscription of soldiers.[8] And in 1929 thousands of women in contemporary Abia state, Nigeria, participated in an extraordinary month-long protest against British colonial authorities. After the end of the colonial era, the 1964 October Revolution in Sudan, the 1974 Ethiopian Revolution, and the protests in southern Africa of the late 1990s all fall outside the three waves, as does the anti-Apartheid struggle in South Africa, a sustained popular movement that strongly influenced subsequent African protests. While we recognize the importance of these episodes of protest, our interest, rather, is in the way in which these major waves revealed continent-wide political developments and dilemmas and led to continent-wide political change.

Chapter 2 introduces and develops the key category of 'political society', which we use to help understand the politics of popular urban protest. The 'Accra riots' of 1948 stand as a seminal event that signals the arrival of political society as the central actor within African protest. By examining the debate between Frantz Fanon and Kwame Nkrumah over how to understand political society's participation in the struggle for national independence, we explore the politics of a constituency whose role in African decolonization has often been marginalized or subsumed within the campaigns of nationalist political parties. The second chapter thus lays the theoretical groundwork for the rest of the book.

Chapter 3 explores the wave of protests in the late 1980s and early 1990s, which began against structural adjustment policies and ended with the broad inception of multiparty politics. It explores the repercussions of the breakdown of the 'developmental' state in Africa and the ambiguities of the celebrated transition to democracy. Here again, political society emerges as the key

11

constituency fuelling the protests, only to find its demands for a transformation of social, economic, and political life co-opted by more formalized actors within civil society who demanded not transformation but mere electoral reforms.

Chapter 4 introduces the contemporary protest wave, charting briefly the crisis of economic neoliberalism and liberal multiparty democracy that is giving rise to today's surge of popular resistance. We document over ninety popular protests in forty countries during the 2005–14 period, most of which have unfolded with little international attention – with the exception of the protests that occurred in four North African states in 2011.

The second part of the book, Chapters 5 through 8, provides detailed case studies of four recent protest movements in different parts of the continent, all of which are part of this ongoing third wave. Chapter 5 explores the 2012 Occupy Nigeria movement (possibly the largest popular protest in the country's history) through a close reading of the tense relations between labour and grassroots activism as the protests came together and then fell apart. This chapter also delves into the complementary relationship between artists and political society, focusing on the imaginative possibilities opened through this engagement. Chapter 6 examines the politics of the 2011 Walk to Work protests in Uganda, which erupted in the wake of disputed elections. To understand these protests as merely the product of opposition machinations, however, ignores the way in which they gained strength only as they transcended party politics and transformed themselves into a focal point around which anger within political society found expression.

Chapter 7 looks at the 2005 protests in Ethiopia, a massive urban uprising that briefly threatened one of Africa's most durable regimes. Put down through a brutal application of force that foreshadowed the repressive tactics employed by many African states in response to the current wave, the protests nonetheless triggered a major shift in state practice. Chapter 8 delves into the ongoing *Girifna* and pro-democracy protests in Sudan, placing them in the context of previous popular urban uprisings. By illustrating the divisions between urban and rural and within the urban that defined the protests, the chapter explores the attempt by students and other civil society actors to marry their efforts with those of political society, and its mixed results. Finally, the Conclusion returns to the question of how the African experience of protest can contribute to debates about today's upsurge of protest around the world.

The future of the current wave of African protests is uncertain; but what is certain is that, even as they ebb and flow, they will not end soon. Instead, they are likely to take an increasingly central political role precisely because there is no end in sight to the conditions giving rise to them. Without fundamental transformations in the state and in the economy, transformations that popular movements have demanded and continue to demand, protest will not fade away. As threats to life and livelihood mount globally, perhaps Africa's experience with popular protest can open up alternative possibilities to intellectuals engaged in the debates over today's global wave of protest. More important, it may point to alternative ways forward for activists around the world who are engaged in the quest for political and economic change.

2 | Mobs or mobilizers? Nkrumah, Fanon, and anti-colonial protest

> On Monday, 24 February 1948 … the Ex-Servicemen's Union
> began their march. … They found a squad of police in their
> way and in the course of the dispute which followed, the
> superintendent of police, a white man, fired at the ring-
> leaders, killed two of them and wounded four or five. …
> [N]ews of the shooting precipitated an outburst of rage. The
> people attacked the European shops and looted them. The
> police were unable to restore order for two days. … There
> was destruction of property by fire and in the two days
> fifteen people were killed and a hundred and fifty injured
> in Accra alone. … These were no ordinary riots of a hungry
> populace over high prices. … The [colonial investigatory]
> commission calls the crowd a 'lawless mob'. That was pre-
> cisely what it was not. (C. L. R. James 1977: 42–5)

The Accra riots, celebrated by C. L. R. James as the spark that
ignited the Ghanaian revolution, left colonial authorities shaken
and nationalist leaders inspired. Despite the small size of urban
populations – Accra had only 135,000 inhabitants by the end of
the 1940s (Israel 1992: 364–5) – cities were soon at the centre of
the struggle for Africa's future.

The Accra riots were by no means an isolated incident, as
the rapid urbanization, rising prices, high unemployment, and
oppressive colonial rule that brought people to the streets in
Ghana were found throughout the continent (Cooper 1996: 252).
Indeed, from the late 1930s onwards, colonialism faced increasing resistance from popular uprisings in urban centres as well
as strikes and protests over working conditions, harsh forms of
labour control, cash crop demands, and forced changes in land

tenure. But these protests were not expressions of a singular anti-colonialist spirit among a unified people. Rather, deep political tensions existed among the various groups of protesters, each possessing distinct tactics and goals. Moreover, different kinds of protest movements led to different paths to decolonization, powerfully affecting post-colonial African politics. In this chapter we trace the history and politics of one key but often neglected form of anti-colonial protest: the popular urban uprising, of which the Accra riots are a prime example. We start by considering the social context of urban colonial rule that made these uprisings possible.

Colonial urbanism, 'detribalized' Africans, and stabilization

Although cities in Africa had thrived for centuries or even millennia prior to European rule, the colonial period saw unprecedented urbanization as people left rural villages and flocked to burgeoning urban centres (Coquery-Vidrovitch 2005; Freund 2007). Colonial authorities, concerned by the transformations they had unleashed, responded by placing rural Africa and urban Africa under different forms of rule (Mamdani 1996). The countryside was seen as Africans' proper locale. There they could be controlled through the rule of despotic 'tribal' chiefs in the name of a 'customary' authority often invented or manipulated by the colonial regime. Rural resistance, consequently, often made those very chiefs their target (Isaacman 1990).

In cities, popular resistance took decidedly different contours. Despite deep reservations about allowing Africans unconstrained by customary authorities to reside in urban areas, the colonial economy made necessary the limited presence of Africans in these primarily European spaces. Some Africans thus became permanent urban residents, but most remained temporary or irregular migrants, subject to intense colonial efforts to restrict access to cities, with the harshest measures in settler colonies like Algeria or Kenya. Despite these policies, livelihood crises in the countryside combined with perceived opportunities in the cities to expand African urban populations far beyond what colonial

15

rulers considered acceptable or the cities' limited infrastructure could handle (Burton 2005). Squatter settlements soon sprang up within the interstices between formal colonial urban spaces (Southall 1967), inhabited by recent arrivals for whom informal, often illegal, employment was typically the only option. In Myers's words, the era saw 'large numbers of the rural poor becoming the urban poor' (Myers 2011: 53).

This incipient urban underclass, with its strong ties to rural areas, provoked self-generated fear among colonial authorities of 'detribalized' urban Africans, disoriented and alienated, who would breed crime, disease, and moral decay (ibid.: 74). From administrators' perspectives, capitalism and colonial rule 'threatened to create dangerous classes without also creating respectable working classes' (Cooper 1983: 20). Violence was thus central to colonial rulers' efforts to control expanding urban populations, as criminalization, police violence, and deportation to rural areas became regular aspects of colonial urbanism. For Africans, urban areas were contradictory spaces: they represented freedom from the patriarchal, despotic rule of the countryside and new livelihood opportunities, but they also entailed precarious living conditions and violent control and discipline by colonial police unmediated by customary authority structures (Burton 2005: 8).

European settlers saw cities as their own exclusive domain, where they could enjoy lives of relative privilege (Elkins 2005). They enjoyed access to a realm of 'civil society' defined by a set of civil and political rights guaranteed by the colonial administration (Mamdani 1996). Urban Africans, meanwhile, were relegated to being subjects, without rights and under direct state control. Most Africans in cities faced an alternation between neglect and intermittent violence perpetrated by the colonial state, unpredictable shifts from being ignored by the law and formal political institutions to suddenly being declared illegal and subject to criminalization and coercion. This precarious existence shaped every aspect of urban life.

Before long, this informal African urban population, under increasing economic pressure, was the source of a continent-wide 'wave of disorder' following World War II, which led colonial administrators to seek new strategies to control the urban centres (Cooper 1983: 35). Faced with protest that drew together urban migrants with more permanent workers and that bridged urban and rural through family and kinship ties, colonial authorities sought to deal with what they saw as an undifferentiated urban mass. One approach could have been to support, regularize, or decriminalize the informal settlements and precarious livelihoods that characterized life for most urban Africans. Instead, colonial authorities took the opposite tack and initiated an urban divide-and-rule strategy known as 'stabilization'.

The objective of stabilization was to separate out a proper working class of Africans and place them under the control of responsible trade unions focused on narrow economic demands, their unruly tendencies disciplined through an industrial relations model. This would stabilize the specific forms of African labour required by the transport sector, in particular railways and docks, and by the lower ranks of colonial state institutions, such as the civil service or schools (Cooper 1996). This incipient working class would be distinguished from the broader urban African population, perceived as useless or even harmful to colonial development. Complementing this model of a proper working class was one of proper urbanism, in which order would be established by formalizing residence and work through mechanisms of architecture and urban planning (Burton 2005: 277; Myers 2011: 54). The most organized and potentially disruptive African city dwellers would thus be managed through unions and through their social, cultural, political, and spatial separation from broader urban and rural populations. Elevated from informality, an urban working class was to be forged and brought inside the law through formal employment, residence, and politics. In practice, however, the divisions within the African population were never as clear-cut as colonial authorities wished or imagined: kinship, ethnicity, and livelihoods connected even the most formal workers into the broader informal milieu, and rural–urban links remained strong (Myers 2011; Mbembe and Nuttall 2008).

The formation of political society

Stabilization, however, was designed to incorporate only a narrow sector of the expanding African urban population. Thus, as a nascent working class was created, so too was a much larger underclass, who found their informal, often illegal, status reinforced. The result was an increasing tension 'between modernist ideas of how cities should look and work – the formal city – that sometimes make little sense, and an alternative, fluid, ambient – informal – city that is getting by on its own, if perhaps barely so' (Myers 2011: 79). Also confirmed for colonial administrations were the supposed threat that this underclass posed to law and order and the continued need for coercion to manage them (Burton 2005: 10). Denied any right to the city, most urban Africans continued to be subjected to regimes of state neglect, control, and violence.

Colonial authorities sought to divide formal from informal urban areas spatially (Cooper 1983: 32). As Fanon explained, the 'compartments' of the colonial world were demarcated by violence, with the extra-legal zone, its 'frontiers ... shown by barracks and police stations', enforced by a regime that can only 'speak the language of pure force' (1963: 37–8). The majority of African urban dwellers thus took for granted 'the impossibility of their entering the city save by hand grenades and revolvers' (ibid.: 130), the tools needed to confront the police who enforced the territorial and legal divisions of colonial urbanism. Colonial regimes increasingly depended on militarized police forces, complete with armoured cars, personnel carriers, and the full panoply of riot control equipment to maintain their imposed order (Brownell 2012), an image still familiar in many African cities today.

These extra-legal inhabitants of the informal city, without access to formal legal or political protections, could find themselves declared illegal at any time. Thus, when not subject to state neglect, the urban underclass was regularly subject to violent 'clean-up' operations in the name of security, hygiene, or development. Squatter settlements were torn down, and those dwellers who refused deportation back to rural areas faced imprisonment

or worse. Violence also defined the line between ci
side, as rural areas faced vicious 'pacification' cɛ
displacements, while pass laws, forced removals, and
attempted to prevent or reverse urban migration anc
distinct from the countryside. At best, the majority
Africans 'simply endured in the interstices between
Europeans wanted from the urban order and the cities
might have been without colonialism' (Myers 2011: 56). Thus,
even under stabilization, the urban majority continued to live
their lives against a backdrop of alternating neglect and violent
repression by the state, extra-legality and illegality.

The urban underclass was a source of constant anxiety for
colonial authorities. Its presence outside formal institutions and
employment, its transient nature and rural ties, and its unpredictable outbursts made it seem dangerous and inscrutable. This
inscrutability, in fact, would also pose a challenge for scholars
(ibid.; Simone 2010). The colonial urban underclass defied traditional class-based categories and has often been defined only
negatively, by setting it off from what it is not: the semi-proletariat,
landless peasants, 'de-tribalized natives', or informal workers.[1]
Even those intellectuals and activists who saw the underclass
as central to the anti-colonial struggle found its identification
difficult: as Amílcar Cabral put it bluntly, 'we have not yet found
the exact term' (1969: 59). Fanon chose to use 'lumpenproletariat',
but only after acknowledging the affront entailed by the Marxist
category and declaring the need to 'slightly stretch' its meaning,
or even for it to be 'thought out again' (1963: 40).

This difficulty in delineating the urban underclass analytically
or politically has led to a blind spot at the centre of descriptions
of urban popular protest. From the colonial period until the
present, accounts of protests tend to describe clearly the political
parties, labour unions, or student groups that were involved, only
then to casually remark that tens of thousands of people took to
the streets but without giving any idea as to who they were, why
they were protesting, or what they sought to bring about. The
urban underclass's participation in protest is typically seen as

Mobs or mobilizers?

...lled by the elite leadership, autonomous only when protest turns violent, and even then its actions are dismissed as mere looting, rioting, or the rage of a shapeless crowd.[2]

But the political identity of the urban underclass can be thought of in a different way, a way that can help make sense of its involvement in protest from the colonial period until the present. When the urban underclass takes part in protest, we argue, its involvement should be understood as a response to its economic status – often one of intense deprivation and insecurity – but even more so as a response to its *political* status. This political status, as we have explained, is determined by the urban underclass's relation to state power, a relation defined by an alternation between neglect and direct violence, between extra-legality and illegality. This is in contrast to the political status of African civil society and the elites, students, civil servants, and formal workers who comprise it and have access to the guarantees and protections of formal legal or political arrangements with the state, whether through legal rights, state employment, trade unions, or professional associations. It is also in contrast to the status of the rural population, subject to customary law and the political authority of chiefs. The urban underclass, without formal legal or political relations with the state, often had to depend upon ad hoc, informal, and personalized negotiations with those in power in order to secure the conditions for survival. The combination of state neglect and violence, informality and illegality, defined all arenas of urban life – work, livelihood, residence, social relations, culture and, of course, politics.

We use the term *political society* to refer to this urban underclass in an effort to emphasize its political identity as it is shaped by the form of state power to which it is subject. Political society, a term we derive from the work of post-colonial theorist Partha Chatterjee,[3] is useful because it emphasizes this urban population's immediately political relations with the state, relations unmediated by the law or by the formal procedures or institutions that are available to civil society. Instead, political society deals directly with the state or with political elites without formal guarantees.

Political society's relations with the state thus often resolve into contests of force, a direct response to the state violence used for urban control. Political society is a category that typically comprises the economically most deprived, bringing together the unemployed, the underemployed, informal workers, and even parts of the petty bourgeoisie. The category of political society also emphasizes the manner in which colonial and post-colonial economies are enforced by, and impossible without, state direction and coercion, so that there is little in the way of an autonomous economic sphere: in the colonial context, as Fanon writes, the 'economic substructure is also a superstructure' (ibid.: 40). From the viewpoint of political society, there is little distinction between the state and the economy.

Different political identities, based on different relations to state power, produce different forms of political action. Civil society, with formalized relations to the state, may seek reform in the shape of further gains in legal rights or a firmer place in a nascent civil society. In contrast, political society faces a different form of power and has different grievances, expectations and modes of action. Its politics are often driven not by an imagination of legal political reform, but by a more radical need to transform the very conditions of life, which are enforced by an arbitrary and violent state power.

Protest, therefore, can mean very different things depending on who takes to the streets. For African civil society, or those Africans aspiring to inclusion in civil society, protest may take the form of non-violent collective action, with clearly stated goals and disciplined leadership. In contrast, when political society takes to the streets, it may not conform to a liberal model of what protest 'should' look like. Instead, it may appear spontaneous, unpredictable, indiscriminate, or destructive. But, as we have emphasized, that does not mean that it lacks politics. Instead, we need a different theorization of protest by political society, one that takes into account the permeating and violent form of state power that forges its political identity. We locate this theorization in the work of Frantz Fanon, the Martinican revolutionary whose

Mobs or mobilizers?

years with the Algerian National Liberation Front provided the basis for his series of seminal works.

In focusing upon the politics of urban protest, it is important not to lose sight of the rural. Given the colonial enforcement of a division between urban and rural, it is no surprise that rural and urban political grievances, modes of action, and expectations would be divergent as well. Political projects may not appeal equally to rural and urban: for instance, rural farmers may see urban demands for lower food prices as a threat to their own interests. Given that rural structures of power often left peasants with significant control over their livelihoods, peasant resistance has often represented a struggle for further autonomy from the state rather than an effort to challenge the state (Scott 1985). Furthermore, when rural resistance did erupt into direct contention with the state, it often took the form of ethnic mobilization, anathema to urban-based nationalist leaders. In this way, the rural–urban divide had an insidious consequence for the politics of urban protest – indeed, all politics – in its politicization of ethnicity.

From anti-colonial to nationalist protest

Colonial stabilization redefined the politics and possibilities of protest. The protests of the pre-WWII period, which emerged out of a generally undifferentiated urban population with strong links to the rural, were largely replaced by the nascent trade movement's strikes and demonstrations over working conditions and by political society's volatile urban uprisings. While both were often explicitly anti-colonial, neither was necessarily nationalist in orientation. Therefore, the central challenge for African political leaders seeking independence for their countries was how to channel anti-colonial protests into a nationalist project.

Nationalist mobilization would require overcoming divisions within the urban as well as those between the urban and rural. In urban areas, nationalist leaders sought to build a popular convergence of urban forces by taming mass urban uprisings and integrating them with protest by civil society's labour unions, professional associations, and political parties–that is, to bring together political and civil society. Even more daunting was the question of bringing together the urban and the rural, for failing to do so would privilege urban political concerns and only deepen the rural–urban divide and the inequalities it involved. One way to bridge rural and urban was to appeal to ethnicity, seen when urban protests drew upon ethnic particularism, such as the pro-Baganda protests in colonial Uganda. This strategy, of course, can turn ethnic politics explosive when it is unleashed in dense, multi-ethnic urban environments. It can also backfire and fragment nationalist movements along ethnic lines. Successful efforts to bridge the rural and urban, such as Nkrumah's, would build upon existing rural–urban linkages of political society and thus give voice to rural grievances within a national political agenda.

To see how African leaders have sought to resolve these dilemmas, we return to the Accra riots of 1948. The Accra riots displayed both the success of colonial stabilization policy as well as its crisis. Stabilization had worked insofar as organized labour stayed out of the riots, leaving political society to take to the streets alone. However, the riots also demonstrated that colonial labour policy could only 'stabilize' a narrow urban sector and left the majority of Accra's residents increasingly desperate and with a long list of grievances against the colonial regime.

The debate between Kwame Nkrumah and Frantz Fanon can illuminate two very different understandings of the politics of the Accra riots and of the role of urban uprisings in the process of decolonization. Each took cognizance of the political dilemmas presented by the divisions within the urban and between the urban and the rural, and each provided a distinct answer by giving a different political role to popular protest. In brief, Nkrumah was the theorist and organizer of a convergence between political society, labour, and the rural population under the umbrella of a nationalist political party, while Fanon was the theorist of the popular urban uprising as vanguard in the nationalist struggle. Both saw anti-colonial protest as needing to be part of a nationalist political struggle if it were to be politically meaningful, even as the visions they had of that nationalist struggle and national independence were significantly different. For Nkrumah, it was a party-led nationalism, in which the political kingdom should first be won and all else would follow. For Fanon, the nationalist struggle should overthrow colonial power in all its forms and domains and not be usurped by a party-led elite project of 'flag independence'. Together, Nkrumah and Fanon provide a framework for understanding the politics of popular protest up to the present.

Nkrumah's Positive Action

If much resistance to the initial imposition of colonial rule was violent – the Mahdist revolt in Sudan, the Maji Maji rebellion in Tanzania, the first Chimurenga in southern Africa – by the time of World War II, non-violent popular protest had taken a central place in anti-colonial strategy for an ascendant generation of nationalist leaders, with Nkrumah at their forefront. Popular protest was showing its power throughout the continent at the same time that colonial states were beginning to be seen as willing to respond positively to symbolic political action and unlikely to unleash crushing violence against protesters. The idea that European powers could be pressured into making good on promises of self-government drew further inspiration from the example of Mohandas Gandhi and the Indian National Congress in South Asia, as non-violent political protest seemed to promise the path to African independence as well.

Non-violent nationalist struggle was given its most prominent support in the fifth Pan-African Conference held in Manchester in 1945. Organized in part by Nkrumah and attended by Kenya's Jomo Kenyatta and Malawi's Hastings Banda, the conference's 'Declaration to the Colonial People' proposed a 'united front between the intellectuals, workers, and farmers in the struggle against colonialism', which would employ 'the strike and the boycott' as 'invincible' tools of decolonization (Addo-Fening 1972: 78; Wiredu 1986). Non-violence would soon be put to the test by Nkrumah with his demand for 'self-government now' for the Gold Coast.

Nkrumah's vision was to build a popular protest movement

led by a disciplined nationalist party that could bridge urban and rural divides. The vehicle of this project was the Convention People's Party (CPP), founded in 1949, and its strategy would be Nkrumah's own coinage: Positive Action. In 'What I Mean by Positive Action', Nkrumah described two ways to achieve self-government: by 'armed revolution and violent overthrow of the existing regime, or by constitutional and legitimate non-violent methods. In other words, either by armed might or moral pressure' (1973: 93). In Ghana's case, given that even the British themselves 'acknowledge the legitimacy of our demand for self-government', only non-violent methods were needed (ibid.). To counteract the rumours spread by the colonial state that Positive Action meant 'riot, looting and disturbances, in a word, violence', Nkrumah insisted on its disciplined character, defining it as:

> the adoption of all legitimate and constitutional means by which we can cripple the forces of imperialism in this country. The weapons of Positive Action are: (1) legitimate political agitation; (2) newspaper and educational campaigns and (3) as a last resort, the constitutional application of strikes, boycotts, and non-cooperation based on the principle of absolute non-violence (ibid.: 93–4).

Positive Action was a strategy that, through popular protest, sought to place direct pressure on the colonial administration and economy. It would also be part of Nkrumah's effort to gain leverage with the British by manipulating the anxiety the Accra riots had provoked within the colonial establishment. Indeed, the British saw the riots as evidence of the general degeneracy and criminality of urban Africans but also viewed them as resulting from manipulation by nationalist political elites. In the words of the colonial secretary, Arthur Creech Jones, in 1948, the most significant danger faced by colonial rule was the 'illiterate and semi-literate population in the towns and urban areas. ... It has seemed to me for some time that many of our most serious difficulties in Africa are going to lie on relations with these detribalized urban people' (Cooper 1996: 254).

By taming urban uprisings and bringing political society within the nationalist party, Nkrumah would seek to convince the British that self-government under his leadership was the only alternative to urban upheaval. By bringing diverse social groups together within the party structure and making national independence the overriding objective, a diversity of anti-colonial protests were to be forged into a singular nationalist political protest, with Nkrumah at the helm. Fulfilling the range of demands by the CPP's constituencies was to be left until after independence had been attained – thus, Nkrumah's famous slogan, 'seek ye first the political kingdom, and all else shall be added unto you'.

Building the protest movement

The CPP presided over a protest movement that brought together the different sectors of the Gold Coast's population around a common immediate objective despite different long-term aims. Nkrumah declared the CPP's Positive Action would find its base of support in the 'politically enlightened masses' (1971: 108). More prosaically, its popular alliance was located in three groups, each with its own legacy of anti-colonial protest that Nkrumah sought to steer towards the nationalist cause.

First, he built support among the trade unions and steered their energies into nationalist politics. Strikes, in particular among railway workers and miners, had culminated in 1947, when 46,000 workers participated in a wave of actions. What Nkrumah and the CPP did for the first time was to take this legacy of labour struggle 'out of its boundaries' of narrow economic demands and push it into the pursuit of political objectives (Cooper 1996: 248). However, these new political objectives were still informed by workers' place within colonial rule, as stabilization policies provided conditions for struggles around claims of legal rights and equality. For workers, self-government often amounted to a demand for entry into the legally defined space of civil society hitherto occupied by Europeans alone. In similar fashion, for many nationalist political elites, demands for self-government were motivated by a desire to have access to the full citizenship and the civil and political rights occupied exclusively by Europeans.

For political society, however, self-determination would not mean entry into civil society. Rather, it had more to do with the fundamental political transformation needed for people's economic, social, and political status to change, for livelihoods and residence to be guaranteed, for employment to be available, and for state violence to end. Political society launched itself into the CPP's protest movement with a diversity of goals, but often in an effort to forge a different relation with the state. As a central constituency of the nationalist struggle, political society became the group with which the CPP has been most associated, as the party sought to tap the capacity for rapid and committed mobilization it had demonstrated in the Accra riots.

Many of Nkrumah's mobilizers were recruited from the so-called 'Verandah Boys' – large numbers of unemployed or informally employed youth who hung around the porches of Accra – who organized in urban areas and whose rural connections were essential for spreading the CPP's activities throughout the country (Rathbone 1999). Other groups within political society were also mobilized. The urban markets would prove another 'social organization of immense power' for the CPP (James 1977: 55) – as Nkrumah put it, 'the market-women made the party' (ibid.: 131). Ex-servicemen also played an important role in Positive Action, working in the countryside and assuming the front lines in demonstrations (Israel 1992: 367).

Through the CPP, Nkrumah managed to mobilize urban populations throughout Ghana within a national political project, and in strikes, rallies, and demonstrations, he proved the CPP's power. Existing formal and informal organization among the urban population was developed by the party, as were existing rural–urban linkages, to create new forms of association and consciousness among the population. Positive Action was to undermine the wide-ranging and often spontaneous protests within political society and build a disciplined, directed form of protest fuelled by the energies of that urban population but maintaining a strategic commitment to non-violence. Taming political society protest and integrating it into a party-led nationalist movement meant suppressing the radical economic, social, and cultural dimensions of political society's uprisings and turning urban populations towards a narrowly political agenda, convincing them to postpone their broader demands for social transformation until after the political kingdom had been won.

Although they were aligned over the demand for self-government, tensions between labour and political society remained. Organized labour made no response to the brutal crackdown on the Accra riots (Cooper 1996: 258), and some argue that the unions remained focused on corporatist economic demands even as they participated in the CPP's nationalist politics (Killingray 1983). Incorporation within the party around a slogan of self-government was not enough to overcome the divisions between workers and the urban underclass imposed by colonial rule (Cooper 1996: 258).

The third constituency for Nkrumah's CPP was rural (Danquah 1994). Once again, this was achieved by co-opting and steering existing forms of protest into the CPP agenda. At the same time, the party's national political weight was used by local political activists to effect change in their own areas. The CPP aligned itself with youth struggles against the authority of older male chiefs (Rathbone 1999), as well as with protests among cocoa farmers against what they saw as illegitimate state interference. It tapped into popular rural grievances against the government to build support, building on a longer tradition of farmers' organization against low cocoa prices (Danquah 1994). By identifying a broad sector of allies among the youth and farmers, the CPP, despite its urban origin, was able to put forth a nationalist agenda that appealed to rural populations.

The continuity of relations between urban and rural areas also enabled mobilization. Many people moved back and forth between the two, maintained economic and social relations based upon kinship, and brought kinship and ethnic ties into their urban associational life. Therefore, it was by activating these rural–urban personal connections that the CPP's nationalist political mobilization was effective. In Mamdani's assessment, 'the only successful attempt yet to bridge the [urban and rural] has been the militant nationalist movements that followed the Second World War' (1996: 297). In short, the party brought nationalist elites, workers, the urban underclass, and the rural population together, redirecting disconnected traditions of protest into a militant nationalist campaign around a strategy of non-violent protest.

Positive action in practice

On 8 January 1950, Nkrumah announced the onset of Positive Action, demanding 'self-government now' and calling for a general strike. 'The response of the people was instantaneous', he recounts; 'The political and social revolution of Ghana had started' (1971: 117). A few days later, according to Nkrumah, 'all the stores were closed, the trains were stationary, all Government services had closed down and the workers were sitting at home. The whole economic life of the country was at a standstill' (ibid.: 118–19).

The British, however, continued to fear that Nkrumah was planning a reprise of the Accra riots and moved quickly in response (Cooper 1996: 257). Within two weeks Nkrumah and other leaders had been arrested and the general strike called off. Nevertheless, Nkrumah declared it an unqualified success:

> Positive Action had not succeeded in bringing down the Government, but it had shaken it to its very foundations, and it never recovered. The hitherto omnipotent colonial administration had been confronted for the first time by organized people's power, and its rottenness and inherent weaknesses had been exposed (1973: 90–1).

C. L. R. James, in his sympathetic account of Ghana's independence struggle, agreed that 'the general strike had defeated the government' (1977: 139). Others, however, have been more hesitant, with Cooper terming it a 'failure' due to the trade unions' 'internal divisions and indecision over whether to join or not' (1996: 433). What seems indisputable, though, is that Positive Action instigated

Mobs or mobilizers?

a precipitous expansion of support for the CPP over the next year, so much so that it won a landslide electoral victory in 1951. By building on a popular urban uprising that grew out of widespread anger over urban economic conditions, as well as a decade or more of protest by labour unions and farmers over corporatist economic demands, Nkrumah brought these forces together to establish the CPP as the leader in the nationalist struggle and to force the British to capitulate on the demand for self-government. Indeed, the British soon reversed their judgement of Nkrumah, coming to see him as a 'responsible' leader with the ability to channel the urban mass's energy into non-violence (ibid.). In 1957, the renamed Ghana became independent.

Nkrumah's success required him to convince his constituencies to leave their own particular economic, social, or political demands until after independence, as per his famous slogan. The dilemma, however, was that once the kingdom was won by a powerful nationalist party, there was no guarantee that the concerns of these constituencies would be addressed. Indeed, the party mobilization needed for winning independence could easily turn to centrally directed demobilization after independence, as previously autonomous associations and organizations were co-opted by the state and external checks on the party were dismantled. This is what happened in independent Ghana through the 1950s, as the urban masses were depoliticized, the labour unions de-radicalized, and rural areas increasingly disregarded by government policy. New laws banned strikes, allowed preventive detention of political opponents, and centralized power around Nkrumah.

For the rest of the 1950s, Nkrumah called for other countries to follow Ghana's path to independence (1971: 290) – even as protest was banned inside Ghana itself. He proclaimed the power of expanding waves of non-violent Positive Action to liberate all of Africa and set the foundation for African socialism. As Nkrumah revelled in his hard-won glory, however, others began to question the significance of his political victory. Most damningly, Fanon argued that independence granted from the outside to a nationalist party – instead of being won from within through a long struggle by urban and rural masses – would be the original sin of African states. Such a mode of decolonization would set the stage for the reproduction of the pathologies of colonial rule after independence, he explained, as ruling parties became networks of informers, tribalism became the dominant logic of rule, and 'the moment for a fresh national crisis' would not be 'far off' (1963: 186).

Fanon's 'lumpenproletariat' uprising

Fanon insisted that the urban uprising would have to be at the heart of the independence struggle for it to produce genuine liberation. His most famous work, *The Wretched of the Earth*, thus provides an indispensable theorization of the politics of political society protest. Fanon begins the book by revaluing the categories of Marxist analysis to apply in colonial contexts. He reverses the roles traditionally assigned to the working class and to what he, perhaps ironically, calls the 'lumpenproletariat', what we are terming political society.[4]

For Fanon the colonial working class, the proletariat, was not revolutionary, but privileged and reactionary, while the lumpenproletariat was not criminal and reactionary, but truly revolutionary. In his words, 'the proletariat is the nucleus of the colonized population which has been most pampered by the colonial regime', and 'has everything to lose' (ibid.: 108–9). Therefore, even though trade unions may 'constitute an impressive striking power' against colonialism's urban core (ibid.: 121), they could not break out of their self-interest in securing additional privilege. So disconnected were they from the broader urban population and peasantry, he explains, that 'if their social demands were to be expressed, they would scandalize the rest of the nation' (ibid.: 122). The nationalist political parties, too, were unable to serve as vehicles of genuine independence. Fanon's most scathing critique is reserved for the national bourgeoisie, organized in elite parties and aligned with wage workers, which, after a negotiated independence granted by the colonial power, would become the

African agents of neo-colonialism. Under the direction of bourgeois nationalist parties, the economic exploitation of African peoples and the repression of urban and rural masses would continue, Fanon argued, as the bourgeoisie stepped into the place vacated by the colonizers.

The lumpenproletariat, in contrast, has nothing to lose and everything to win. As Fanon writes,

> It is within this mass of humanity, this people of the shanty towns, at the core of the lumpenproletariat, that the rebellion will find its urban spearhead. For the lumpenproletariat, that horde of starving men, uprooted from their tribe and from their clan, constitutes one of the most spontaneous and the most radically revolutionary forces of a colonized people (ibid.: 129).

Fanon illuminates the political imagination of the lumpenproletariat, of political society, which faces a permeating form of state power, one that involves subjugation in political, economic, and social domains. Throughout these domains, the mode of subjugation alternates between neglect and direct violence, between treating African urban dwellers as extra-legal and illegal. The lumpenproletariat alone faces the full extent of colonial power, Fanon argues, a violent force that runs so deep that it denies humanity itself to the urban masses. Thus, to defeat this total form of coercive power requires an equally radical and all-encompassing politics by the lumpenproletariat, a direct assault on all its parts. Their political action seeks fundamental change in all realms of their lives, with the result that their 'minimum demands' would be for nothing short of total transformation. As Fanon explains, urban uprisings demand the 'whole social structure being changed from the bottom up. ... The need for this change exists in its crude state, impetuous and compelling, in the consciousness and in the lives of the men and women who are colonized' (ibid.: 35–6). He sums up the programme of decolonization 'in the well-known words: "The last shall be first and the first last"' (ibid.: 37).

Anything associated with the colonial regime is a legitimate target because everything must change for anything to change. Political society protest targets all aspects of life – political, economic, social, and cultural – as the lines between different realms make little sense for a group facing such totalizing, violent state power.[5] This was clearly on display in the Accra riots, during which all the perceived agents and symbols of colonial power were targeted.

The 'spontaneous' urban uprising becomes an emancipatory act, producing mental freedom and humanization for those acting directly against the colonial regime in any of its parts. The directly and intensely political character of mass urban uprisings is clear: political society takes to the streets not for limited economic claims, as with labour protest, nor to pressure the government into political reforms, as with elite nationalist protest, but to make the last first, to reject the entire colonial system in its fused political, economic, social, and cultural dimensions. Urban space had to be occupied and its compartments broken down physically. It is not a project of seeking recognition or effective representation, but one of direct action (Al-Bulushi 2012). Political society's action is not oriented around a realm of rights or perhaps even the possibility of rights, but rather around political negotiations and contests of force, in which intense state violence is always a ready possibility. Given political society's experience of the state as a predatory, violent force, popular uprisings are also opportunities to push it back, to clear out its agents and symbols, so that when the protest ends the state finds its capacity for coercion greatly diminished. Protests can even amount to demands for increased state neglect, efforts to force a vicious, predatory state out of neighbourhoods and economies.

The social and cultural aspects of political society protest are particularly important for Fanon. Indeed, cultural action can be as 'political' as direct challenges to the state and often evolves into contests of force. He describes how uprisings represent a cleansing and redeeming power for individuals as they become part of a larger collectivity. In revolutionary moments, he writes, 'You can no longer be a fellah, a pimp, or an alcoholic as before' (1963: 88).

Mobs or mobilizers?

Rebellion 'invests their characters with positive and creative qualities' (ibid.: 93), and these 'new men', with 'a new language and a new humanity', come together to form a new nation. A new morality emerges, for 'they won't become reformed characters to please colonial society, fitting in with the morality of its rulers'; instead, they 'are rehabilitated in their own eyes and in the eyes of history' (ibid.: 130). This cultural transformation through rebellion reaches into ethnic identity as well, as the fragmenting ethnic divisions imposed by colonial rule are replaced by a new, unifying, national culture. For there to be a 'liquidation of regionalism and of tribalism', explains Fanon, it is necessary that militants 'show no pity at all toward ... the customary chiefs. Their destruction is the preliminary to the unification of the people' (ibid.: 94). Thus, urban uprisings represent projects of internal moral transformation as well as external political change. They are efforts at constructing alternative political, social, and cultural orders and arrangements beyond the state, based within the informal social networks comprising political society.

The violence of colonial power helps set the terms in which political society's struggle for humanity and liberation takes place. The turn to violence is forced upon Africans by the colonial regime. 'The native's challenge to the colonial world is not a rational confrontation of points of view' (ibid.: 41), Fanon explains – not because the colonized masses cannot reason, but because it is pointless to try to reason with the colonizer, who uses and understands only the language of force. Violence and destruction by political society protest is not a sign of its meaninglessness, but a response to state violence and the need for total transformation. Fanon declares that, 'You do not turn any society ... upside down with such a program if you have not decided from the beginning ... to overcome all the obstacles that you will come across in so doing. The native who decides to put the program into practice, and to become its moving force, is ready for violence at all times' (ibid.: 37). Destruction can also be an effective way – sometimes the only way – to carve out spaces free from the state's presence.

Political society's uprisings may lack clearly articulated, strictly political or economic demands, a fact that its detractors invoke to dismiss its politics. However, explicit demands are lacking not because those taking to the streets lack the ability to make them, but because the urban masses understand the nature of the colonial regime all too well. They understand the absurdity of making demands in a context in which no one with power will listen to reason and in which force alone brings results. Political society's goals are starkly clear in the decision as to whose property is targeted, what areas are occupied, and what slogans are chanted or sung.

To see political society's protest as a violent deviation from what protest 'should' look like is to ignore the form of state power being protested against. When political society takes to the streets, it is in a context in which the regime has already declared reform impossible and force to be its response to any challenge. Accepting promises by the state to reform or deferring improvements to the future are out of the question.[6] The horizon of political action is now: it is all or nothing, because faith in the possibility of reform requires faith that the state will follow through on its promises once it is no longer threatened by people in the streets – a faith political society has learned it cannot afford. Political society protest may seem to begin and end unpredictably, a result of the existing and often localized forms of everyday organization that comprise it. These networks may suddenly be activated, bringing people into the streets with little planning, but may be de-activated just as quickly, leaving the streets empty again. Huge protests calling for the end of the regime may be quelled by lowering food prices, while protests over taxes may escalate until they end in a contest of force and a change of regime.

Spontaneous urban uprisings have their strengths but also their weaknesses, as Fanon makes clear in the second chapter of *The Wretched of the Earth*. The weaknesses derive from the political structures of colonial society, in particular the rural–urban divide. Indeed, Fanon does not see the spontaneous urban uprising as being able to deal with the political dilemmas imposed by colonial rule or bring about genuine decolonization by itself. One problem is that popular uprisings on their own will dissipate into uncoordinated violence when met with the overwhelming violence of the colonial state. Another is that the urban uprising alone cannot bridge the rural–urban divide and break down the ethnic divisions imposed on the countryside by colonial rule.

For these dilemmas to be overcome, the urban uprising must become part of a national struggle, one anchored ultimately in rural areas and organized by a nationalist leadership. Only extended struggle can bridge the rural–urban divide and overcome the weaknesses of spontaneous urban uprisings. The national revolution, for Fanon, thus involves a complex interplay of urban and rural. He values the urban character of the revolution since it is the lumpenproletariat who have experienced colonial power most directly and have the most at stake in its overthrow. The urban perspective is also key because it is needed to see beyond the fragmenting tribalism of the rural and demolish such divisions for the sake of national politics (ibid.: 94). At the same time, however, it is in the rural that the revolution finds its energy and base of support and in the liberation of the peasantry that it finds its ultimate objective. In this sense the lumpenproletariat is a peasant displaced to the city, the urban agent of a rural revolution. To do justice to both urban and rural, urban uprisings must be part of a prolonged independence struggle, anchored ultimately in rural areas and organized by a nationalist leadership. Only in this way can the urban bias and rural ethnic divides imposed by colonialism be overcome.

In the process, the nationalist leadership, whose estrangement from the masses was another divisive consequence of colonial rule, must itself be disciplined so that it does not become a national bourgeoisie, taking the benefits of independence for itself alone. This disciplining can happen only through a 'backward surge of intellectuals toward bases grounded in the people' (ibid.: 46), leading to a political consciousness of solidarity among those engaged in nationalist struggle. As Fanon writes, in areas 'sufficiently shaken by the struggle for liberation' (ibid.: 48), '[t]he people have the time to see that the liberation has been the business of each and all and that the leader has no special merit' (ibid.: 94). Where this struggle occurs, the people 'will allow no one to set themselves up as "liberators"' and will rebel 'against any pacification' (ibid.: 94; Nzongola-Ntalaja 1984).

Fanon sought to chart a way for urban uprisings to be part of a larger nationalist struggle that would overcome the colonially imposed divisions within the urban, the cleavage between the urban and the rural, and the fragmenting power of ethnicity within the rural. In doing so, he dismissed the workers as agents of political transformation, demanded the liquidation of tribal identity, and insisted that the nationalist leadership commit 'class suicide', in Cabral's phrase (1969). Political society became the privileged group, being the only one whose position in the colonial structure of power meant that it faced all forms of domination and therefore would seek to overthrow the whole of colonial power in all its dimensions. It is the perspective of political society that must lead the nationalist struggle if it is to achieve genuine liberation. Only through a struggle that bridges rural and urban and that attacks a permeating colonial power in all its aspects – political, economic, social, and cultural – will post-colonial states avoid the pathologies of colonialism. If liberation is only political – winning the political kingdom – other forms of colonial domination will remain, inevitably reintroducing political domination as well.

Post-colonial trajectories

Two different visions, by two different champions of de-colonization and national independence, both premised upon transforming anti-colonial protest into nationalist struggle. For Nkrumah, let the political kingdom be won by a nationalist party and all else will follow; for Fanon, political independence that is granted from above to national elites will leave untouched the structures of colonial power. Indeed, for Fanon, once the political kingdom has been won, it may already be too late. Ghana's experience showed how those divides could be overcome in the period of nationalist mobilization, only to re-emerge after the political transition.

As the era of decolonization proceeded, Fanon's diagnosis and warnings appeared increasingly prescient. If the 1945 Fifth Pan-African Conference was where non-violent anti-colonial struggle had been most prominently articulated, and if Nkrumah's Positive Action campaign was where it was proven, the 1958 All-African People's Congress, held in Accra, was where it came under its first significant public challenge (Ahlman 2010; Young 2005). The congress was held at a moment when anti-colonial leaders around the world were questioning whether imperial powers were really ceding control or merely finding new ways to exert their domination. In some places colonialism showed no sign of giving up power at all. Algeria was just such a case, and Fanon came to Accra to request support from militant African leaders and intellectuals for the National Liberation Front's war of independence against the French. As Nkrumah continued to espouse non-violence and an 'almost mystical humanism' based on the 'African Personality' (Ahlman 2010: 73), Fanon described the incessant French brutality faced by Algerians since the beginning of the war in 1954: 'we tried this method [non-violence], but the French came to the Casbah, broke down door after door and slaughtered the head of each household in the center of the street. When they did that about thirty-five consecutive times, the people gave up on non-cooperation.'[7]

By 1961, in response to the continued violence of remaining colonial regimes, the political crises of independent African states, and specific events including the assassination of Patrice Lumumba and the Sharpeville massacre, a sea change had occurred (Young 2005: 36–7; Wiredu 1986). Over the course of the 1960s, armed struggle came to be seen as the norm for decolonization, epitomized by the African National Congress's turn to violence through the formation of Umkhonto we Sizwe and the liberation wars against the Portuguese. As the remaining colonial regimes held on with increasing violence, and the political failings of independent African states became more apparent, faith in the political potential of non-violent protest was widely abandoned among those engaged in Africa's liberation (Ahlman 2010: 78; Prashad 2008).

Despite this inhospitable terrain, popular protest remained present, even if sporadic and often ineffectual, in African political life in the decades after independence. The 1964 October Revolution in Sudan, the 1974 revolution in Ethiopia, the 1977 protests in Egypt against rising food and fuel prices, the 1979 'rice riots' in Liberia, the uprising in Tunisia in 1983 and, perhaps most significant of all, the South African township protests of the 1980s – these were just some of the most notable large-scale popular uprisings. Labour, too, remained active in many places, testified to by general strikes in Ghana in 1961 and 1966, Nigeria in 1964, and Senegal in 1968, among others (Cooper 1996: 461). However, it was not until the 1980s that, under external and internal pressure, a new wave of popular protest would erupt, reshaping the political landscape once again.

3 | A democratic transition? Anti-austerity protests and the limits of reform

The first widespread challenge to post-colonial African states erupted in the late 1980s, when popular protest swept across the continent on a scale not seen since the end of European rule. Sudan's 1985 revolution was perhaps the first place this second protest wave broke (Chikhi 1995; El-Affendi 2012), but smaller workers' strikes, student protests, and demonstrations had arisen throughout Africa as economic conditions worsened over the course of the 1980s.

Although the protest wave was most dramatic in Francophone west and central Africa, over two-thirds of African states saw major protests during the late 1980s and early 1990s, as the frequency of protest quadrupled by 1991 from just a few years before (Bratton and Van de Walle 1997: 6). The political reforms that followed this wave were equally widespread: in 1990–94 there were competitive elections in thirty-eight African countries, up from only nine in the previous five years (ibid.: 7). Before 1990 no African leader outside of South Africa or Mauritius had been removed from office through elections, but eighteen were removed within the next six years (Nugent 2004: 369). Whereas in 1989, thirty-one states were under single-party rule and eleven under military rule, by 1994, only two *de jure* single-party states were left.[1]

Benin came to be seen as the paradigm for this wave of political transformation. Its relatively orderly course of events fitted the standard 'democratic transitions' model well, and it established a 'script' adopted by those pushing for reform elsewhere (Robinson 1994). In 1989, protest erupted in Benin over state-imposed austerity measures demanded by the international financial institutions (IFIs). Students demonstrating against worsening conditions were joined in the streets by state workers, who were unpaid by the cash-strapped government. As this initial bout of protest – 'spontaneous, sporadic, disorganized, and unsustained' (Bratton and Van de Walle 1997: 84) – was joined by wider urban constituencies, economic demands increasingly merged with political demands for democratic elections. A national conference was convoked by President Mathieu Kérékou, only to have the conference declare itself sovereign, suspend the constitution, and instal Nicéphore Soglo, a former World Bank official, as prime minister. Elections followed, as Benin transformed from a single-party state into a multiparty regime and from the personalized rule of Kérékou to the elected technocrat Soglo. This basic pattern would soon be repeated in many African countries (ibid.; Clark and Gardinier 1997).

By the mid-1990s, however, discussions of the protest wave and the multiparty elections it had ushered in had already come to be marked by a tone of disappointment. Electoral reforms had failed to produce either the properly functioning multiparty democracies sought by liberals or the substantive changes to inequality and exclusion sought by radical critics. The result, in Ihonvbere and Mbaku's words, was that 'many regimes, including those that came into power in the late 1980s and early 1990s with a reformist agenda, have become authoritarian, exploitative, and as corrupt as their predecessors' (2003: 8). In some cases, incumbents even pre-empted protests by organizing multiparty elections to assure their own victory and gain international legitimacy (Bayart 2009). Benin itself came to epitomize what had gone wrong, as technocratic expertise failed to translate into changed reality. Corruption and patronage continued, and 'the same practices which had characterized Kérékou's much loathed "authoritarian dictatorship" were very much present after his downfall' (Nwajiaku 1994: 442; Bayart 2009). Indeed, the anticlimactic end to the reform process saw Kérékou himself return to win the presidential election in 1996. A decade after the protest wave, analysts and activists were again proclaiming the need to 'rescue' the faltering project of democracy (Ihonvbere and Mbaku 2003: 7–8).

A democratic transition?

Some seek the answer to 'what went wrong' in the political economy of neo-colonialism, locating Africa's woes externally. In this narrative, political reform was introduced, but in a context strictly determined by global capitalist institutions. Multiparty elections were little more than a new way to obtain popular consent to the same neoliberal policies and elite rule (Abrahamsen 1997). The result was 'choiceless democracy', in Mkandawire's words (1998), in which elections were accompanied by worsening socio-economic conditions (Lumumba-Kasongo 2005: 5). Samir Amin is equally critical, declaring electoral democracy to have 'always constituted the effective means for blocking any threats' posed by radical movements (2014). Others place the blame internally on the 'neo-patrimonial' character of African politics. In this narrative, personalized rule, rent-seeking, 'big man' politics, and corruption plagued opposition elites as much as incumbent regimes, and so opposition leaders, once in power, proved more interested in 'struggles over spoils' than ideological differences (Bratton and Van de Walle 1997: 86). Multiparty democracy was the newest guise of the neo-patrimonial state, as patronage remained the route to state power and personal enrichment its reward.

Here we take a different approach and do not ask 'What went wrong?', a question that tends to measure African politics against a presumed universal standard of democratic transitions. Instead, our focus is on how the protest movements that drove the transition were constituted and on how the internal and external dilemmas they faced shaped their capabilities to effectively put their demands into practice or to reveal new political possibilities. What was the imaginative and organizational work being done to rethink those dilemmas, to find ways of going beyond the terms in which they had set politics for decades? By examining how economic duress undermined state authority in the late 1980s, we hope to make sense of protest as well as of its outcomes. We begin the chapter with an account of the post-independence developmental state and the social order founded upon it, the crisis of which would set the stage for this second wave of protest.

Developmental states and societies

Despite a contemporary tendency to cast the history of independent Africa as one of decline, the first decade of independence often saw nationalist regimes preside over significant progress, against massive odds, in the economy, infrastructure, and social welfare.[2] These state developmental projects set the terms of post-colonial politics, and, even where progress was stymied by corruption and maladministration, the promise and possibility of national progress were very real.

Through its expansive civil service, military, state industries, and parastatals, the 'developmental state' was the primary route to economic well-being and political power. Access to state munificence, or, even better, a permanent, salaried position within it or one of its institutions, were the prizes sought after by Africans aspiring to social advancement. African universities assumed the role of nurturing this urban class of politicians, civil servants, and managers, as government scholarships and guaranteed state employment were the concrete benefits of independence for select youth.

African civil society thus comprised this largely urban, relatively privileged, population, which enjoyed formalized, legally or politically guaranteed access to the government and its distribution of resources and benefits (Mbembe 2001: 45). African civil society was thus forged not on a Western model, in which a set of civil and political rights guarantee a realm of economic activity and political association relatively autonomous of the state. Rather, the overwhelming presence of the developmental state in the economy and society meant that civil society in Africa would be tied tightly to the state and thus have a different material base and different politics than in the West (ibid.: 39).[3] This African civil society, clustered around the developmental state, gained key importance due to the stabilizing role it played in the wider social order. With access to state benefits came an inescapable responsibility to one's networks of kinfolk and dependents. Civil society's privileged members would thus preside over a further redistribution of state largesse throughout urban political society and rural villages. The redistributive developmental state was thus two-sided: redistribution allowed a path to social stability in the face of intense internal and external pressures, but it also opened the way for corruption and personalized patronage politics.

Organized formal labour was also incorporated into the developmental state through state industries and parastatals. The independent unions that had been part of the push for independence were largely demobilized through patronage and purges, replaced by state-run unions and professional associations. Organized labour, like wider civil society, enjoyed access to state redistribution and to a share in political power through corporatism rather than through a guaranteed set of legal workers' rights. Workers' salaries reinforced social stability as wage labour became one part of broader economic structures inhabited by urban Africans seeking to ensure livelihoods (Cooper 1996: 467).

Political society largely found its status hardly changed with independence, as colonial structures of urban rule were maintained by post-colonial states (Burton 2005: 4). Political society continued to be defined as extra-legal or illegal, subject alternately to neglect and to bouts of intense violence (ibid.: 270). Destruction of squatter settlements, for instance, was a common occurrence. A 1970 clean-up campaign in Nairobi left 50,000 homeless; the Ivorian government destroyed the homes of 20 per cent of the population of Abidjan between 1969 and 1973; and entire neighbourhoods were bulldozed in Dakar, Senegal (Stren 1989: 63).

In many cases, developmental states mounted efforts to provide basic services and benefits, such as subsidized food prices, to the urban poor, usually in exchange for political support. Personalized, informal patron–client relations became prevalent between political elites and urban populations, activated especially around elections or other times of political contestation (Mbembe 2001: 44). This ad hoc and limited provision of benefits, however, made cities even more attractive to the urban and rural poor, swelling urban populations further. Just as the colonial fear of 'over-urbanization' (Miner 1967) resulted from the gulf between the colonial model of 'proper' urbanism and the reality of African cities, so were post-colonial states permanently anxious over seemingly inscrutable, dangerous urban masses and the challenge they posed to plans for urban modernization. A post-colonial African city had indeed been formed – but too often 'the wrong kind of city' from the perspective of the state (Cooper 1983: 32), and so the perception of permanent urban crisis lived on (Burton 2005: 277; Demessie 2007; Myers 2011).

The developmental state's demobilization of the labour unions, political parties, and urban associations – the bodies that had driven the independence struggle – would exact a significant political price. The nationalist alliances fragmented, and a multitude of constituencies emerged around different particular interests, all seeking state intervention or a place in distribution networks. For those within civil society, relations with states could be formalized politically or legally, bringing significant guarantees and political influence; for political society, where such relations existed, they were ad hoc and always set against the backdrop of extra-legality and state violence.

States under the leadership of a single or dominant party soon became the prevalent mode of power. Independent political organization was forbidden, and political activity was concentrated within the single party and its intra-elite factional struggles. Fanon's warnings increasingly resonated as many countries came under authoritarian and corrupt rule presided over by a powerful individual, whether Milton Obote in Uganda, Mobutu Sese Seko in Zaire, or Jomo Kenyatta in Kenya (Anyang' Nyong'o 1987). The military also took an increasingly important role in the decades after independence, which often brought violence to the forefront of state–society relations. More importantly, as states came to depend upon coercion to maintain internal order, the military frequently became a competitor for state power itself, and so anyone trying to reform state power without taking the armed forces into account would do so at their own peril (ibid.: 22; Bratton and Van de Walle 1997: 243–5).

The economic and social advances of the 1960s were short-lived, however. The 1970s saw price collapses in extractive industries coupled with deindustrialization, divesting many formal workers of their jobs. Weakened workers' associations found their protests shut down by overwhelming force (Wiseman 1986: 509). By the mid-1980s, even the most optimistic analysts and activists were lamenting the political disengagement of urban populations (Anyang' Nyong'o 1987: 20). But the possibility of popular politics was by no means moribund: only a few years later, the second protest wave would sweep across the continent, directly and successfully challenging political and economic order.

State and society in crisis

Africa's developmental states were hit hard by the debt crisis of the 1970s, which struck in the context of declining terms of trade for the continent and an international economic order that stymied efforts at industrialization and diversification. Debt brought the World Bank and International Monetary Fund (IMF), willing to loan money to African states but only if their strict conditionalities were met. The resulting neoliberal structural adjustment programmes (SAPs) removed states' room to manoeuvre and imposed austerity measures deeply harmful to urban populations. State and parastatal workers – a 'bloated labour force [employed] at relatively high wages', as the World Bank dismissively referred to them (1983: 4) – were laid off or had their salaries slashed, and the subsidies upon which urban workers and the poor were dependent were abolished.

From the World Bank and IMF's perspective, these wrenching reforms were the cure for post-colonial states' supposed 'urban bias'. According to the Bank's now-infamous Berg Report, changes had to be forced through by African governments even if resisted by 'bureaucratic inertia or vested interests' (1981: 123) such as 'consumers and producers, parastatal managers, civil servants, and industrialists [who] have an interest in maintaining existing policies, however inefficient' (ibid.: 7). Economic recovery required that the state be insulated from its former constituencies and that it 'be willing to take firm action on internal problems' (ibid.: 8). The call for 'firm action' gave international approval for adjusting

African states to practise what has been termed 'repressive dissent management' (Onimode 1992: 67), that is, the repression necessary to silence labour unions and students, to retrench the civil service and parastatals, and to suppress urban unrest. As Ake wrote at the time, 'there is no way of implementing the structural adjustment programme without political repression. Even so, the programme is so hostile to popular interests, so prone to cause suffering that the use of repression has not always been able to prevent popular insurrections against these programmes' (1989: 62).

Those 'popular insurrections' were not simply in opposition to declining economic conditions. Rather, protest was a political reaction against the violation of the social pact that developmental African states had made with their populations. Austerity did not clean up corruption and bloated state payrolls, as the World Bank liked to believe. Rather, it swept the ground out from under an entire socio-political order that reached deep into urban and rural settings and that had, when it was functioning, offered a significant degree of stability. The exit of the state from wide domains of life under neoliberalism left the previously privileged groups at its core, especially government workers, students, and unions, facing significant uncertainty and unable to maintain the broader urban and rural networks dependent upon them. The crisis was accompanied by a widespread disillusionment with the 'historic memory that accompanied the nationalist generation's rise to power' (Diouf 1996: 226).

Structural adjustment intensified the hardship already faced by the urban poor. Many African cities had seen rapid and un-controlled population growth throughout the 1970s and 1980s, which contributed to the breakdown of services and to increasing inequality. Those urban residents who had managed to negotiate service delivery from the state were generally a minority compared to those who remained outside the state's purview. The privatiza-tion of service delivery, especially in informal settlements, had made livelihoods even more precarious. The urban poor were deeply vulnerable to unpredictable price swings for the key com-modities needed for survival (Stren 1989).

Rapid social change, including a major demographic shift towards youth, exacerbated difficulties for populations with little prospect of employment. And while the newly laissez-faire approach to cities sometimes opened opportunities for urban dwellers to find livelihoods outside the state, the privatization or elimination of previously public goods narrowed the available possibilities dramatically. Furthermore, state apathy was, as always, paired with sporadic violence against political society, whether the informally employed, unemployed, youth, or squatters (Burton 2005). By the late 1980s, 'the moment for a fresh national crisis', in Fanon's phrase, was indeed 'not far off'.

Civil society uprising?

'Among the forces that dislodged entrenched authoritarianism in Africa and brought about the beginnings of formal democracy in the early 1990s,' asserts Gyimah-Boadi, 'the continent's nascent civil societies were in the forefront' (1996: 118). This dominant liberal interpretation of the protest wave tends to consider civil society, in Harbeson's words, to be the 'missing key to sustained political reform, legitimate states and governments' (1994: 1). Others have questioned this enthronement of civil society, however. They point out that liberal paeans to African civil society obscure the diversity of forces and interests that were involved in the protest wave and mistakenly take one elite, urban faction as representative of all African society (Mamdani 1996; Nugent 2004: 369; Shivji 2007). Celebrations of civil society hide the possibility that civil society's interests may in fact be antithetical to those of political society and rural populations or that civil society's triumph may be a defeat for more democratic and inclusive possibilities.

From Benin onwards, multiparty democracy provided the rallying cry for the second wave of protest movements throughout Africa. However, liberal slogans and agendas were often little more than the vehicles for efforts by political elites, labour, NGOs, and students to halt the neoliberal dismantling of developmental states and to regain the relative privilege they had enjoyed. Political parties, often created and led by insider elites, were one

48

instrument through which these groups sought to advance their interests using the language of democratization. Opposition parties mobilized mass constituencies to take to the streets around demands for fundamental political change. They used popular protests to force the state into liberal reform and then stepped in as contestants in multiparty elections (LeBas 2011: 7). Opposition elites were thus often securing their own interests by taking advantage of a 'mass constituency ... ripe for appropriation by ambitious leaders who could articulate an appealing message of political change' (Bratton and Van de Walle 1997: 103). Once in power, opposition leaders would offer little substantive change from the incumbent regime they had displaced, demobilizing the very forces that had helped carry them to power. In extreme cases, political transitions looked to be little more than a hijacking of popular uprisings by self-interested elites.

Labour unions also sprang to life at the end of the 1980s as political space opened and livelihoods collapsed. Worker demonstrations became a central part of the protest wave (LeBas 2011). Seeking to avoid a descent into urban poverty, labour endeavoured to use the language of democracy and civil society to hold on to the guarantees they had enjoyed through state employment or formal labour markets. Thus, labour often aligned itself with political elites seeking a reinstatement of the benefits of state developmentalism instead of with popular constituencies. This further enabled the demobilization of popular protests and their demands for substantive change (Dwyer and Zeilig 2012: 36–7).

Students, meanwhile, were facing the transformation of university education from a government-provided right that guaranteed employment after graduation, into a privatized investment with a decreasing possibility of repayment through formal employment (Mamdani 1995; Harrison 2002: 119). Students were by no means a homogeneous category, and their politics reflected considerable internal diversity (Zeilig 2012). Some already found themselves in political society, while others retained the possibility of entering the elite. Some identified with the demands of popular constituencies, while others sought to pursue particular interests (Arnaut

2005; Bathily et al. 1995). Furthermore, their politics were riven by the same tensions that affected popular politics more broadly, and so the violent assertion of 'tribalism' or religious particularism could easily fragment student politics (Konings 2005: 175).

The NGO sector became a prominent actor towards the end of the 1980s – the group most often self-identifying as civil society. Some analysts made much of these donor-funded associations, giving them significant credit for the wave of democratization (Ndegwa 1996). NGOs themselves, however, seem to have played a relatively small role in the eruption of protest, and too much focus on them obscures many longer-standing social organizations that played a more integral part. Churches and mosques, for example, were often involved in demanding democratization either at the beginning of the transition, as in Malawi, or as openings occurred, as in Zaire. It is precisely the lack of a popular constituency on the part of NGO-based civil society that often restricted its role to participating in the formalized dimensions of the reform process rather than engaging with the protests in their more popular phases.

Each of these civil society groups joined the protest wave, making demands for an end to corruption and mismanagement, for multiparty democracy, and for political liberalization. All were to some extent concerned with resecuring the political and economic benefits that had characterized the post-colonial developmental state. All fought bitterly, given that the alternative they faced was to lose their status and descend into political society with its economic and social deprivation and lack of guarantees. Their challenge was to get political society on board so as to provide the driving force for protests, focusing its grievances on unseating the incumbent regime, while retaining the capacity to demobilize the urban masses once their objectives had been won.

Political society in protest: the case of youth

The fundamental role of political society in the protest wave is widely recognized. In Wiseman's words, the sheer size of the crowds – hundreds of thousands in several cases – 'clearly shows that these cannot reasonably be portrayed as elite, middle class even. Genuine mass participation was clearly occurring' (1996: 63–4). Little attention, however, has been given to the politics of political society's participation, despite the fact that it provided the crowds in the streets and the force behind the political transitions. Political society's lack of a stated political agenda that fitted into the democratic transition model meant that, outside of a few cases such as vendors protesting tax increases in Ghana or Senegal (Nugent 2004: 380), the question of whether political society had its own politics was generally ignored by mainstream narratives. Instead, most analysts subsume political society's actions under the strategies of the groups that were seen as the proper agents of democratization – parties, labour, students, and NGOs. Others frame the upsurge of political society as part of a single, long-standing popular democratic struggle, but equally miss the divergent goals, ideas, and resources of the different constitutive parts of political society. Youth, squatters, the unemployed and under-employed, different ethnic groups and neighbourhoods – there was no guarantee that they would converge in political protest.

A useful approach is to build upon this diversity of political society's involvement in the protest wave. The most pressing factor was clearly the increasingly precarious lives and livelihoods of the urban poor under structural adjustment. Given the fused nature of economic and political power in post-colonial states, responsibility for economic deprivation was seen to lie squarely with the government (Abrahamsen 1997). And given what little discernible difference existed between the state, the ruling party, and the incumbent ruler, economic grievances could easily be steered by opposition leaders into protests against the corruption of incumbent regimes. Drawing a firm line between economic and political protest is therefore simply not viable.

Some political society protesters may have been seeking to establish patronage relations with rising opposition political parties as the chances for securing benefits from cash-strapped sitting governments fell away. But others took to the streets not to forge new relations with state agents, but to push back the state, establish alternative orders outside the state's purview, or overthrow the whole system and all its parts. As Amadiume (1995) makes clear, it should not be taken for granted that protest movements were seeking power or formal political transformation; indeed, they may only have been defending their autonomy. Nwajiaku confirms this, pointing out that for popular constituencies, democracy may mean 'subverting, by-passing, and/or even openly attacking the state' and not reforming its institutions or distribution networks (1994: 437). And Fanon has already provided a theorization of the popular uprising as an attempt to overturn the entire social and political order.

Political society protest grew out of the informal networks which, in the midst of increasing hardship, vulnerability, and state neglect, had often flourished through new forms of associational life at the most local levels (Adetula 2002; Myers 2011: 70–103). Under the pressure of neoliberalism, the informal realm required extensive organization so that those within it could eke out a living (Abdoul 2002). Most such informal associations were organized around livelihoods, but they could also become instantly political when they took to the streets in popular uprisings. Simone has described the informal urban realm as one of multiple publics, actualized, for instance, through feasts or riots – a challenge to liberal analysts' more comfortable visions of the public sphere as exclusively inhabited by organized civil society (2004; 2005). Others characterize informal associations as representing alternative urbanisms in what Abdullah calls the 'reconfiguring' of cities 'from below' (2002). Nevertheless, these informal modes of organization should not be romanticized: intense material poverty and political society's migratory character, combined with heavy-handed state repression, often limited organization to networks of basic solidarity for survival (Trefon 2004).

A closer look at youth can help illuminate the politics of political society. Youth politics is most often characterized as two-sided: agents of change and hope but also repositories of rage and destruction (Abbink and Van Kessel 2005; Honwana and De Boeck 2005; Philipps 2013). Structural adjustment hit this post-independence generation hard, as widespread unemployment, lack of social mobility, and the concomitant inability to assume adult social roles – leading to what Honwana (2013) has called a status of permanent 'waithood' – took on political force in the context of increasing material impoverishment. Nationalist images and rhetoric, which had helped hew previous generations to the state, instead made a mockery of youth's living conditions, provoking further alienation (Harrison 2002: 115–19). African states did not fail to note that young men made up the bulk of urban protests just as they did of armed groups, and so the 'urban youth who were not "captured" in any formal organization' (Nugent 2004: 380–1) became a significant concern, as they had been in colonial times. But youth, like political society, were by no means a unified group, as differences between elite youth, students, and poor or unemployed youth can themselves lead to political conflict (Kagwanja 2005).

Diouf provides a seminal account of urban Senegalese youth politics in the late 1980s. These young people, he argues, stood excluded from 'postcolonial munificence and its sites of sociability … the rights to free speech, work, and education' (1996: 229). For this group, 'the government has always reserved repressive treatment' (ibid.: 233), and so they saw 'no possibilities other than confrontation and negotiation' (ibid.: 228). The gradual liberalization of politics only exacerbated youth alienation, as urban youth who had never benefited from the developmental state found multiparty democracy equally incapable of addressing their core interests of jobs, services, and political voice (ibid.: 229).

Excluded from relations with those in power, whether in government or opposition, youth increasingly acted outside conventional political frameworks and engaged in distinctly non-liberal forms of politics (Diouf 1996: 234). Taking to the streets in riots or joining militias enabled recourse to violence and the direct destruction of symbols of post-colonial statehood. When youth did align with political parties, it was often little more than a temporary alliance, a vehicle for the realization of other interests.

An agenda of social cleansing familiar from Fanon – known

as '*Sopi*', or 'change', in Wolof – was at the centre of the wave of youth riots and protests in Senegal starting in 1988. Youth were 'reconstructing urban spaces and practices' through moral strictures, new religious and ethnic associations, service provision, job training, and collective security arrangements (Diouf ibid.: 240). These arrangements were independent of political patronage relations and irreducible to liberal models of politics, according to which contestations over citizenship, welfare, and urban space must remain within a civil society framework. Instead, protest movements such as *Sopi* are often exclusivist and highly localized, rejecting liberal notions of citizenship and civil society. It can take violent forms, such as the outbreak of deadly nativist attacks against Mauritanians in Dakar. In sum, Diouf argues, a new imaginary beyond developmentalism and liberal multipartyism had been activated 'through protests, clean-up campaigns, murals, and memorials', marking 'their possession of urban spaces to oppose the state' (ibid.: 249).

The protest wave of the late 1980s was thus far more complex and internally riven than the liberal civil society narrative suggests. African civil society did indeed take to the streets with multiparty democracy their stated agenda – which translated in practice largely into an effort to regain lost privilege. Political society, as described, took to the streets as well, but with a variety of motivations. So, even if political society gave voice to civil society's rallying cry of multiparty democracy, that does not mean that the two constituencies meant the same thing by it – often, the temporary convergence around a narrow demand masked very divergent objectives and visions. Indeed, just as new possibilities emerged, long-standing dilemmas would reassert themselves.

Even more damaging to the protest wave's chances at introducing political change than the divisions within the urban were the divisions between the urban and the rural. The economic crisis of the late 1980s was largely an urban crisis, and so the cities were the 'crucibles of political opposition' (Nugent 2004: 368). Whereas, for the urban poor, inflation, economic downturn, or a breakdown in state services would be immediately disastrous, this was less the case for rural dwellers, who often could rely on their access to land. Fiscal crises thus did not produce sudden change for a population already expecting little from the state and whose prevalent response to state depredation was further withdrawal from state control (Harrison 2002: 80). Civil society-led protest movements had little incentive to seek support from rural populations, and the protest wave would do little to democratize the rural–urban relationship.

By focusing on these dilemmas, the debate over whether or not the protest wave and resulting political reform represented a 'democratic transition' can be historicized. Democracy is not just a formal question of multipartyism or liberal institutions. Instead, democracy in African contexts would have to entail popular political participation based on a national agenda that cuts across the civil society–political society divide within the urban as well as the rural–urban divide. Otherwise, even the most liberal reform agenda will remain essentially undemocratic. Most literature on protest fails to situate it within national political questions and thus has difficulty explaining why there seemed to be so little substantive political or economic change only a few years after the protest wave. We argue that contextualizing protest within a set of national political questions helps to make sense of why protests arose and also, depending on the answers protest movements gave to those questions, why they had their particular consequences. Again, to return to Ake's approach, we are concerned less with the formal political transformations that were brought about – largely a story of civil society taking advantage of popular mobilizations to usher in multipartyism – and more with new possibilities, other political visions and imaginations, that emerged through popular collective action, even if they did not produce tangible political reform. We illustrate this approach with the following case studies of Niger and Zaire.

Niger: the national conference model

In 1974, the Nigerien army seized power from the single-party Parti Progressiste Nigérien regime. Like the civilian government it overthrew, the Supreme Military Council was characterized by the political dominance of the Jerma ethnic group. The Hausa community, despite comprising around half the population and possessing significant economic resources, found itself widely excluded from state power (Gervais 1997). From the late 1970s onwards, the discovery of uranium provided an influx of money for state redistribution to the urban centres. By the early 1980s, however, declining uranium revenues helped spark a debt crisis, and Niger initiated its first adjustment programme in 1986 (ibid.: 89). The austerity measures hit what had been a relatively privileged urban population and provoked a series of strikes and other disturbances in 1990. The protests were met with state repression, and in February, two students were killed and ninety-one injured by security forces (Robinson 1994: 597). The trade unions, which had existed under the military regime but without independence from the state, were radicalized 'virtually overnight' by the killings, and the previously dormant union started its own wave of strikes and demonstrations (ibid.: 599). Thus, workers – mostly civil servants organized in the Union of Nigerien Workers' Unions (USTN) – and faculty and students – organized in the Union of Nigerien Scholars (USN) – were the main instigators of the protests and became the main voices within the national reform process (Riley and Parfitt 1994).

By June, workers and students, building on the incipient move away from military rule already begun by President Ali Saïbou, politicized their demands and called for a multiparty system 'as the only real guarantor of democratic freedoms' and for a national conference on the Benin model (Robinson 1994: 598–600). Strikes and demonstrations continued, eventually bringing political society out into the streets alongside the workers and students. One hundred thousand people took part in a demonstration in Niamey in November in conjunction with a five-day general strike (Nugent 2004: 379). Unable to wield the military as a tool against these urban uprisings, a weakened President Saïbou introduced a series of political reforms, including a multiparty system and the softening of some austerity measures (Gervais 1997: 92). He then announced a national conference for 1991 and multiparty elections in 1992.

From July to November, the national conference met. It is important to note who was included and who excluded from this 'national' body. The unions' and students' insistence on a national conference was a key moment: previously diffuse and divergent demands were given a single political articulation. Political society, however, was excluded, as was the rural population. The historic divisions within African society, between rural and urban and within the urban, were not ameliorated but entrenched by the national conference process.

The case of Niger signals the broader problem of urban bias within this wave of protest movements. Urban protest typically had little resonance in rural areas. This is because, in the economic sphere, demands by urban constituencies were frequently antithetical to the interests of rural farmers. Politically, the rural population suffered under despotic local government as well as the domination of urban interests over the rural. National-level multiparty democracy alone would not address their more fundamental needs: reform of the rural structures of power and of the urban–rural relationship itself (Mamdani 1996). Often, questions of ethnicity were also ignored by urban-led transitions, thus compounding pressing national questions instead of helping to resolve them. Even if some analysts were more optimistic about the possibility for urban protesters to address rural grievances (Wiseman 1996: 64), in practice urban distrust of the rural typically prevailed.

From one perspective, the failure to incorporate rural society or urban political society into the reform programme was self-serving on the part of Niger's political elites, workers, and students. By framing the political solution to the economic crisis as multipartyism through a national conference, they were pushing for one option among many. Unsurprisingly, this was the option that presented civil society activists with the best chance to secure their own ends by engaging in political negotiations within an institutionalized framework that they could manage.

57

This is not to say that their engagement was cynically instrumental. As Robinson (1994) makes clear, urban activists bought into the idea that multiparty democracy would have an automatic, self-evident base of legitimacy and that liberal democratization was almost a historical necessity. A multitude of new urban-based parties also sprang up to gain entry to the conference, each of which 'tended to defend the interests of only a tiny minority' (Gervais 1997: 99). These parties failed to take into account the need for a more substantive reform in rural areas beyond establishing multipartyism, and they also failed to take seriously the importance of the military in the de facto power structure (Robinson 1994: 608). The result was that representation at the national conference clearly reflected the interests of the main convoking forces. Informal sector workers whose 'activities account for 80 percent of Niger's economy' were excluded (Gervais 1997: 94), even though they provided the mass presence for many of the urban protests.

Whatever their intentions, the national conference and the power of the discourse of liberal democracy allowed the reformers to legitimize the re-establishment of their own privileges through a national framework. It enabled them to avoid the more difficult questions of national political reform and to present their own preferred changes as representing the interests of all. It also allowed economic hardship to be blamed entirely on corruption and mismanagement by the existing regime instead of on the international economy and the demands for austerity.

Meanwhile, representatives from rural areas, where 90 per cent of the population lived, were relegated to non-voting observer status, in large part due to the urban constituencies' fear that rural areas would support the regime. Voting power was divided up by civil society alone, specifically between the trade unions, the student union, employers and CEOs, government, political parties, associations, and non-affiliated unions. Eventually rural areas were given a place, but one so small as to be negligible (Robinson 1994: 603).

The unintended outcome of this arrangement was that President Saïbou and his representatives at the conference could claim, not without justification, to represent the excluded rural and urban majority (ibid.: 604). The urban representatives, instead of putting forth a national programme to address the lack of democracy in the countryside, chose to leave it unaddressed. The rural was excluded from what amounted to an urban process of reform. Thus, when the conference declared itself sovereign, the act appeared to be a 'mechanism for civil society power seizure by constitutional coup' (Young 2012: 198–9). Narrow, relatively privileged urban constituencies declared themselves to represent the people as a whole, a claim that many observers accepted by identifying those constituencies as a nationally representative 'civil society'.

Others, however, were not so charitable. The national conference model has been characterized as little more than a 'civilian putsch' or as 'an essentially antidemocratic exercise in which elites from a highly fragmented civil society spoke mainly for themselves' (quoted in Bratton and Van de Walle 1997: 112). Not surprisingly, the conference in Niger focused on formal, technical political reforms and the corruption and crimes of the previous regime, while those subjects that were central to the country's divisive national politics – 'ethnicity; regionalism; Islam; and, to a lesser degree, gender', were 'off limits' (Robinson 1994: 609). Political issues outside the concerns of the urban centre were excluded.

As the conference proceeded, the particular interests of the main players became more central. According to Gervais, the delegates were motivated by the idea that if they recovered the embezzled funds of the previous regime, the fiscal crisis would be resolved and the second round of SAP would be avoided (1997: 97). They saw corruption and mismanagement as the problem and seemed to believe that they could return to the status quo ante if they just rooted out the corrupt officials. Therefore, the conference refused to reduce the benefits that students, state workers, and other urban constituencies enjoyed while also refusing to ameliorate the conditions of the urban or rural poor; this led to the 'maintenance of the status quo in basic economic policies' (ibid.: 99). Moreover, in rural areas, the new parties struck deals with the customary chiefs, just as the previous regime had in order to secure rural votes – signalling no change in the political relations between rural areas and the central government. Elections were held in 1993 but represented little more than 'the reversal of alliances within the dominant class' and the continued marginalization of most of the population (ibid.: 102).

The sequence of events in Niger cast doubt on the idea of a 'democratization process'. Instead, multiparty democracy, driven by donors, political elites, and unions and professional organizations in their more corporatist mode, can be seen as a way of disciplining long-standing demands for radical change from political society. The democratization process also represented a tool for promoting urban interests at the expense of the rural, and urban elite interests at the expense of the poor. The 'regime transition' might better be seen as an effort to contain the protest of political society, not as representing an affirmation and realization of that protest. The national conference itself thus played a central role in this containment strategy. By the end of the process, disappointment was such that citizens of Niger were quoted as declaring that they wanted to 'change the change' (Harrison 2002: 101).

Zaire: from protest to armed struggle

The political upheavals in Zaire in the early 1990s reveal the way in which even sustained, widespread protests, when concentrated in urban areas and when captured by civil society, can fail to bring about change – in this case the downfall of Mobutu Sese Seko – and instead leave the terrain ripe for armed struggle. As Nzongola-Ntalaja (2002) documents, struggles against political oppression stretch back to the country's colonial beginnings and, during that time, have employed the entire range of tools and tactics. Protest has played a major role. The Leopoldville riots of January 1959, for instance, were a factor in pushing the Belgians towards decolonization. Under Mobutu, however, mass public participation in politics was typically limited to pro-government rallies (De Villers and Tshonda 2004). The massive wave of protest of the 1990s emerged from a society under severe stress as the Zairean state came under major economic pressure (Young 2012). As the massive corruption of the elite bit further into the livelihoods of the poor beginning in the 1970s, and as state institutions and the formal economy began to break down, survival in Zaire's cities, in particular the capital Kinshasa, became more and more difficult. IMF-imposed stabilization and austerity measures of the 1980s made matters even worse for formal workers and for the urban poor.

As elsewhere, there was controversy over the degree to which the state's corruption and mismanagement, rather than the austerity programmes, were to blame for people's dire conditions (Renton et al. 2007: 148), but the results were clear. In 1985, workers launched a strike in Matadi Harbour for a rise in wages, and Mobutu himself was said to have called Kinshasa a 'powder keg' (Riley and Parfitt 1994: 160). While labour began to voice its demands for improved conditions in the 1980s, the formal political opposition also organized, primarily around the (illegal) Union pour la démocratie et le progrès social (UDPS) and its most prominent leader, Etienne Tshisekedi wa Mulumba (Nzongola-Ntalaja 2002: 185). In January 1988, on the anniversary of Lumumba's assassination, Tshisekedi led a demonstration of thousands in Kinshasa. Similar demonstrations were organized in 1990, followed by student protests in Kinshasa in April, and demands for Mobutu's departure began to be heard (Renton et al. 2007: 152).

The protests created a context in which Mobutu, seeking to pre-empt opposition demands, held a 'popular consultation', collecting the views of Zaire's citizens on the state of the country. Instead of dampening enthusiasm, this exercise 'created a popular expectation of political change' in Kinshasa (Riley and Parfitt 1994: 161). The country quickly entered a cycle of protest and state repression, starting with students protesting after what they saw as inadequate concessions by Mobutu in early April. Later that month, Mobutu responded by declaring a multiparty system and the legalization of the UDPS; but he seemed to backtrack in early May, sparking renewed student protests in Lubumbashi. The state responded with massive force, killing dozens of students and provoking demonstrations throughout Zaire's urban areas (Renton et al. 2007: 53). This proved to be a watershed moment, as a wave of protests and strikes erupted among workers, professionals, and civil servants, mostly over economic issues but also over massive state corruption (Riley and Parfitt 1994: 162). Mobutu responded to the demonstrations by agreeing to a national conference – only to manipulate the opposition and place obstacles in the way of the meeting. Sporadic protests by opposition supporters would continue for the next two years, to which Mobutu would react with a combination of concessions, manipulation, and brutality.

In the first years of the 1990s, a deteriorating economic situation for the urban population turned into disaster as hyperinflation struck. In December 1990, political society took to the streets in several major cities in often violent protests over food prices. In that same month there were episodes of looting of foreign-owned stores in Kinshasa (De Villers and Tshonda 2004: 150). These mobilizations, too, seemed to produce political concessions from Mobutu, as he declared unrestricted multipartyism after the looting. The '*ville morte*' (dead city) strategy, by which all activity was brought to a halt, was also a significant tool used by the opposition (ibid.: 146).

As the political order began to fracture, rank-and-file military began to loot – which many assumed was orchestrated by Mobutu, though the soldiers were joined by large crowds of civilians. Members of political society in particular turned from economic looting to destruction of the symbols and property of the state and of the privileged, with over a hundred people dying in the chaotic protests of September 1991 (ibid.: 142). Political society protest was not limited to rioting, however. In early 1992, the 'March of Hope' featured tens or even hundreds of thousands of people peacefully taking to the streets of Kinshasa to demand the reopening of the national conference, closed by Mobutu in late 1991. Organized by parish committees within the Catholic Church, which, due to their extensive reach and proximity to the people, possessed a unique ability to marshal political society, the march was successful and the conference reopened soon after. Political society had here demonstrated a significant capacity for organization and for coherent, peaceful action, but, as in Niger, that action was directed entirely towards the liberal multiparty agenda put forth by Zaire's elites. Those years saw a constant interplay between civil society protest, political society protest, and machinations by Mobutu to contain the uprisings. The contingency and unpredictability of protest politics were clearly on display.

Despite the protests, strikes, riots, and uprisings from all sectors of urban society, the goal of unseating Mobutu was not achieved. One reason for this was Mobutu's firm control of the security services and state institutions, especially provincial administration (Turner 1997: 256). The institutionalization of opposition power was focused almost entirely on the national conference and on political parties. This points towards a deeper reason: despite the fact that 'there were several moments between 1990 and 1994 when Mobutu could have been removed' (Renton et al. 2007: 168), the opposition failed to do so and, as time went on, seemed less and less interested in doing so. The disappointment was a result of what Nzongola-Ntalaja refers to as the 'unresolved tension between the people's aspiration for democracy and the politicians' concern for their narrow class interests' (2002: 189). For those politicians, the national conference was the site where they could jockey for position, using popular protests to pressure Mobutu into reforms that would help support their own bid for office. Renton et al. argue that the elite 'regarded mass mobilizations only as a means to an end, as a method to pressurize the dictatorship to share power' (2007: 158).

This strategy of using the national conference to align opposition energies behind elite interests was effective, for as soon as the national conference was a possibility, it became the focus of political demands by the opposition and by political society, as even the March of Hope demonstrated. It appears that demands by protesters for Mobutu to go, or for fundamental political or economic change, were replaced by demands for the national conference to proceed. No alternative political agendas were put forth by the opposition and none was sought: 'Nowhere was there a politics that put the organization of the street, community and workplace at the centre of change' (ibid.: 170). The result was that no sustained alliance emerged between the organized urban constituencies of civil society, whose demands often boiled down to recouping the losses they had experienced in the 1980s, and political society, whose impressive power for protest was visible in sometimes violent protests or in the more peaceful March of Hope. One positive outcome was found in the flourish- ing of certain forms of associational life within both civil and political society after the upheaval, as popular disappointment in political reform gave rise to community organizations, NGOs, and prominent 'street parliamentarians' (Nzongola-Ntalaja 2002: 197; Trefon 2004).

As in Niger, rural interests were left out of the elite-led national conference process. The failure to address the divides between urban and rural and between civil society and political society came back to undermine the struggle's potential for political transformation. Given the massive economic deterioration and the collective anger at the Mobutu regime, the intra-urban ten- sions were occasionally resolved sufficiently to allow collective political action and to enable a shared objective, but not enough to ensure that the conference would become a site of real politi- cal change. Even if the political upheaval had led to the fall of Mobutu, it is uncertain whether urban-based change would have introduced sufficient reform to address the armed uprisings in the east of the country. Without substantial change at the centre, the neighbouring states of Rwanda and Uganda, working through rural proxy military forces, stepped in, driving their own effort at armed political reform in 1996 and leading to the massive devastation that continues to define the country.

Beyond the 'democratic transition'

Did the outcome of the protests of the late 1980s and early 1990s amount to a 'democratic transition'? Some argue that it did; others argue that it was a stalled democratic transition that needed completion; others declare it a liberalization without democratization. Our preference is to reframe the question by avoiding the term 'democratization' in describing the changes that occurred during this period. Democratization obscures more than it illuminates by implying a unity of interests and objectives among the very different social constituencies that were demanding change (Mamdani 1987; Nwajiaku 1994). Applying the label to the protests and their aftermath assumes that multipartyism was indeed a step on the way to full democracy. It ignores that the political inclusion of one constituency – even a constituency calling itself civil society – may come about at the cost of excluding the majority.

It is important to see the contradictory nature of the processes that occurred and to assess the democratic content of the changes in a contextualized fashion. As Riley and Parfitt put it, the 'relationship between austerity protests and the democratization pressures in Africa is thus complex and locally conditioned' (1994: 168). We also avoid placing these episodes in the context of the so-called 'Third Wave' of democratization popular among some commentators. This framing rehearses the tired question of why Africa did not follow the trend of the rest of the world and seeks pathologies internal to Africa to explain its deviation – usually in Africa's supposed incapability of escaping neo-patrimonial politics.

Using a democratization lens interprets the events of the mid-to-late 1990s as a rollback of democratic gains and occludes the possibility that those later developments may be more integrated with the advent of multipartyism than some liberal commentators wish to admit. Furthermore, denominating this period as the era of democratization ignores the multifaceted struggles for democracy that have taken place for decades and restricts the category to those events that seem to conform to a liberal democratic

65

model. Indeed, the relation between these longer-term struggles and the events of the late 1980s and early 1990s is by no means self-evident. Finally, the focus on democratization as the primary trend of the era, and the casting of African history as a story of the progress (and occasional regress) of democratization, prevents us from seeing the other trends, such as state militarization, that may in fact be dominant.

Once the democratization model is put aside, space is opened for alternative interpretations of the protests and their aftermath. Though the protests ended up being oriented towards multiparty-ism, this was not pre-determined. Instead, it was one route among other possible routes. Protest, in short, is to be understood as political not only when those at its head articulate a concise demand for state reform. The politics of protest and the politics of democracy are open to a much wider set of possibilities, imagined and enacted by people as they take to the streets in efforts to bring about transformations in diverse domains of life. These possibilities will always be structured by the conditions in which people live, but they can also go far beyond those conditions in unanticipated fashions, often through the act of protest itself.

4 | The third wave of African protest

From multiple directions, crowds converged on Burkina Faso's National Assembly on 30 October 2014. For days, massive protests of tens or even hundreds of thousands had mounted against President Blaise Compaoré's effort to push a constitutional amendment through parliament that would allow him a third term. Finally, frustrated at the lack of response from the government, thousands of protesters smashed their way into the parliament compound, setting ablaze vehicles and ransacking the building. Soon, flames flickered up the sides of the white-tiled structure as soldiers stood by and watched. Other government buildings were soon burning, and, despite the military's attempt to put down the uprising, Compaoré had no choice but to announce his resignation on the following day.

A new wave of protest is sweeping across Africa today. The multiparty regimes and neoliberal economies that emerged from the upheavals of the late 1980s and early 1990s have proved unable to meet popular aspirations for fundamental change. Starting in the late 2000s, what we identify as the third wave of African protest has posed dramatic challenges to the established order in over forty countries across the continent. This chapter introduces this ongoing third protest wave and sets the stage for the case studies that follow – Nigeria, Uganda, Ethiopia, and Sudan – which together provide an illustrative sample of the diversity of contemporary African protests. Indeed, Burkina Faso's uprising, occurring just as this book is going to press, has led to the resignation of its president and to an ongoing transitional period. The Burkinabé uprising, in which political society was once again at the forefront, is a powerful reminder that this third wave of African protest retains its strength and will continue as long as the conditions giving rise to it are not resolved.

TABLE 4.1 List of African protests, 2005–14

Country	Year
Algeria	2011, 2012, 2013, 2014
Angola	2011, 2013, 2014
Benin	2011, 2014
Botswana	2011
Burkina Faso	2011, 2014
Burundi	2014
Cameroon	2008, 2012
Central African Republic	2006, 2013, 2014
Chad	2010, 2014
Côte d'Ivoire	2010, 2011
Democratic Republic of Congo	2011, 2013
Djibouti	2005, 2011, 2014
Egypt	2008, 2009, 2010, 2011, 2012, 2013, 2014
Ethiopia	2005, 2006, 2013, 2014
Gabon	2009, 2011, 2012, 2014
Guinea	2007, 2009, 2013, 2014
Kenya	2008, 2010, 2013
Lesotho	2011
Liberia	2011
Libya	2011, 2013
Madagascar	2009, 2010, 2013
Malawi	2011
Mali	2012, 2013
Mauritania	2011, 2012, 2013
Mauritius	2011
Morocco	2011, 2012, 2013
Mozambique	2010, 2012, 2013
Niger	2009, 2013, 2014
Nigeria	2012
Senegal	2011, 2012

Somalia	2010, 2014
South Africa	2009, 2010, 2011, 2014
Sudan	2011, 2012, 2013
Swaziland	2011, 2012, 2013
Tanzania	2011, 2012, 2013
Togo	2005, 2010, 2011, 2012, 2013, 2014
Tunisia	2011, 2012, 2013, 2014
Uganda	2011
Western Sahara	2011
Zimbabwe	2005, 2007, 2008

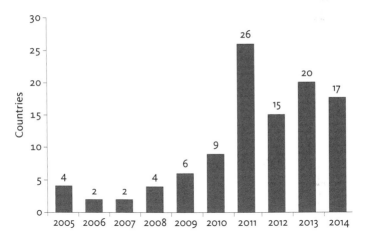

FIGURE 4.1 African protests by year, 2005–14

Note: The list comprises popular protests from 2005 until November 2014. We include all those protests that involved significant political society participation. Protests that narrowly focus on specific goals were excluded. For example, student protests that focus on campus living conditions; labour strikes that demand improved wages for industrial workers; human rights campaigns targeting specific internationally derived demands; and ethnic protests that demand benefits for a particular community, were all excluded. The full list of protests and coding criteria is available at http://faculty.vassar.edu/zamampilly/.

Political society in the global economy

The precarious livelihoods of urban political society is one of those unresolved conditions, and today's protest wave represents a vehement rejection of the neoliberal economy by Africa's poor. The structural adjustment programmes and integration into the global economy demanded by the Washington Consensus and imposed by donors throughout the 1990s and 2000s largely failed to improve living conditions for the majority of Africans.[1] Even where GDP numbers did rise, they were often paired with increasing poverty. As Bibangambah summarizes, 'on the one hand there is impressive economic performance and on the other there is deepening abject poverty, human deprivation, vulnerability and inadequate social services' (2001: 128–9). The promised structural transformations in Africa's economies have also failed to materialize. Instead of industrialization, deindustrialization has become the norm: today, industrial output in Africa represents a smaller share of GDP than it did in the 1970s (Stiglitz et al. 2013: 9). A flood of cheap manufactured products, primarily from China, has further undermined the possibility of meaningful industrialization. New investments in extractive industries, while occasionally driving impressive growth rates, have done little to reverse this trend and have maintained Africa as an exporter of raw materials. Africa's much-heralded growth has thus predominantly been jobless, accompanied by rising inequality, unemployment, and underemployment.

Exacerbating the plight of the urban poor have been continued high rates of urbanization. Africa is home to more than a quarter of the world's one hundred fastest-growing cities, with over fifty African cities already claiming more than a million people each. The majority of Africans, it is predicted, will live in urban areas by 2035, as will the majority of the continent's poor (UN Habitat 2014: 23). Already, 40 per cent of Africa's population is urban, higher than in India, undercutting the claim that Africa is too rural for urban protest to effect meaningful change (Ford 2012). Africa's urbanization has been magnified further by rural displacement. Rather than being pulled into the cities by employment opportunities, Africa's rural poor are being displaced from or dispossessed of their lands by governments seeking to make way for infrastructure projects or land grabs by foreign investors. Today's rural 'development' thus often takes place at the expense of the rural poor and adds to the urban plight.

As has been the case since colonial-era urbanization, new-comers to the city are rarely able to establish secure livelihoods. Urbanization without industrialization means that formal employment is not an option for most, and so urban Africans turn to the long-standing informal or illicit sectors for survival. Housing evinces a similar pattern, as the population of squatter settlements and slums grows twice as fast as that of cities, and peri-urban areas expand rapidly as urban and rural spaces blend together (Davis 2006: 8–11). Adding to this volatile urban mix is Africa's growing youth bulge. Over two-thirds of the continent's population is under the age of twenty-four. This expanding youth population is faced with contracting opportunities, characterized as a condition of permanent 'waithood' (Honwana 2013). A growing political society of frustrated youth is a recipe for urban uprisings and other forms of possibly destructive political action, a reality not lost on African governments.

As international markets increasingly determine the cost of basic items, including food, needed by urban (and often rural) populations, African lives are at the mercy of price fluctuations made even more unpredictable by the hegemony of global finance capital. When those price swings threaten the survival of already precarious populations, it is no surprise that political society may rise up in protest, as was seen in the series of large-scale urban uprisings in Africa and elsewhere in the global south in 2007 and 2008 (Holt-Giménez and Patel 2009). To reduce these protests to 'food riots', however, is misleading. Neoliberalism has solidified the popular understanding of the state's responsibility for economic deprivation, and so economic demands and political demands merge, as they did in previous bouts of protest. In one analyst's words, 'Although the demonstrations and riots were sometimes precipitated by food price rises, the protests usually

71

included demands to reduce political repression, promote political reform and curtail the influence of international firms' (Bush 2010: 122). African states, recognizing the political threat represented by these protests, tend to meet them with force: in Guinea, for example, more than two hundred protesters were killed in 2007. Despite brutal crackdowns, however, the protests of 2007 to 2008 would prove to be just the start of the wave that continues today.

The limits of multiparty democracy

A second condition giving rise to today's protest wave is also familiar: the unaccountable and violent state power faced by Africa's urban poor, often still unreformed under multiparty democracy. This raises the question of why the political status of Africa's political society has not substantively improved even with the advent of multipartyism, which itself was a result of the last wave of protest. Why do elections in Africa so often fail to represent the 'periodic staging' of civil liberalism anticipated by the proponents of Western-style representative democracy (cited in Young 2012: 29), and instead represent the periodic staging of uncivil revolt by political society? Why are multiparty elections so often the occasion for mass uprisings that challenge the political system as a whole?

There are many debates around the lack of fit between multiparty electoral democracy and African social and political realities, as there are around the fact that elections seem often to provoke more conflict than they quell.[2] Some answer these questions by appealing to a supposedly patrimonial African political culture, while others answer them by invoking the limits imposed by the global economy. Our approach is to frame the politics of multiparty elections in Africa within the context of the deep political dilemmas we have discussed previously – the rural–urban divide, the political society–civil society divide, the prevalence of state violence, and a constraining international order. We argue that multiparty democracy, in a context where these underlying, long-standing dilemmas of African politics have not been substantively addressed, let alone resolved, will tend to entrench those divides instead of mitigating them. At the same time, elections represent charged moments when a confluence of political and social factors set the stage for masses of people to take to the streets for a variety of motives, often outside the control of political parties or civil society organizations.

By framing today's wave of protest in this way, what may appear to be a divergence between the 2011 North African protests and protest elsewhere in Africa can be corrected to some degree. Some analysts have argued that the Arab Awakening represents North Africa's 'catching up' to sub-Saharan Africa on the democratic transition path, as single-party and military regimes are overthrown in the north as they were in the rest of Africa over twenty years ago. In their view, sub-Saharan Africa no longer requires revolutionary uprisings but rather a 'slow-burning' transition towards genuine liberal multiparty democracy (Juma 2011). We argue, however, that if the evolutionary narrative of a single, universal democratization trajectory is dropped, then formal differences between single-party and multiparty regimes become less relevant. The presence or absence of multiparty elections in different countries may be less important in determining where protest occurs than the common experience of violent state power and economic deprivation. To comprehend the contemporary politics of election protest in the context of multiparty democracy, therefore, it is necessary to look to the current status of Africa's long-standing political dilemmas. To this end, this section briefly sketches political developments among Africa's elites in the 1990s and 2000s, while the next section looks at civil society's changing role in protest during that time.

The second protest wave, as explained above, was joined by political elites, middle-class professionals, and formal workers, often in an effort to regain the privileged status they had enjoyed under the developmental state. In the twenty years since the protest wave, elites have largely maintained their privilege – but with key differences. Whereas in the post-independence period it was the developmental state that distributed benefits throughout society, thus stabilizing a broader social order, under neoliberalism the origin of economic resources has shifted beyond national borders.

African elites benefited tremendously from the donor-mandated privatization sprees of the 1990s, at the expense of the state and the public. Now, in many countries, the elite gains its wealth through access to foreign aid or from foreign investment, both licit and illicit. Many African states have been turned into conduits for aid monies that flow into the hands of top political operatives, usually with the tacit complicity of donors. At the same time, as extractive industries expand, driven by Asian investment, opportunities for elite enrichment have grown exponentially through formal employment and through less formal routes. Foreign investors place well-connected African elites on their payrolls in order to ensure that contracts are awarded and an 'enabling environment' for investment is promoted.

Under neoliberalism, the flow of resources to elites does not lead to social stabilization, as it could under the developmental state. Rather, it increases inequality and social fragmentation, as massive and permeating corruption comes to characterize many African regimes. Redistribution to political society, when it does happen, typically has the limited objective of mobilizing client groups in intra-elite conflicts. The urban underclass has been stuck with the bill for neoliberal adjustment while elites have managed to use external funding and state resources to secure their own positions.

The result is that partisan differences during elections can hide a basic commonality of interests among a clique of political and economic elites. African intellectuals had offered prescient warnings of this trend in the early 1990s, immediately following Africa's democratic transitions: Mkandawire (1998) denounced 'choiceless democracies' in thrall to corrupt regimes and capitalist economic forces, and Ake declared multipartyism in Africa as tantamount to 'voting that never amounts to choosing, freedom which is patently spurious, and political equality which disguises higher unequal power relations' (1996: 1–2). Ten years later, Lumumba-Kasongo's assessment was equally bleak: 'liberal democracy is failing the majority of Africans' (2005: 202–3). Elections represent times when corruption-fuelled elite conflicts can take on popular dimensions, as competing elites bring their supporters or crowds for hire into the streets. Despite this inhospitable environment, however, there are occasions when political parties can go beyond anti-incumbency and articulate broader anti-neoliberal agendas in conjunction with social movements, giving election-time protests a more productive political dynamic, as we see in the case studies below.

The Africa Rising narrative declares that a globalized and professionalized African elite will provide a counterweight to this entrenched, corrupt state elite, driving on an inevitable democratic transformation. However, in practice, this globalized elite is rarely significant enough to provide an alternative, and its interests are often bound up with the state itself. Even the largest international companies find it difficult to operate without close ties to the state. This globalized African elite's political capacity is undermined by its highly tenuous status, and, in those places where a substantial global elite independent of the state has emerged, its oppositional politics are typically limited to calls for more efficient technocratic governance. Rarely will it join its voice with the demands for justice and equality coming from political society or the rural poor. The populist politicians that draw huge crowds in urban marketplaces are typically seen as a threat to order by Africa's rising elite. The chasm between it and political society and the rural poor should thus give serious pause to those proclaiming its redemptive political role.

In some African cities, this globalized elite is pushing forward a new model of urbanism in conjunction with the state. The violently policed divisions of colonial cities are resurrected, as, across the continent, private security regimes, gated communities, fortified malls, and militarized public and private space expand along with the surrounding slums. Neoliberal urbanization pairs the dispossession of the many with the concentration of wealth in a few, as the former are left living, often literally, in the shadow of the walls protecting the latter. In this context, popular protest can frighten the elite into building those walls between themselves and the poor even higher.

The new 'civil society'

The neoliberal aid economy has also led to a reconfiguration of the politics of middle-class professionals. Once drawn to the stability of state employment – whether within the expansive government bureaucracy, parastatals, or university employment – today, as the state and its institutions are carved up into personalized fiefdoms and the formal economy continues to provide few middle-class jobs, those seeking secure, middle-class livelihoods flock to opportunities offered by NGOs and international organizations. Donor funding has created a professional, NGO-based service sector commonly going under the name of civil society. Its sphere of political action is restricted by its financial base, as many donors forbid NGOs from involvement in overtly partisan or oppositional activities. The politics of the NGO sector are further restricted as many who seek employment in civil society view it as an opportunity for a secure lifestyle and not as part of a commitment to an oppositional or even liberal politics. The language of civil society, democracy, and rights may be used because that is what the donors require; however, those pronouncing such values may have little stake in their realization because their own livelihoods are fulfilled through foreign aid.

As a consequence, when today's self-proclaimed civil society gets involved in protest, it may have little political importance. For instance, witness the spectacle of well-ordered marchers from a Western-funded pro-democracy or human rights organization, placards aloft with clear messages referencing international protocols. If the state actually responded to their demands, it would come as a shock. These groups are able to hold marches for human rights or peace only because both state and society are aware that such protests are without political power. By contrast, if large numbers of peasants or unemployed youth were to take over the city centre to demand their rights, they would bring down the violent wrath of the state. Civil society, in practice, is often the name given to a class of professionals who have managed to secure access to resources that had, in an earlier era, been provided by the developmental state – but without the broader social pact. Instead, today donor funding exacerbates urban civil society's alienation from the urban and rural poor.

It is true that this new civil society does engage directly with the urban poor, as the latter are designated the 'beneficiaries' of development or capacity-building programmes run by the former. The politics of this engagement can have different meanings. The impressive influx of NGOs, national and international, over the last two decades into urban Africa has, in some cases, ameliorated the welfare crisis of the poor, but often at a significant political cost. For one thing, neoliberal states can absolve themselves of responsibility for their own citizens, passing them off to the NGO sector. New forms of patronage relations can emerge between populations and NGO donors. Further, new development ideologies trumpeting the 'entrepreneurialism' and 'resilience' of the poor as the primary 'resources for development' – epitomized by microcredit lending schemes – steer NGOs' urban beneficiaries away from collective political action and towards individualized profit-seeking as the path to social and economic improvement.[3] Significant changes are occurring in popular associational life (Englund 2006, 2011), often with the result that political society is being depoliticized, managed in its poverty by new non-governmental forms of regulation and control.

Civil society's engagement with political society can lead in other directions as well: for instance, some NGOs are engaged with organizing slum dwellers or informal market sellers, which can set the stage for political action or protest among those constituencies (Lindell 2010; Mitullah 2010). In Nairobi, middle-class activists are leading important efforts to merge their organizational savvy and technical expertise with broader popular movements. This was given its most recent impetus with the concerted response to the 2007/08 post-election violence. Issue-based campaigns such as the recent effort against a new value-added tax – called the 'No Unga Tax' campaign in reference to the Kenyan staple maize flour – successfully brought together workers, urban slum dwellers and middle-class activists through organizations like Bunge la Mwananchi (the People's Parliament), defeating the proposed tax.[4] New

77

experiments in inclusive urban politics bridging civil and political societies are being explored in Kenya and elsewhere; where such initiatives are not pursued, however, the division between Africa's middle classes and urban poor may grow only deeper.

Organized labour, despite having been a major part of the second wave of protest, has seen its fortunes wane further in the neoliberal era. Where it is politically active, labour is often able to reanimate its organizational structures and capacity for disciplined collective action and can play a key role in protest (Harsch 2012), as Occupy Nigeria demonstrated. However, organized labour may seek to protect what little privilege it still enjoys relative to informal workers. Its effort to keep itself from slipping into the informal economy and losing the guarantees it still retains can lead it to remain aloof from popular politics, preventing alliances between it and political society. In Uganda, for instance, none of the few existing workers' organizations – such as those for teachers or civil servants – came out to support the demands of the urban poor during the 2011 protests. Additionally, in many cases massive unemployment means that those few who do have steady jobs are unwilling to risk their livelihoods by taking to the streets. In other cases, however, organized labour has entered into creative alliances with informal labour in efforts to prevent the further degeneration of common conditions (Andrae and Beckman 2011; Lindell 2011; Bond and Mottiar 2013).

Patterns of protest

Political society protest has taken on new importance today in this context of increasing economic insecurity, unaccountable, militarized states, political elites who benefit from devastating systematic corruption, an anaemic middle-class NGO sector, and a gutted labour movement. We identify two patterns of political society protest: 'localized protests' and 'general uprisings'. Both erupt from within political society, but they differ according to whether they are able to overcome political society's internal fragmentation to achieve mass mobilizations.

Localized protests occur when particular constituencies, whether organized around neighbourhood, housing status, occupation, gender, ethnicity, age, or otherwise, take to the streets to make demands of an unresponsive state for improvements in their own conditions. These localized protests represent efforts to force the state to address a specific constituency's problems without necessarily addressing the conditions of the rest of society. Conforming to this pattern are so-called 'service delivery' protests, which have arisen most prominently in South Africa (Bond and Mottiar 2013) but also in unexpected locations like Khartoum. Although focused on the lack of social services, these protests often have a greater political salience, as Trevor Ngwane, a Soweto activist and researcher, makes clear:

> If you look at the media, the government, even academics, the protests in South Africa are labelled service delivery protests, which suggest that they are about the provision of basic services, water, electricity, housing, roads. This is very true, but our study also shows that over and above that people are worried about unemployment, are worried about their crime, domestic violence and, more importantly, are worried about the quality of democracy in post-apartheid society. (SACSIS 2014)

These localized protests are structured by the character of relations between the state and political society, as protesters seek to increase pressure on power brokers or to demonstrate the seriousness of their demands by using the tools that seem most effective. And when the state still refuses to respond, the direct seizure of needed resources can be the next step.

At first glance, localized protests may appear to lack organization or leadership; however, many neighbourhood-level protests have complex organizational structures and strategies. Ngwane describes a tripartite division of labour within one protest:

> [I]n Kagiso, they had quite a worked out system. They had three community structures. One called 'The Commanders', like the executive, which was in charge of the whole protest. Another called 'The Intelligentsia'. These were people dealing with

79

lawyers, with the legal issues, getting contacts with journalists, writing press statements and also working out strategy. And then a third group called 'The Commandos', which is like the action combat squads, people who set up barricades. (ibid.)

Localized protests can emerge out of various kinds of social organization, ranging from entirely informal networks, to disciplined community-based organizations, to groups facilitated and guided by international NGOs. Protest can be a strategy used by social movements that are themselves shaped by existing political relations of violence and patronage, giving rise to what De Waal and Ibreck (2013) have called 'hybrid social movements'. Thus, localized protests can take place within clientelistic relations between political society constituencies and their elite patrons; alternatively, they can seek to reject or break out of those structures. Furthermore, as Philipps (2013) has explored, in many contexts there is a blurred line between youth groups that engage in clientelistic political mobilization and those that engage in criminal activities at the expense of the urban poor, revealing another dimension to protests' hybridity.

Localized protest can also, on occasion, represent not an effort to negotiate with the state or elites but rather a rejection of the state and its political order. Committed groups may refuse the corruption and patronage that undergird party politics and seek to drive the state out of neighbourhoods or markets. Protest can represent efforts at social cleansing, leading to the enforcement of alternative social and political orders through the eradication of perceived moral corruption. In all these cases, however, localized protests tend to be restricted by the many divisions within political society.

The *general uprising* is the second type of political society protest seen today. It goes beyond securing benefits for, or changing the immediate conditions of, specific constituencies. Rather, general uprisings occur when the divisions within political society begin to dissolve and the presence of protesters in the streets draws more and more people out, swelling protesters' numbers and creating the conditions for anything up to revolution. The degree to which such general uprisings draw upon or go beyond existing social organization varies, as does the degree to which protesters share visions, objectives, and tactics. Sometimes, common conditions, such as unbearable increases in food or fuel prices, bring political society out all at once. Other times, a common rallying cry resonates throughout the informal markets and slums. Elections can provide the opportunity for diverse existing grievances to suddenly find a single target in the sitting regime. In other cases, what brings people out into the streets is more opaque and may become manifest only during the uprising itself as popular protest opens new vistas, makes possible new convergences, and invents imaginations beyond the existing limitations of political society.

Even where there is a single event that mobilizes political society, such as a rigged election, general uprisings will represent an at best tenuous convergence of multiple visions for political change. These visions may be divergent or even contradictory, as some protesters seek changes to material conditions, some call for policy reform by the sitting government, others demand the respect of multiparty democracy and an end to corruption, others reject all political parties as equally corrupt, and still others reject multiparty democracy itself, seeking democratic alternatives to a political liberalism that does not seem to be working. General uprisings can be more about challenging the very parameters and foundations of social and political order, including the subjugation of political society, than about improving one's position within it. Some may imagine nothing less than the overthrow of postcolonial power and its attendant grip on social, cultural, and economic life as a whole – to make the last first, as Fanon says. This internal complexity of general uprisings is compounded by the fact that the process of protest itself can transform motivations, help new agendas emerge, and make possible new solidarities, so that divisions present at the inception of protest are overcome. Alternatively, new divisions can emerge during protest to fragment popular coalitions, or popular demands can degenerate into violent assertions of autochthony (Neocosmos 2011).

Towards new visions

Bridging the divide between political society and civil society in the midst of popular protest is no less fraught than bridging the divides within political society. NGOs, intellectuals, or elites may put themselves forward as the spokespersons for popular uprisings, framing protesters' demands in terms of civil and political rights, democratization, anti-corruption, or electoral rectitude. However, that does not mean that the motivations of those in the streets are accurately represented. Also important to note is the fact that the politics of election-time protest cannot be reduced to competition between parties or to elite manipulation of protesters. Political parties often try to mobilize and instrumentalize protest but can soon find themselves on the sidelines of uprisings that go far beyond their intentions or capabilities. Protest can catch elites by surprise, rupture lines of clientelism, reform political structures, and give rise to demands far more fundamental than the replacement of incumbents with new elites. Despite these challenges, general uprisings will always represent charged moments when the dividing lines between political and civil society, between organized workers and informal workers, or even between rural and urban may suddenly collapse, giving entirely new and unforeseen answers to long-standing political dilemmas.

Today's lack of accessible unifying political ideologies or programmes makes maintaining alliances within political society or between political and civil society even more fraught with tension. During the first wave of protest, demands could converge on independence, and during the second wave, demands could focus on multiparty elections. Today, however, there are no clearly viable alternatives to the dominant political order. Political parties offer little help, since their repression, their often elite and self-interested nature, and their desire to curry favour with Western donors have kept them from coming up with new, popular agendas. Civil society, focused on development and anti-corruption, equally has little to offer. Socialism as an alternative is out of fashion, and broad critiques of neoliberalism are infrequently heard. The only readily available political language is the liberal, donor-supported discourse of 'good governance' – which, in practice, often has no room for popular or even democratic politics. Thus, protest tends to home in on the easiest, and most limited, way to translate economic grievances into a critique of the state: anti-corruption and anti-incumbency.

This lack of alternatives to the current order obscures the relation between political grievances and objectives.[5] What exactly needs to change in order to bring about desired transformations in people's lives is often unclear. Even the demand that 'the regime must go' raises questions: who or what is the regime, exactly? Is it the president, the dominant party, the military, the economic elite, or the entire state itself? One consequence of the diversity of motives and lack of clarity that characterize general uprisings is seen when militant demands for fundamental change are heard in the streets, but protests demobilize quickly in response to minor concessions. Or, conversely, when concrete demands – such as for the ousting of the incumbent – are met, but nothing substantively changes as a result, protest can re-emerge and turn even more radical. Žižek captures this possibility well in speaking of today's global protest wave: 'the demand for social and economic justice was spontaneously integrated into the demand for democracy – as if poverty was the result of the greed and corruption of those in power, so that it would be enough to get rid of them. But if we get democracy and poverty still remains – what *then*?' (2012: 74). This is the question that many protesters are asking right now in African cities: the second wave of protest brought multiparty democracy but little substantive political or economic change, and in today's wave, even where incumbents have fallen, the conditions giving rise to protest have persisted.

In Burkina Faso, for instance, the popular ouster of President Compaoré opened the way for the military to attempt to seize control. Protesters, recognizing the danger to their recent victory, took to the streets again, effectively preventing a military takeover and forcing a transitional period until new elections could be held. However, tension between protesters, the opposition, and the military has continued, as protesters remain rightfully wary of complacency in a context where there are no easy victories, as the examples of Egypt, Libya, and Tunisia at present, and Nigeria and Sudan in the past, make clear. The challenge facing African protesters is stark: where to turn when yesterday's independence and today's liberal democracy – proclaimed as solutions to Africa's structural problems – have been tried and found wanting.

The prevalence of popular protest in the midst of multiparty democracy also presents a dramatic challenge to the state's ability to manage opposition. As discussed previously, multipartyism arose often not as a realization of popular demands, but as an effort to contain those demands, as states or self-appointed civil societies seized the political initiative from political society. The multipartyism of the 1990s was, in this sense, the state's attempt to co-opt popular dissent and to regain Western support in the process (Peiffer and Englebert 2012). Now, however, as multi-partyism itself is often under challenge from protesters, states have little left to offer beyond more bribery or coercion. On top of this, state militarization and the quick resort by regimes to overwhelming violence when faced with resistance are making it even more difficult for protests to develop or to give rise to new political programmes or visions. Protesters find themselves targeted by state security regimes in the name of anti-terrorism, anti-extremism, or some amorphous commitment to 'protec-tion'. Neoliberal urbanism's focus on policing, surveillance, and violently enforced spatial divisions makes sustaining protest an even greater challenge. The Africa Rising narrative, premised on the promise of progress through good governance and human security, neoliberalism and anti-corruption, and social media and entrepreneurship is out of touch with the reality of politics in Africa. Worse, it can easily be used as an alibi for ignoring or crushing popular political projects.

Popular protest today must contend with the new African urbanism, which is no longer based upon a vision of stable work-ing and middle classes and the provision of state services to the poor. Now, the urban model is based upon the dominance of global finance capital, in which a small sector of African elites is physically separated from the urban poor, who in turn are to be managed through state violence and NGO discipline. The inner cities may even be abandoned to rebellious political society and militarized riot police. Cairo, Johannesburg, Nairobi, or Lagos are the new exemplars, in harmony with a worldwide effort by states to respond to popular political pressures through the intensive militarization of urban space (Graham 2011). This is a new urban political modernity, one in which protest is condemned as a threat to security and order, not lauded as a path to change.

Such an urban modernity is increasingly supported by foreign forces as external pressure for liberalization diminishes. Western aid is being replaced by Asian capital unattached to even minimal reform agendas, while Western donors themselves are less interested in democratization and more interested in security and stabilization (Schmitt 2013). Indeed, the international context continues to help determine the direction that protest takes and the political possibilities emerging from it, as the internal assaults on protest are almost always enabled and compounded by damaging external involvement. In blunt terms, the fact that Uganda or Ethiopia, as opposed to Malawi, can consistently repress political opposition and use massive force against protesters, all the while maintaining international support, is a significant influence on the future of protest and political struggle.[6] A skewed international order serves to shut down democratic possibilities and restrict the terrain of political action for protesters in Africa.

Yet today's lack of clear political alternatives also represents a political opportunity. There is an opening today for new visions, strategies, and programmes to be put forth by, and in conjunction with, popular struggles. There are novel alliances forming between political society, organized labour, middle-class activists, NGOs, and political parties. These experiences build upon each other, resonating ever more widely. As the third wave of African protest marches on, people throughout the continent will continue to draw lessons and inspiration from each successive dramatic experiment in popular democracy.

5 | The precipitous rise and fall of Occupy Nigeria

Armed robber came to your house
'E no take money, 'e no rape your wife
Went straight up to your bedside
Six feet, now you are down
Which armed robber no want money?
Which armed robber no want jolly?
Na political armed robber be that
Na wetin dey kill Nigeria o
Nigeria jagajaga
Everything scatter scatter
Poor man dey suffer suffer
Gbosa! gbosa!
Gun shot inna de air
What you are say
Africa, make you love your land
Africa this na motherland

Eedris Abdulkareem, 'Jagajaga'

Chanting slogans and waving placards denouncing the government, people flooded on to the streets of Lagos and Abuja. Banging drums, singing protest songs, and performing street art to the beat of anti-government music, including Eedris Abdulkareem's banned hit, the crowds moved slowly through the streets, bringing daily life to a standstill. The Occupy movement had arrived in Nigeria.

In September 2011, people from all walks of life gathered in tiny Zuccotti Park, an undistinguished concrete patch in lower Manhattan. Relying on little more than committed volunteers, social media, and a widespread sense of national outrage, activists constructed a slapdash redoubt from which they called on the 99 per cent to 'Occupy Wall Street!' Drawing inspiration from the events unfolding in New York, Occupy protests quickly metastasized across the planet. By October, similar calls began appearing in blogs and other media urging Nigerians to 'Occupy Nigeria'.[1] On 1 January 2012, unaware of the turmoil he was about to unleash, President Goodluck Jonathan removed the fuel subsidies that many of Nigeria's poor, who comprise almost half the country's 170 million people, depended on for their daily survival. Though cheered on by influential Western economists like Jeffrey Sachs and IMF chief Christine Lagarde, the decision was widely condemned by the Nigerian public and provided the spark for one of the largest mass protests in the country's history (Sampson 2012; Sowore 2013).

In this chapter, we consider Occupy Nigeria, a potent demonstration of people power that, for two weeks in January 2012, brought political society and civil society together in a powerful, but fragile, coalition that briefly threatened to topple the government. The urban poor, popular artists and musicians, and pro-democracy groups and trade unions together managed to achieve an unprecedented nation-wide reach. Members of political society first took to the streets, reacting angrily to Jonathan's withdrawal of fuel subsidies. Nigeria's innovative artistic community, moved by the energies of political society, then provided the imaginative capacities that accelerated the protests, transforming them from a dispute over a fuel price hike into a call for fundamental political change. Civil society groups also entered the fray, providing organizational acumen and expanding the political and economic reach of the movement. Yet despite the scale of the protests, most participants and commentators today bemoan how little they actually accomplished.

Drawing on interviews with key participants in the protests, this chapter examines the internal debates between its central protagonists. By looking within the movement at the specific motivations of its constituent parts, we illustrate how the coalition came together and why it broke apart. Why did Occupy Nigeria, despite its size and scope, fail to produce even the minimal changes that the vast majority of participants demanded? We argue that infighting within civil society doomed the movement from the outset. The ambiguous and often conservative position of the labour movement came into direct conflict with the more ambitious agenda of the messianic Save Nigeria Group, a loose coalition of actors promising national salvation and capitalizing on the mobilization of political society. The government inserted itself within this ideological and logistical divide in order to split the movement, cutting it short and usurping its tremendous potential.

To understand the government's strategy, we return to the arguments developed earlier concerning the challenge of mobilizing mass movements within political society that rely on the organizing savvy of civil society. The labour movement provided the underlying organizational infrastructure that allowed the protests to achieve their dramatic scale. However, decades of state meddling had divested Nigerian labour of its more militant tendencies, and so it did not share the ambitions of more radical elements of the Occupy coalition. This led to conflict and disarray within the movement and ultimately inhibited its potential to bring about transformative change. When labour withdrew its support, there was little the rest of the coalition could do to sustain the protests. Still, the movement stands as a powerful indicator of the unceasing oppositional energies of the Nigerian public.

Though Nigeria has experienced relatively few national protests, Occupy Nigeria was not the first time a truly popular movement came to the fore. Like many other regimes in Africa during the second wave, Nigeria's military dictatorship reached a crossroads in the late 1980s following the implementation of a structural adjustment programme that failed to buoy an economy plagued by financial crises. Austerity measures did little to curb the widespread proclivity for high-level governmental corruption; instead, their punitive effects fell on those least able to withstand the economic downturn. Structural adjustment initiated a cycle of popular protests calling for democratization and the end of military rule. That protest movement was successful in forcing the dictatorship to hold elections, and when those elections were cancelled by the regime, mass protests broke out across the country again in 1993. Despite their scale, however, they, too, failed to force the government to respect the will of the people. Instead, the military made a brutal grab for power, initiating one of the darkest periods in the country's post-colonial history.

Comparing Occupy Nigeria with the 1993 protests illustrates the common structural challenges that any protest movement must overcome to be successful in this, Africa's most populous country. The Nigerian government has honed a counter-protest strategy that relies on a fluid mix of coercion and co-optation. While force is an essential component of the equation, more important has been the state's ability to fragment the various social forces that would have to converge for any movement to have a chance at success. By comparing the role of different actors in both sets of protests as well as the fragile negotiations that brought them together – and eventually rent them apart – we can learn much about the chances of future movements.

Mobilizing political society: the 1993 pro-democracy protests

Between 1960, when it became independent, until 1978, Nigeria achieved enviable growth rates on the back of rising oil prices. This enabled the regime, like many developmental states across Africa during this period, to pour money into colossal infrastructural schemes. The spiking oil demand of the 1970s was not to last. It was soon replaced by a global glut of crude oil that pushed prices down from a peak of around $35 a barrel in 1980 to just over $14 by 1986. This prolonged depression in prices sent the Nigerian economy into a decade-long slump, relegating the country to the low-income category for the first time. Nigerians first experienced the pain of austerity during the regime of Shehu Shagari, who initiated a series of economic adjustment programmes beginning in 1981. These measures did little to boost the country's finances, and so Shagari's civilian regime was overthrown in 1983 by the military, which proved similarly inept in staunching the economic crisis. Faced with massive external debt, uncontrolled inflation, and a depreciating currency, the military government of Ibrahim Babangida was forced into enacting a structural adjustment programme between 1986 and 1988. Babangida, an infamous kleptocrat, put in place harsh austerity measures without any succour for the country's most vulnerable groups, stoking widespread anger (Ihonvbere 1996: 196–7).

Soon after Babangida announced economic reforms, students under the aegis of the National Association of Nigerian Students (NANS), took to the streets. The state had long tried to curtail the independence of students, but unlike its more successful efforts to co-opt labour (recounted below) and the academic faculty, the state met with stubborn resistance from students.[2] In 1988, at the height of the anti-austerity protests sweeping the continent, students at the University of Jos engaged in a peaceful protest against an IMF-endorsed fuel hike. As the protests spread beyond the confines of academic institutions, the initially non-violent protests quickly descended into riots as the government cracked down on student activists. NANS was proscribed, its leaders arrested, and the government shut down thirty-one educational institutions (Shettima 1993).

Though the students were able to garner some support from the working poor, especially market women and commercial drivers, without the broad support of political society and the rural masses the incipient movement struggled to transform itself into a truly national affair. Instead, the combination of government repression and concessions seemed to quiet student agitation. Only a year later, however, students protested again, setting off a pattern of student revolt. By 1990, the regime issued a decree banning NANS and instituted harsh penalties for any student organizers, many of whom were expelled because of their activism. Having experienced their own strength, however, students continued to push the administration towards a democratic transition.

Babangida was acutely aware of the shifting dynamics in the region, having witnessed democratization processes unfold in several neighbouring West African countries. Facing pressure at home and from Nigeria's international creditors, he announced the initiation of a national electoral process, which he intended to oversee closely. Rather than turning the country over to civilian rulers, Babangida wanted to ensure that the army remained the dominant political institution in the country. Towards this end, he carefully managed the election process, establishing two centrist political parties and handpicking the politicians who would be allowed to participate.

On 12 June 1993, Nigerians flocked to the polls to elect a new president, having already elected a new parliament and state governors and assemblies. After ten years of military rule, the country was perched on the threshold of a democratic transition, albeit one engineered by the generals who had run the country since 1985. Despite the historic power struggle between the north and south of the country and between Christians and Muslims, Moshood Abiola, a wealthy southern Muslim businessman and philanthropist, won a landslide victory over Bashir Tofa, a northerner. Abiola managed to defeat Tofa in both regions in an election deemed free and fair by most national and international observers. His political independence and landslide victory, however, posed a threat to the country's military establishment. Two weeks after the election, on 26 June, Babangida annulled the results, banning both Abiola and Tofa from further participation in the transition. The annulment of the election triggered widespread outrage and provided the impetus for an unprecedented national coalition between civil and political society.

Prior to the election's annulment, with the exception of some student initiatives, Nigerian civil society was largely divided, with different parts articulating narrow projects and rarely convening to push a 'national' reform project that would address the concerns of political society (Ihonvbere 1996: 201). Ahead of the election, a coalition of thirty-five groups came together as the Campaign for Democracy to oversee the transition process. The Campaign was formed in 1989 through the auspices of the Civil Liberties Organization, a leading human rights organization in Lagos. Under the direction of the late Chima Ubani, it was initially created to push for a sovereign national conference.[3] Ubani's experience as a student organizer had primed him to the importance of building a mass movement.

With the election annulled, the Campaign decided to focus on a single transformative goal: removing the military from power. Along with allies drawn from labour unions, student groups, and professional associations, it called for Nigerians to take a firm stand against the military dictatorship and demanded that the Babangida regime respect the original handover date of 27 August. Unlike earlier civil society efforts, the Campaign recognized the importance of bringing the broader population into the movement. In rural areas, traditional leaders were contacted and encouraged to motivate their constituents. To reach out to political society, the coalition distributed hundreds of thousands of leaflets in popular venues, such as soccer stadiums, calling for 'one week of national protest to force Babangida to go and to enforce the result of the June 12 election'.[4] Organizers called on all Nigerians to participate in rallies, demonstrations, strikes, and other acts of civil disobedience. The leaflets explicitly rejected violence and invoked unity across ethnic and religious lines.

Five days of mass protests – the largest in Nigeria's post-Independence history – followed from 5 to 9 July. Crossing ethnic, regional, religious and class lines, millions participated in collective actions throughout rural and urban areas, paralysing economic and political life. The success of the movement was attributed to the coalition's preparatory groundwork and the fact it had 'done its homework by having meetings with special interest groups – meat sellers, market women, shop keepers, students, trade unions, and road transport workers – and by enlisting their cooperation and support' (ibid.: 202). By reaching out to both political society and the rural masses in a targeted fashion, an opposition movement was able to reach a mass scale for the first time in the country's history.

The response by the military junta was swift. Security agents arrested the leading organizers, shut down universities and media houses, and sought to infiltrate the protest movement. However, for reasons that are still debated, Babangida did not – or could not – throw the military into an all-out assault to crush the uprising. Instead, he agreed to leave power on 26 August on his own terms. In his final act, Babangida signed a decree establishing an interim government with a civilian, Ernest Shonekan, the former head of the transition council, at its head. The movement, however, was not placated. Protests and strikes continued, plunging the country into a political and economic morass. In November 1993, Babangida's defence secretary, General Sani Abacha, used the disorder as a pretext to seize power, leading Nigeria into one of its darkest periods.

The failure to bring to power an elected civilian government had devastating effects on the pro-democracy movement, splintering the coalition and sending former allies in divergent directions. Several key figures from the movement supported Abacha's power grab, stunning those who became targets of the government crackdown. Sensing the uprising's waning strength, Abacha announced a national conference, which he promptly packed with the most conservative elements of the movement. Simultaneously, he cracked down on its more progressive factions within civil society, including trade unions, human rights activists, students, and journalists. By targeting key opposition organizers while demonstrating his regime's coercive force to the wider population, Abacha was able to stifle the broader uprising.

In 1994, with smaller actions continuing across the country, including strikes within the key oil sector, the regime abandoned any pretence of overseeing a democratic transition. As a last-ditch effort to resurrect a dying movement, Abiola feebly declared himself president on the one-year anniversary of the cancelled election. He was promptly arrested and thrown in jail.[5] Abacha accelerated his campaign of repression and soon consolidated power by either co-opting or destroying each individual faction of the once mighty pro-democracy coalition. Over the next five years, Abacha gained notoriety for imprisoning or killing off a wide variety of anti-regime elements, which pushed the remaining pro-democracy forces deep underground or into exile. The country would only return to its aborted democratic transition in 1999, following the mysterious death of Abacha in June 1998.

The legacy of 1993 and the rise of Occupy

The 1993 pro-democracy uprising left a two-sided legacy. Most importantly, Nigerian civil society realized that military rule could undermine their privileged status relative to the urban underclass and, hence, that they needed to incorporate political society and the rural population in any future attempt at national political change. Prior to 1993, the sole effort to mobilize nationally in Nigeria had been during the independence struggle, which had run aground on deep regional differences. The brief unity among Nigerian elites at that time was short-lived, and their fragmentation paved the way for the first of the many military coups which have defined politics in the country.

But the legacy of 1993 was mostly negative. Five years of repression of pro-democracy forces denied the movement continuity as leaders were arrested, assassinated, or exiled. The breakdown of the coalition left those who remained few options beyond co-optation by Abacha's military junta. Some important civil society initiatives bravely struggled on within the country, most notably the United Action for Democracy, led by Olisa Agbakoba, and the Joint Action Committee of Nigeria, a coalition of forty groups under the charismatic leadership of Gani Fawehinmi. These groups, led primarily by middle-class professionals and restrained by the heavy repression of the Abacha regime, were ineffective in assembling broader movements and saw their activism limited to Lagos and its environs (Lewis et al. 1998: 93–5).

When the entrenched military elite decided to hold elections in 1999, therefore, popular movements could take little responsibility for having compelled the government's change of course. Rather, Nigeria's democratic transition was recommenced by the regime due to the intense pressure it was under from the international community, which was itself driven largely by the activism of Nigerian exiles.[6] The 1999 elections, widely condemned as unfree and unfair, returned the former military leader Olusegun Obasanjo to the presidency. Obasanjo had first held power in 1976 in the wake of a military coup, and for three years he had presided over an extended oil-driven boom in the country's finances, eventually handing power over to an elected civilian president. Within Nigeria, however, Obasanjo was known equally for his political repression.

Notably, Obasanjo was considered responsible for the death of Funmilayo Ransome-Kuti, a legendary activist who did much to forge the distinctive mix of culture and politics that has characterized Nigerian popular movements across generations. A brief detour through her and her family's lives can help illustrate the central role that artists have played in crafting the Nigerian political imagination. As the head of the Abeokuta Women's Union (AWU), Ransome-Kuti played a central role in organizing women during anti-colonial protests in the 1940s and 1950s, and her progeny have remained at the artistic forefront of Nigeria's pro-democracy movement to the present day. Educated in England in the 1920s, she returned to Nigeria where she led the AWU, an organization established to foster cross-class solidarity between working-class market women and their middle-class counterparts. AWU organized a series of creative protests against British colonial authorities through the latter half of the 1940s. Despite the state repression they faced, the protesters developed novel methods, such as deploying popular music, to motivate and unify protesters and to shame the all-male colonial administration.

Women activists frequently employed a mix of raunchy humour and direct threats to communicate their message. In songs from the period, they targeted colonial administrators and collaborators for abuse, denouncing them as crooks and thieves. One song reminds a haughty male administrator of women's power: 'It is from the head of the vagina / that you males are born'. Another identifies its target by name: 'If your hand should catch Ajibodu / Kill him, do not spare him / demolish him as you would demolish a good meal of *eba*' (Shonekan 2009: 135–8). The AWU achieved several milestones for women's representation in colonial Nigeria before going on to play an important role in the

95

nationalist movement. Ransome-Kuti herself even served on the team that negotiated independence from the British.

Ransome-Kuti's activism continued into the post-independence period and her family emerged as vocal critics of Nigeria's venal rulers. Her husband, Oladotun, had served as the first president of the Nigerian Union of Teachers, which played an important role in the anti-colonial struggle. Her son, Beko, is still remembered as one of the most fearless human rights campaigners in the country for his work with the Campaign for Democracy. She was the aunt (by marriage) of the Nobel Laureate and pro-democracy activist, Wole Soyinka, and, most famously, the mother of Fela Anikulapo-Kuti, the legendary creator of Afrobeat and an untiring champion of Nigerian political society.

Fela's music bears strong influences of his mother's work with AWU. Like the songs of the women activists before him, Fela's anthems targeted capricious state power with bold challenges and mocking wordplay. Afrobeat, a potent mix of American funk with Nigerian rhythms, resonated strongly with Nigeria's urban youth, and Fela emerged as a popular hero and leading critic of the military regime. Fela set up the Kalakuta Republic in 1970, a communal compound that featured a recording studio, health clinic, and living space that became a refuge for young members of political society. Declaring Kalakuta sovereign and beyond the authority of the Nigerian state, he used it as a base from which he mocked the military regime. In 1977, he released *Zombie*, a four-song album that included the eponymous single, a contemptuous reference to the mindless behaviour of Africa's soldier-rulers. In it, he excoriates the Obasanjo regime, deploying the familiar mix of humour and disgust that characterized the songs of the AWU a generation earlier. Fela's subversive lyrics, combined with his acts of political theatre, unsettled the Obasanjo regime. In February 1978, Obasanjo sent a thousand troops to the Kalakuta Republic in a show of force. In the ensuing chaos, Kalakuta was destroyed and his beloved mother, Funmilayo, was thrown from a second-storey window by rampaging soldiers, dying soon after. Fela followed her to an early grave in 1997 during the dark days of the Abacha regime. In the lead-up to the 1999 elections, it was widely rumoured in Lagos that, had Fela lived, he would have prevented his old nemesis, Obasanjo, from retaking the presidency. As we will see, Ransome-Kuti's grandsons, Femi and Seun, have emerged as central figures in the Occupy Nigeria movements alongside their uncle, Soyinka.

Upon his return to office in 1999, Obasanjo was hailed as the reformed leader of a global anti-corruption movement, having served as the Chair of the Advisory Council of Transparency International, an anti-corruption advocacy group. Yet his record in office never lived up to his vaunted reputation with the international community. Opponents accused him of allowing graft to fester at high levels within his regime and of deploying anti-corruption investigations selectively. Obasanjo did preside over an impressive increase in Nigeria's annual growth rate, which rose to over 6 per cent during his rule. But, as is the case with today's economic boom, the gains were distributed narrowly, while the vast majority failed to see substantive improvements in their lives. In 2006, despite a constitutional provision that limited presidents to two terms, Obasanjo, following the examples of Yoweri Museveni in Uganda and Idriss Deby in Chad, sought to modify the constitution to allow him a third term in office. Due to significant condemnation both nationally and internationally, his efforts failed (Timberg 2006).

Instead, Obasanjo installed the younger brother of his former vice-president as the candidate of the ruling People's Democratic Party. Umaru Yar'Adua, the scion of a Nigerian political dynasty, came to power in a 2007 election of dubious integrity. The election was delayed multiple times, and observers from both inside and outside Nigeria recorded widespread incidents of vote rigging, ballot box theft, and voter intimidation. Over seventy people were killed. Still, the election marked the first time in the country's history that an elected government passed power to a non-military regime.

In November of 2009, Yar'Adua suddenly flew to Jeddah, Saudi Arabia, for treatment of a heart condition. After three months abroad, a sickly Yar'Adua returned to a country roiled by debates regarding the power vacuum at the top. In February, with no word on Yar'Adua's condition, the government announced that Goodluck Jonathan, the vice-president, had been declared acting president. Yar'Adua died on 5 May, and Jonathan was sworn in as president the next day.

Jonathan was the son of a canoe carver, who earned a doctorate in zoology before turning to politics, where he rose steadily through state and national positions. Upon taking the presidency, he declared that he would step down in May 2011, the end of Yar'Adua's original term, only to then declare himself a candidate for the 2011 elections. Competing against entrenched political interests, Jonathan emerged as the surprise victor in what were considered singularly fair elections. Despite his rise from humble beginnings to the highest office in the land, however, Jonathan had no intention of challenging the deep structures of Nigerian politics. Instead, his government continued the system of intra-elite negotiation that has characterized the country since independence. As his popularity waned, he provoked widespread anger by attempting to extend the term of president from four to six years. He was viewed as inept in dealing with Boko Haram, an Islamist movement that continues to wreak havoc in the country's north, and his continued soft treatment of Nigeria's powerful oil sector reinforces the widespread perception of his weakness as president (Busari 2012).

The fateful incident that would trigger one of Nigeria's largest popular uprisings in history occurred just a few months after Jonathan's 2011 election. Though the country's economy had risen at a steady clip since 2003, averaging between 5 and 8 per cent growth annually, that growth has not led to substantive improvements for the vast majority of citizens. As even the World Bank – a firm supporter of pro-growth policies despite evidence of their harmful impact on the country's poor – acknowledged, Nigeria represents 'a puzzling contrast between rapid economic growth and quite minimal welfare improvements for much of the population' (2013: 2).

In December 2011, Christine Lagarde, the newly appointed IMF Managing Director, made a high-profile visit to Nigeria. She arrived in the midst of the European Union's financial crisis, as austerity measures had failed to reverse the traumatic effects of the 2008 recession and threatened the continued viability of the EU and the Euro. Her speech, which drew a crowd of leading business people and government officials, emphasized the risk of the Euro crisis contaminating the Nigerian economy through a drop in oil prices, reductions in remittances, or other financial links. Pointing out the relatively small size of Nigeria's foreign currency reserves, she urged the government to adopt immediate austerity measures so as to insulate itself from the Eurozone crisis (*Business Day* 2011).

Imposing austerity programmes in a country with sustained growth rates and increasing inequality makes little sense to anyone but the most devout adherents of neoliberal dogma, especially given the long history of popular resistance to such policies in Africa. Jonathan, however, bowed to pressure and began by announcing that subsidies on fuel would be removed on 1 January 2012. To understand the significance of the fuel subsidies and the outcry that followed, it is essential to grasp the particular dysfunction of Nigeria's oil-dependent economy. The country is Africa's largest oil producer and consistently ranks among the top producers in the world. Yet the moribund state of the country's refineries means that they cannot produce a sufficient amount of oil to meet domestic demand. Instead, the government exports what it extracts and then imports what the country uses, paying full price on the international market and reselling this imported oil to domestic consumers at a highly subsidized price.

Jonathan's decision to remove fuel subsidies was not the first time the government had manipulated oil prices for political reasons. Indeed, manipulating fuel subsidies as a means to reward or punish the population has a long history (Kperogi 2011b). Almost always, the hikes are justified by claims of improving governance performance and macro-economic stability – Obasanjo himself had the reputation of being a particularly egregious practitioner of this dark art, reducing subsidies eight times during his regime (Anikulapo-Kuti 2012). Abacha, too, hiked oil prices in the 1990s, claiming that the financial savings would be used to improve the country's infrastructure and service delivery. His regime went as far as establishing a Petroleum Trust Fund intended for national development, but instead of improving the country's governance crisis, the Fund became another site of government corruption. Indeed, the manipulation of fuel prices rarely produces hoped-for improvements in a country's fiscal picture; instead, they are more likely to provide the spark for anti-government agitation.

Occupy Nigeria: the unsustainable convergence

Jonathan's removal of oil subsidies proved to be the final provocation that brought political society on to the streets. The price rise struck during the holidays, when many people were out visiting their hometowns or villages to celebrate the New Year. It left large numbers literally stranded, unable to return due to the skyrocketing cost of transportation.[7] Civil society had been organizing against the Jonathan regime for some time, but had failed to catalyse any popular movement behind it. The removal of the subsidy provided the necessary tinder to set the country ablaze. As one participant explained, 'the fuel hike was the trigger, but the gun was loaded over a period of time'.[8] On 2 January, the day after the fuel subsidies were withdrawn, political society – especially unemployed youth and the working poor – took to the streets in Abuja and Lagos to register their anger.[9]

Just as musicians played an indispensable role in Tahrir Square during the Egyptian uprising, participating in marches and offering support to those injured in Mubarak's crackdown, Nigerian artists quickly joined in the swelling crowds. Performances by musicians and actors were woven throughout the demonstration sites, giving the protests the feel of a music festival, according to one observer.[10] A broad sweep of performers, ranging from obscure acts to Fela's famous children, Femi and Seun, were regular participants in the protests.[11] Seun's presence gave the movement international visibility through his media interviews and written statements, in particular a critical essay published just days into the protests on the CNN website (Anikulapo-Kuti 2012).

Musicians composed songs mocking Jonathan and condemning the fuel hike, while street performers educated the public about the chronic governance problems in the country.[12] Indeed, artists helped transform the focus of the protests beyond the fuel hike towards a broader critique of the political system (Anikulapo-Kuti 2012). DJs played a broad selection from the past and the present, with Fela's 'Shuffering and Shmiling' proving especially popular alongside more contemporary songs such as 'Mr. President' by African China and 'Jagajaga' by Abdulkareem, all scathing critiques of Nigeria's governing class. In the Ejigbo neighbourhood, Jelili Atiku, a Lagos-based artist, performed 'Nigerian Fetish', a dramatic example of the highly political street performances that often accompanied the protests. Draped from head to toe in the green and white colours of the Nigerian flag in the manner of a traditional masquerade performer, Atiku adorned his body with dozens of placards demanding political reforms and marched through the streets accompanied by sign-waving children. Artists' involvement invoked the long history of musicians and performers serving at the front of popular movements in Nigeria, their commitment fuelling broader participation, especially among youth. Even the regime itself seized on the music as a way to dismiss the importance of the protests: President Jonathan claimed that it was not the politics but the performances that brought protesters out into the street (Odebode et al. 2012).

While artists brought crowds to the streets in a largely uncoordinated fashion, several civil society factions, each pursuing its own goals and strategies, struggled to position themselves within the protests. Moving quickly to capture the swelling popular outrage, these actors were able to impose a structure upon the movement, giving it a fearsome cohesiveness, at least initially. The two most prominent civil society factions were a loose coalition of pro-democracy groups known as the Save Nigeria Group (SNG) and Nigeria's robust labour unions.

Occupy Nigeria

The SNG was led by Pastor Tunde Bakare, an Evangelical Christian preacher and one-time colleague of the noted pro-democracy activist, Gawi Fawehinmi. Pastor Bakare had initially brought together a variety of individuals and groups in early 2010 with the goal of monitoring the 2011 election. With the crisis of leadership triggered by Yar'Adua's departure, Bakare outlined fourteen steps for ensuring a fair election, steps that resonated among voters still burnt by the experience of the 2007 election.[13] In the lead-up to the 2011 election, Bakare's group initiated a number of actions against perceived government malfeasance and recruited several prominent figures to its cause, most prominently Wole Soyinka, the Nobel Laureate. The group released a lengthy 'Contract to Save and Transform Nigeria', a major critique of almost every aspect of Nigerian politics. As President Yar'Adua's mysterious absence in Saudi Arabia grew longer, SNG organized 'Enough is Enough' protests to pressure the National Assembly to resolve the presidential crisis. Soyinka and other prominent Nigerian activists would address gatherings which rarely numbered more than a few hundred people, reflecting the inability of SNG to penetrate political society.

In January 2011, frustrated by his lack of progress, Bakare announced that he would stand as the running mate of the former military leader, Muhammadu Buhari, in the rapidly approaching election. Bakare's decision was met with outrage among both his supporters and the broader Nigerian public. But following his and Buhari's defeat by Jonathan in the April election, Bakare refocused his attention on SNG. He reoriented the group around an agenda for the broad transformation of Nigeria led by civil society. Having generated considerable attention with his electoral campaign, Bakare and SNG were thus among the best-organized groups ready to capitalize on the anger triggered by the fuel hike.

Bakare's group was not the only civil society actor primed for action. Following Jonathan's decision to cancel the fuel subsidy, the country's largest labour unions came together as the Joint Action Front (JAF) and announced that they would hold a protest rally on 3 January. The front was comprised of the powerful

Nigerian Labour Congress, a national federation of industrial unions founded in 1978 at the behest of the military government that still claims over four million members, and the Trade Union Congress, a federation of senior staff associations. A day later, JAF announced that it would begin a strike on 9 January that would last until the subsidies were reinstated. By 6 January, protests had spread to the national capital, Abuja. The Federation of Informal Workers' Organizations of Nigeria (FIWON), along with other civil society groups, organized rallies that shut down the capital.[14] Mass actions also spread to smaller towns and cities across the country – by some counts, over seventy locations saw protest during those days. On 9 January, the labour front began its nation-wide strike, bringing the economy to a halt.

Not to be outdone, Bakare and his allies within SNG also moved into action. Calling not only for a reinstatement of the subsidies but for the end of the Jonathan regime, SNG staged protests throughout Nigeria. Initially, SNG and JAF worked together, building on a history of cooperation between pro-democracy organizations and labour.[15] Though the moniker 'Occupy Nigeria' first arose in reference to the members of political society who started the nascent movement by taking to the streets, SNG and JAF quickly embraced it as the name for the burgeoning convergence of civil and political society.

Gani Fawehinmi Park, a dilapidated green space in the Ojota neighbourhood of Lagos, quickly became the central focus point of the movement, with many protesters dubbing it 'Freedom Park' after Cairo's Tahrir Square. However, tensions between the two key civil society forces flared over both logistical and ideological concerns (Ahiuma-Young 2012). Logistically, divisions over who would lead the movement emerged, with an especially vitriolic debate over the appropriate methods for the agitation. While labour openly sought to reduce the possibility of clashes with the regime, SNG embraced a more confrontational approach. Ideologically, labour leaders shied away from SNG's demands to go beyond a reduction of oil prices and calling for the overthrow of the Jonathan regime. SNG, which had slyly positioned itself as more in tune with

Occupy Nigeria

political society's rage, benefited from its maximalist demands, confrontational posture, and theatrical leadership. In contrast, labour leaders came across as overly conservative and were viewed by political society as too concerned with their own interests.

On 9 January, the day the strike commenced, these divisions split the movement. Finding Freedom Park occupied by SNG and its supporters within political society, labour leaders had little choice but to direct their followers to position themselves outside the crowded green. Instead of manning the frontlines of the protest, labour activists were instructed to focus on monitoring work places to ensure the strike order was being followed. Though an essential task, JAF leaders and members were annoyed that SNG had taken the most visible leadership position at the forefront of the massive protests.

The killing of a protester, Ademola Aderinto, by the police on 10 January quickly ratcheted up tensions with young members of political society, who made up the bulk of the protesters. Youth leaders promised 'to invade the [police] station and get our pound of flesh', before being talked down by neighbourhood leaders (Anofochi 2012). Far from an atavistic response, the youth call for violence articulated a clear structural critique of the justice system. 'Records show that the victims of extra-judicial killings in Nigeria never get justice', one explained to the media; 'We wanted to get justice for Ademola' (ibid.). Once the spectre of violence had been released, however, it would unravel the coalition in highly unpredictable ways.

Labour leaders had articulated concerns about the potential for a violent crackdown by the state. The Nigerian military had been deployed to quell the protests, and the presence of uniformed troops raised tensions, pushing labour organizers to hasten their backdoor negotiations with the regime (Sowore 2013). During one such meeting on the fifth day of the strike, Jonathan shared with labour leaders security reports that purported to show that Boko Haram, the country's violent Islamist insurgency, was intending to use the strikes and protests as cover for an assault against the regime. Jonathan's warning fitted a pattern. By playing on the legitimate fear of terrorism among the country's anxious working and middle classes by deploying the discourse of counter-terrorism, he was able to divide and undermine the protesters. Though several informants claimed that Boko Haram had declared a unilateral 'ceasefire throughout the duration of the protests', others took Jonathan's warning to heart, fearing, not without reason, that the religious and political elites who are thought to manipulate Boko Haram for their own ends might use the protests as cover for a violent settling of scores.[16]

Boko Haram's relationship to the protests is a challenge to tease out. Commonly framed as a radical movement seeking to impose sharia on the country, Boko Haram is equally a manifestation of the state's chronic inability to provide opportunities to its rural and peri-urban youth populations. Mohammad Yusuf, a Muslim cleric, founded the group in 2002 in the north-eastern city of Maiduguri and quickly drew followers from among the region's unemployed youth by speaking out against police violence, corruption, poverty, and poor governance. In 2009, after hearing reports of members accumulating weapons, the government brutally cracked down on the sect, killing at least eight hundred and pushing its leadership underground.

The state has tried to frame Boko Haram as an outside force, treating it as the tool of a transnational Islamist movement. Yet many Nigerian analysts understand it as the rural expression of the very same structural forces that give rise to urban protests (Kaci 2011; Kwaja 2011; *Sahara Reporters* 2012). For these analysts, Boko Haram is a direct product of a political system in which elites continually manipulate ethnic, class, and religious identities in order to sustain power at the local and national levels (Kwaja 2011). Defining what the 'authentic' position of Boko Haram was regarding the Occupy protests, therefore, is impossible to discern, as it is a product of often contradictory local, national and transnational forces. Protest organizers, especially those with SNG, did attempt to draw parallels between the struggles of the urban poor and the conditions that gave rise to Boko Haram (*Sahara Reporters* 2012). Others directly linked popular protest and armed violence, suggesting that ignoring the former would fuel the latter. As Gbenga Komolafe, general secretary of FIWON, put it in an interview: 'protests could erupt any time over a whole number of issues from the economic, political, developmental to security, and this would be the better scenario. The more ominous scenario is that of sectional armed insurrection already being foreboded by the Boko Haram violent armed campaign.'[17]

At the meeting with labour leaders, Jonathan reportedly agreed to reduce the price of oil by reinstating the fuel subsidy, but without specifying a price (Ahiuma-Young 2012). Within hours, labour leaders announced that they had accepted Jonathan's offer, and, without consulting other civil society groups, let alone political society, they called off the strike with immediate effect. On Monday 16 January, Jonathan gave a nation-wide address during which he committed himself to reducing the price of fuel from N138 to N97 – a significant reduction, but still far from the N65 per litre price that was in place prior to the removal of subsidies. Jonathan's announcement was received to the chagrin of labour leaders who felt duped by the government's manoeuvres.

SNG and the young members of political society decided to push ahead with the general uprising. But without support from labour, and with the army moving into Freedom Park and other neighbourhoods, the protests petered out in their second week (Ogunseye 2012). The decision by labour to cancel the strike was met with outrage from a broad section of protesters who felt that, at the very least, 'Bolder unionists would have insisted that the president listened to the voices of Nigerians and revert the pump price of petrol to the pre-January 1, 2012 price of N65 per litre', as one of the less severe critics put it (Ahiuma-Young 2012). Others took a harsher tone, suggesting that labour 'scuppered the protests by selling out to the government', in the words of one organizer, giving voice to a common assessment among non-labour informants.[18]

Labour's acquiescence and willingness to engage with the regime, even against the wishes of their allies in the protest movement, can be illuminated by a glance back at the origins of the Nigerian Labour Congress (NLC), the coalition of unions at the forefront of the protests. Under military rule in the 1960s, political parties and communal associations were banned. Nigerian trade unions emerged instead as the most potent site of autonomous resistance to government power, reassuming the role they had occupied during the anti-colonial struggle. Fearing their prowess, the military regime of Yakubu Gowon worked to curtail labour activities. In 1969, his regime placed a ban on union strikes, which was repeatedly defied. In response, Gowon sought to demobilize Nigerian labour by separating industrial unions from professional staff associations and placing them under the ambit of the government-controlled NLC. Though initially unsuccessful, by 1978, the NLC emerged as the sole central labour organization, with authority over the 1,000 previously autonomous unions that were reorganized into forty-two industrial unions. Under subsequent administrations, the NLC gained a chequered reputation for its close relationship with various dictatorships and lacklustre support for the pro-democracy movement.

Despite efforts to centralize control of labour within a single organization, the NLC did not always command the loyalty of all of its members. Serious disagreements between its national command and state councils were a regular feature of labour activism. Following the annulment of the 1993 elections, for example, the NLC coordinated a crucial national strike that mounted considerable pressure on the interim government, only to cancel it three days later to the shock of most working-class Nigerians. Accusations of bribery of the top NLC leadership were rife (Ihonvbere 1997: 80–5). This pattern of confrontation and collusion with the regime came to define the labour movement at least until Abacha's crackdown on union activity during the mid-1990s, which spurred NLC leaders to seek a more autonomous position. The NLC's behaviour also had the effect of splintering the labour movement as newer unions, like the Civil Service and Technical Workers Union (CSTWUN) and the Nigerian Union of Petroleum and Natural Gas Workers (NUPENG), adopted more radical positions against the wishes of the NLC leadership.

Occupy Nigeria

During the transition to democracy in 1999, the NLC was initially proud of its closeness to the Obasanjo regime and touted its ability to negotiate effectively with the new government. Yet Obasanjo's repeated manipulation of oil prices and his efforts at claiming a third term soured the council's enthusiasm, and so the relationship deteriorated substantially. In 2004, following the decision by the federal government to increase fuel prices again, the NLC organized a series of nation-wide strikes within the oil industry. The government tried to prevent the strikes and even arrested the NLC president, Adams Oshiomole. But the strikes continued and the NLC proved itself an increasingly independent force within Nigerian political life. Suspicions about the motives of labour leaders nevertheless lingered, arising again in the 2012 protests.

In interviews, key leaders of the labour movement repeatedly cited the impossibility of the radical political transformation called for by the Occupy movement's leadership as the justification for their decision to call off the strike. They worried that, by seeking near-revolutionary change, SNG and political society would initiate a violent backlash that would set progressive forces back even further. For example, Denja Yaqub, an assistant secretary of the NLC, offered the following analysis:

> There were no achievable political issues because even if some groups among the civil society groups advocated for system change, some among them were louder with the agitation for regime change. These are two different things. And in Nigeria, we all know we don't have the organization capabilities to achieve such demands. We don't even have an alternative that is popular and acceptable to all the groups in the opposition. We lack ideological coherence and clarity to pursue such demands.[19]

In a separate interview, Abiodun Aremu, the secretary of the Joint Action Front, reaffirmed this analysis, contrasting Nigeria's protests with those of Egypt:

> There was nothing different in the mass character of the

Jan. 2012 protests than previous massive protests [in Nigeria] other than the international profiling and public expectations that it would have gone in the direction of the so-called Arab Spring. The misplaced assumption about the gathering by local and international media ... showed a clear misconception of the concrete realities ... across the country. Hence the errors being committed by many in correlating the political power contestation in Tahrir Square, Egypt with the [January 2012] mass assemblage that posed no real political threat to the neoliberal puppet government in Nigeria.[20]

Aremu continued by arguing that 'system change' is the real goal of the JAF and that 'mass resistance is our vehicle to attain it'. He suggested that the structural advantages possessed by the Nigerian state – including its military prowess and rising global economic status – prevented Occupy Nigeria from posing a genuine threat.

While labour leaders claimed that the absence of a common platform and the lack of awareness regarding the structural challenges facing the movement limited the effectiveness of the protests, other interviewees focused on labour's own shortcomings. For many, the willingness of labour leaders to negotiate directly with the Jonathan regime without consulting their partners within the broader Occupy Nigeria movement was in line with labour's historic proximity to government power. Ogaga Ifowodo, a Nigerian author who was a student leader and former acting head of the Civil Liberties Organization, offered this assessment:

> I believe that the protest not only failed but set the left, the progressive movement, back a great deal. Just when the coalition of forces had successfully taken control of the streets, particularly in Lagos where it matters most, the labour movement (the Nigerian Labour Congress and the Trade Union Congress) behaved true to its more recent history in similar circumstances and betrayed the public's confidence. The moment they began negotiating with the government, everyone feared the worst. And the worst indeed came to pass when they demobilised

the forces arrayed in the streets by asking them to go home to recharge – or some such inane idea.[21]

The convergence of political society, civil society, and artists that constituted the movement was forced to rely on labour's organizing prowess to achieve its national reach. Yet, as the government intervened in the protests, seeking to pick apart the fragile coalition, the gaps between the objectives and strategies of political society, SNG, and labour proved too large to bridge. Beyond the recriminations levelled against each side, the relative ease with which the government was able to undercut the protests points to the challenges facing any future popular movement in the country.

The aftermath of Occupy

Though the protests did not effect substantive structural transformations, Nigerians heralded the movement for a variety of reasons. Beyond the fact that Occupy was among the largest popular protests in the country's history, what impressed many was the extraordinary diversity of participants. Conventional wisdom about Nigeria suggests that the country's nearly four hundred distinct ethnic communities and deep regional and religious cleavages inhibit truly popular movements from taking hold. Though civil society actors like the NLC and SNG were key in organizing the protests, they comprised a relatively small portion of the actual protesters, the bulk of whom were drawn directly from political society, comprising a wide range of citizens across generations, ethnicities, religions, and regions. Nigerians in the diaspora also carried out demonstrations in solidarity at Nigerian embassies around the world, illustrating the global appeal of the movement and its potential for forming transnational alliances.

Most significantly, the movement was able to stretch beyond the major urban centres of Lagos and Abuja, spreading across the country into smaller cities and towns and forging novel alliances. For example, some of the most strident protests that continued even after the Lagos protests died out were held in the northern city of Kaduna. Kaduna, a city of a little over half a million people, is perhaps most famous for its recurring bouts of Muslim–Christian violence. Yet organizers were able to muster a multi-religious coalition that brought together an unexpected assortment of religious leaders and human rights activists (*Daily Post* 2012; Sowore 2013).

Artists did much to ensure the mass character of the protests, relentlessly offering arguments that prodded political society to think beyond the fuel subsidy and focus on the failure of the state to improve living conditions. After labour called off the strike, artists returned to the vanguard, working to ensure that the movement did not end after the streets were cleared.[22] Less than ten days after the end of the protests, Wole Soyinka addressed a town hall meeting in Lagos. 'A new citizenship spirit has emerged', he told the crowd, declaring that 'the organisation and spontaneity of the protests is worthy of being adopted by other countries' (Oladesu 2012). While the protests have subsided for now, Nigerian artists continue to nurture this spirit of resistance. While their position within the country's unique mélange of social forces may not always be recognized, they will continue to play a central role in fostering oppositional political imaginations and pointing the way for movements yet to come.

Many informants shared their belief that the protests would arise again. Pointing to a common pattern of dysfunction that afflicts African countries, Chido Onumah, a journalist based in Lagos, suggested that, despite the protests, the government has yet to take seriously the demands made by the movement and should expect further uprisings: 'Africa's youthful population are getting radicalized by the persistent levels of underdevelopment and the seeming gross incompetence of the ruling elites to address the challenges.'[23] Indeed, many view conditions on the ground as ripe for another outburst from within political society. As Ayodele Olofintuade, a writer who organized protests in Ibadan, put it, 'Nigeria is presently sitting on a keg of gunpowder that the most innocuous thing can trigger'.[24] Most informants viewed another outbreak of popular action as a necessary disruption to continued political and economic malaise. 'The future of popular protest in Nigeria is the future of Nigeria,' one participant explained, 'We know the price of what we desire and we shall be ready to pay it. No matter the shortcomings of the last [protest], we can only get better.'[25]

6 | Political walking in Uganda

A screaming came across the sky, as MiG fighter jets buzzed the tops of Kampala's green hills, leaving behind long trails of inexplicably orange smoke. 'Perhaps they're going to crash?' one lecturer remarked, ducking as the jets zoomed down over Makerere University. Nothing of the sort – the government's blatant display of power over the city's two million inhabitants went off without a hitch, a capstone to the brutal military force used to crush the urban protests that had rocked the country for the previous month.

The fighters were a mocking display of state impunity. The government of President Yoweri Museveni had, without debate or approval, spent $740 million on the planes, a significant chunk of the entire yearly national budget. This in a country where hospitals and clinics are regularly without power or running water, let alone drugs or doctors, where youth unemployment is around 80 per cent, and where malnutrition stalks the expanding slums. While its people suffer under a breakdown of social services and livelihoods, the Museveni regime expands its military force – which the state then uses when the people rise up to protest their deprivation.

Indeed, it was another five years of Museveni's rule that the MiGs' maiden flight was celebrating. Uganda's third multiparty presidential election had been held in February 2011, and 12 May was inauguration day. The ceremony itself was being put on at a cost of several million dollars – again over denunciations by activists and media – and a number of African state leaders were in town to congratulate Museveni on winning his fourth term as president. Added to his unelected time at the helm from 1986–96, it made a quarter-century in power and the promise of at least five more years.

113

In the midst of the state-orchestrated celebration, however, news started to filter up from Entebbe airport, twenty miles to the south. Kizza Besigye, the main opposition presidential candidate and catalysing figure of the recent protests, was on a flight back from Nairobi, where he had gone for medical treatment two weeks earlier after having a canister of pepper spray emptied into his eyes by a state security agent. Now he was making his return, and huge crowds came out to line the road between Entebbe and Kampala to welcome him back. After landing and struggling past airport security, Besigye set off for Kampala, and a one-hour drive stretched out to eleven as the jubilant crowds swelled and riot police and military tried to scatter them with tear gas, bullets, and armoured vehicles.

As Besigye's car crept closer to Kampala and the roads filled with throngs of people, many of Kampala's residents wondered aloud if the country would see a second inauguration that day. Would Besigye declare himself president in front of tens – or hundreds – of thousands of supporters? Would the government be able to crush an uprising that large? Would it be a Tahrir Square moment for Uganda, the overthrow of a dictator through peaceful mass action, the culmination of the urban uprising known as 'Walk to Work' that had shaken Uganda to its roots over the last month?

None of this was to be. Besigye finally made it to Kampala, only to give a speech and go home. The crowds dispersed, and Besigye's return, instead of being the climax to what had perhaps been the most important unarmed opposition movement of post-independence Uganda, revealed only the movement's political exhaustion. The large-scale protests were over, opposition leaders were arrested, and Kampala became a 'garrison city', in which an expansive network of informants and infiltrators represents the hidden side of a security regime whose visible side occupies every open space – parks, roundabouts, major roads – in a permanent deployment of riot police and armoured vehicles.

While it lasted, however, Walk to Work presented a fundamental challenge to understandings of politics in contemporary Uganda. The movement managed to achieve a unique, though tenuous, convergence between urban political society and civil society and between different ethnic groups and regions around a set of political and economic demands. Walk to Work had demonstrated the continued possibility of non-violent political change in Uganda while also illuminating the obstacles that any movement would have to overcome to realize that change. The protest movement had shown one way out of the dilemmas of national politics in Uganda, igniting imaginations as had not happened since the National Resistance Movement (NRM) took power – before the uprising itself fell victim to those very dilemmas, fragmenting into particularized constituencies without a common vision for progressive political change in the country.

The dilemmas of Ugandan politics

For the significance of the 2011 protests to be clear, they need to be framed within the broader and long-standing dilemmas structuring Ugandan politics over the previous decades. One place to start is with a brief account of the three national questions that have largely defined the context of post-colonial Ugandan politics: the Northern question, the Buganda question, and the Asian question. All three national questions are the legacy of colonial indirect rule and the politicization of ethnicity and race on which it was founded (see Mamdani 1976; Gingyera-Pinycwa 1989; Branch 2011; Golooba-Mutebi 2011). The sitting NRM government has built its power on managing these questions through a blend of co-optation and force. Together, they pose serious dilemmas for any effort to challenge the NRM's hold on power.

The Northern question emerged from Uganda's post-colonial regional politics. From independence in 1962 until 1986, Uganda was ruled by leaders from northern ethnic groups despite the fact that the south of the country, and in particular the Buganda region where Kampala is located, was the seat of economic and social power. Resentment by southerners against what they saw as a quarter-century of northern dictatorship gave rise to the Northern question: how to end northern domination and bring the north into a more inclusive national political arrangement. This resentment helped spur the southern-based National Resistance Army (NRA), led by Museveni, to victory in 1986 after a five-year guerrilla war.

Once in power, the NRM gave its answer as to how to deal with the north: crush its military power and eradicate its political capacity to mount a coherent challenge to the NRM state. In the north of the country, NRM power took the form of a counter-insurgency state, as a series of brutal civil wars erupted and the northern populations found themselves subject to social and economic devastation for over twenty years. The result is that today the Northern question has itself taken a new shape: how to deal with that legacy of state violence and how to reincorporate the north politically and economically into the country so as to prevent armed violence from being seen by northerners as the only route to political change.

The Northern question and the Buganda question were closely linked. Although the core of Museveni's NRA came from the south-west of Uganda, it waged its guerrilla war in the central Buganda region and drew many of its rank-and-file fighters from there. The Baganda (the ethnic group that inhabits Buganda), though far from a majority, are the largest group in Uganda and had been privileged under British colonialism due to their centralized political organization under their 'king', the Kabaka. From the late colonial period onwards, therefore, the question of what Buganda's place should be within a national political structure loomed large. So too did the problem of the role of the Kabaka in regional and national politics, as well as a set of historical grievances of the Baganda. With independence, the Buganda question was effectively answered in practice through the repression of the Baganda by the succession of militarized northern regimes. In 1986, however, with the ascension of the NRM to power, the terms of national politics were suddenly reversed. Political power was now based in the south, held by a government that depended on a strong relationship with the Baganda and that saw a need to guard that relationship into the future.

The NRM's answer to the Buganda question thus was to manage the Baganda through a trickle of concessions – key among them the restoration of cultural kingdoms and the reinstatement of the Kabaka – and a delicate balancing act with the Baganda leadership. NRM power in the south was thus diametrically opposed to its long counter-insurgency in the north. In the south, the NRM built support through reconstruction, the guarantee of security, and the promise of future development. The NRM was able to expand its base and thus avoid having either to depend too much upon the Baganda or to capitulate to demands for Baganda privilege, which would have been deeply unpopular in the rest of the country. The challenge for any national opposition movement is to represent northern grievances and cultivate support in Buganda without alienating the rest of the country.

The third national question, the Asian question, originated in the economic privilege granted to the Asian population under colonialism, part of British efforts to prevent the emergence of an African nationalist bourgeoisie or cross-racial anti-colonial movements (Mamdani 1976). The result has been that, since colonialism, popular grievances over economic inequality have often been racialized, with the Uganda Asian community the scapegoat. Most dramatically, this led to Idi Amin's 1972 Asian expulsion. As Asians have been invited back by the NRM as part of the regime's effort to attract foreign investment, they have had to depend upon the regime for security (Hundle 2013). Reports of Asian business leaders providing financial support or services (including money-laundering) to the regime are common. Today, Asians are again targets of popular economic grievances, especially as the regime presides over increasing inequality. Urban popular protest has a strong tendency to degenerate into anti-Asian violence, as it has since the colonial period and as was seen most recently in the Mabira riots and the 2009 Buganda riots, discussed below. As the NRM business-political-military elite profits from widespread state corruption, the urban population grows more frustrated and resentful. In this situation, a racialized scapegoat is useful to divert attention from the state's role in economic deprivation. Any protest movement, therefore, would need to de-racialize and repoliticize economic grievances if it is to avoid another turn to anti-Asian violence.

The NRM state and political opposition

Recognizing the many centrifugal forces at work in Ugandan politics, Museveni gave little room to opposition. Once in power, his 'broad base' strategy co-opted most armed and unarmed opposition leadership, while the 'no-party' Movement system allowed political parties to exist but not to compete in elections (Mugaju and Oloka-Onyango 2000). Rural areas were key to Museveni's strategy as a bastion of votes and a counterweight to possible urban dissent. Under the NRM, customary rural authority was dismantled, and in its place a hierarchy of elected resistance councils was formed. The councils were soon transformed into components of the security apparatus, however, and a dense web of centrally appointed administrators and security personnel reached from the capital to the district headquarters down to the village. This rural administrative-security apparatus ensured that Museveni and the NRM continued to win the vote and prevented organized opposition. The 'broad base' was a powerful effort to forge support for the NRM throughout the country, whether by coercion, consent, or clientelism. Competing with that national structure presents a continuing challenge for any opposition force.

The political economy of the NRM state, as it was consolidated in the 1990s, was one of expansive corruption and donor dependence in the context of a neoliberal policy framework (Branch 2011: 80–7; Sjogren 2013). A military-political-business elite around Museveni emerged at the heart of the regime, which has held increasing power in the country ever since. Massive donor support, despite those donors' constant refrains of 'good governance', has only further enabled and exacerbated corruption. Since the mid-1990s, despite the corruption and abuse, Uganda has been a donor favourite and has enjoyed an influx of foreign aid amounting to 80 per cent of its development expenditures (Reno 2002).

The consistently high levels of donor support are the product of several factors. First, Uganda's reputation is tied strongly to

Museveni himself (Mwenda 2007; Tripp 2004). By the mid-1990s, he had been named by President Bill Clinton as one of the 'new leaders of Africa' who would lead the 'new African renaissance' that was dawning on the continent. Museveni has cultivated close personal relations with a number of European politicians and has managed to retain important political support from significant sections of the US establishment.

Uganda's reputation among donors has also been ensured by its image as a success story of economic neoliberalism. But, as has been the case in other countries undergoing neoliberal restructuring, the consequence in Uganda has been strong economic growth numbers alongside weak social services and deepening poverty (Bibangambah 2001: 128–9). These changes hit the swelling urban population particularly hard, contributing to the conditions for protest.

Uganda's willingness to engage in neoliberal reform played an important role in helping the government to ensure that any donor criticism of its human rights record or of its militarization would be short-lived. It has also ensured that Uganda would be able to continue to use donor funding at its own discretion, as donors are wary of doing anything that might threaten Uganda's reputation and put the efficacy of their own policies into doubt. The military budget is itself key to the consolidation of power: while donors extended their sway over most of the national budget, they left military expenditure under Museveni's discretionary control and thus available to the regime for its own ends. Despite donor complaints, in Mwenda's words, 'Museveni always won; the donors always lost' (2010: 50–1). The defence budget has consistently increased under Museveni, from $42 million in 1992, to $110 million in 2001, to $260 million by the end of the decade (2010). Therefore, as Mwenda and Tangri conclude, 'donor reforms have reinforced rather than reduced the propensity of political leaders to use the state and its resources to maintain themselves in power' (2005: 451). Museveni's enlistment in the war on terror, in particular his willingness to deploy Ugandan military in Somalia and to serve as the key regional security broker in Central African Republic,

Democratic Republic of Congo, and South Sudan, has made him even more indispensable to the US government. A statement on the United States Agency for International Development website leaves no doubt about the relationship: 'Uganda has been a model in the fight against HIV/AIDS, poverty reduction, and economic reform, and is a strong ally in the war against terrorism.'[1]

The year 1996 saw the first presidential elections under the NRM, which Museveni handily won. By the late 1990s, however, cracks were emerging in the NRM's machine caused by Ugandan involvement in the Congo war and accusations by Besigye, Museveni's former close ally from the guerrilla war, about NRM corruption. In the lead-up to 2001, Besigye broke with the regime and launched his own presidential campaign. Despite the significant support gained by Besigye, Museveni, with the state security apparatus at his disposal, again easily triumphed. In 2005, multiparty elections were reintroduced, and Besigye, whose brutal treatment after 2001 had forced him into exile, returned and stood for president under the Forum for Democratic Change banner. The 2006 election was marked by intense state violence against opposition supporters as well as the high-profile arrest and trial of Besigye on treason, terrorism, and rape charges. Besigye lost the election but garnered 37 per cent of the vote, winning Kampala and most of the north and east of the country, often by huge margins.

By the time of the 2011 elections, the Ugandan political landscape had taken on a distinctive hue. Museveni depended largely on rural areas for his votes, where opposition political parties were ineffective in organizing because of their own shortcomings and the state's security apparatus, which kept them restricted to urban areas. Organized labour, which played an important role in politics elsewhere in the region, was almost entirely absent in Uganda, restricted largely to transport associations and teachers' associations, which were subject to intense state control and intimidation. The main Kampala traders' association would play only a limited role in the protests. A substantial donor-funded civil society had emerged in Uganda, but one that had little interest or capacity to engage in politics. Donor pressure combined with state repression to keep NGOs from taking overtly political positions. Their mandates focused more on depoliticized development and governance than explicitly political issues, and the class interests of urban NGO employees made employment in civil society an opportunity for a secure middle-class lifestyle instead of a commitment to an oppositional or even liberal politics.

By 2011, Besigye, once again the candidate of the Forum for Democratic Change (FDC), could count on an enthusiastic following in urban areas, in particular Kampala. Every arrest would provoke demonstrations or small riots, and his rallies produced huge crowds. As the elections drew near, the opposition had a firm grip on the urban centres and benefited from a visceral anti-Museveni protest vote in the north and east. However, the violence and bribery accompanying almost every Ugandan election, the opposition parties' incapacity to build rural support, and the judiciary's refusal to impugn government vote-rigging all left the opposition increasingly despondent about its chances of capturing power through elections. Meanwhile, conditions in urban areas were increasingly explosive, as unemployment and inequality became more glaring in the face of the disjuncture between the celebratory rhetoric of good governance and the sordid reality of state corruption, social service collapse, police brutality, and disintegrating infrastructure.

The dilemmas that faced any protest politics, therefore, were stark. Protest would have to deal with a continued rural–urban divide, a dearth of organized labour, poorly organized political parties whose support was limited to urban areas, and an urban political society that was ready to take to the streets but had little capacity for a sustained presence or strategic action. It would have to address a northern region that seemed on the verge of another bout of armed conflict. It would have to deal with a swelling population of poor, frustrated Baganda youth in Kampala and other urban areas who rallied around the Kabaka and had the potential for rapid and violent political mobilization along ethnically chauvinist lines (Golooba-Mutebi 2011). It would also have to deal with a largely non-political civil society, a state which had managed to build support through expansive webs of corruption in which almost all formal political and economic institutions were complicit, and an economy and politics dependent upon the support of donors who continued to champion Museveni. Most threateningly, protest politics would have to deal with a highly militarized regime, one that depended upon a militarized police force and, in the extreme, upon the military itself to maintain order – a regime that did not hesitate to use violence against the population.

The first urban explosion would come in September 2009, when days of violent protests by Baganda, in particular Baganda youth, gave Museveni, according to Kalinaki (2009a), 'the biggest test of his career'. The 2009 Buganda riots demonstrated the fragility of the political settlement established by the NRM, but also revealed the need for political opposition to effectively address difficult national political questions in order to succeed.

The 2009 Buganda riots

As part of their divide-and-rule strategy against the Baganda, the NRM encouraged smaller communities to identify as distinct 'tribes' and to assert independence from the Kabaka. The Banyala had done so, and when the Kabaka announced a visit to the Banyala region in September 2009, the government refused him permission in the name of preventing conflict. When a representative of the Kabaka tried to visit on 10 September, he was blocked by security services. As news of this undignified treatment spread via radio, Baganda activists launched into action. That same day, protests exploded in Kampala and other urban centres throughout Buganda.

In Kampala, protests were sparked by a petty traders' march from Kampala's Kisekka market – which had a significant history of protest over recent years – to the State House. As Florence Brisset-Foucault makes clear, the protests were 'first and foremost a strike' (2014: 21), which quickly expanded into other modes of political action. As news of the march spread through Kampala's crowded markets and slums, Baganda activists erupted into the streets. Youth set up barricades, lit bonfires and, once the riot police and military had gone on the attack with tear gas, armoured vehicles, and live ammunition, counter-attacked with stones and whatever else was at hand, engaging in running battles. A police station was burned down, and, by 13 September, over forty civilians had been reportedly killed by security forces, over a hundred injured, and five hundred arrested (HRW 2012).

The protesters' often violent direct action had a number of dimensions, all ultimately tied to the defence of the Buganda kingdom against the NRM state. First, protest had an immediately anti-state dimension that focused on the state's security services, institutions, and agents. Police posts were burned, and individuals or businesses thought to be affiliated with the NRM were targeted for looting or beatings. Second, protesters intimidated or physically accosted those Baganda who were not visibly supporting the protests and thus were not good subjects of the Kabaka (Brisset-Foucault 2014). The protests represented a mode of internal ethnic discipline, marking the boundaries of and cleansing a 'genuine' Baganda community.

Third, violence was turned outwards against those ethnic and racial groups seen as aligned with the government. For many Kampala residents, especially non-Baganda, it was this often vicious pro-Baganda chauvinism of the riots that stood out. Stories abound of Baganda activists stopping people on the street, pulling them out of vehicles, and beating them if they spoke Luganda with an accent. Targeted also were those who could not sing the Buganda national anthem, or women wearing trousers instead of the dresses favoured as 'proper' Baganda clothing. The protesters homed in on two groups: those who supposedly looked as if they were Banyankole, members of Museveni's own ethnic group from the south west of the country; and Asians, seen as aligned with the NRM, whose shops were looted or burned down and many of whom, according to reports, were forced to seek refuge in police stations. Radio stations played a role in fanning the flames of the violence, which was given expression by popular songs from the period.

It was a violent populist cleansing of perceived moral corruption within the Baganda community and of the Buganda kingdom's perceived external enemies. An alternative political and social order was being imposed in the streets, one in which the true authority, the Kabaka, was returned to his rightful place above the Museveni regime, even if only temporarily.[2] In the process, protests spread outside Kampala and the division between urban and rural was tenuously overcome by appealing to Baganda ethnic commonality. Urban grievances among working, underemployed, and unemployed youth, who were subject to the heavy hand of NRM state power, found expression in Baganda identity. But overcoming the urban–rural divide through an appeal to ethnic belonging led to inter-ethnic conflict and a reinforcement of ethnic fragmentation. The urban was not a site for overcoming ethnic and racial divisions, as Fanon had hoped, but a place where rural ethnic divisions were been inserted into urban areas through an exclusivist ethnic discourse, with violence its consequence.

The state's response was to blame the violence on the opposition political parties. Museveni declared that 'these riots have been caused by the same opposition opportunistic elements using the Mengo [Buganda] Kingdom. … The security forces always contain those criminal actions' (*New Vision* 2009). Others who did not see a conspiracy saw the riots instead as 'mindless mayhem and predatory plunder posing under a thin veneer of politics' (Kalinaki 2009b). Some saw the riots as signalling a breakdown between the Baganda establishment and the NRM, but, in hindsight, this seems less germane, given that the NRM did well in rural Buganda in 2011. Instead, the key factor, as Nabudere (2009) pointed out, was the role of poor urban youth, who would escalate their violence, he argued, as long as the state continued to use force against them. As rural divisions were violently inserted into the dense urban setting, the protests represented urban grievances expressed through the language of ethnicity. Political society rose up but showed its internal divisions at the same time. In 2011, protests would draw on this same poor urban constituency, but would be able to overcome, at least tenuously, ethnic particularism and forge a national political agenda.

2011: planning for protest?

Things did not look good for the political opposition in the lead-up to the 2011 elections. The NRM government was funding Museveni's presidential campaign from state coffers and preventing the opposition from organizing in rural areas. The violence that had characterized the 2006 elections had lessened, and the government turned instead to an unprecedented campaign of bribery, often carried out publicly by the president himself, who would hand out fat envelopes and even fatter promises to thankful villagers. The north, a guaranteed opposition vote bank during the war, now, with peace, seemed open to voting for the NRM. Western donors made no sign of halting their twenty years of expansive support to the regime.

The opposition did little to help its own cause. A trumpeted 'Inter-Party Coalition' broke apart through squabbling. Besigye remained the only viable candidate, as others struck out on their own, relegating themselves to irrelevance. No clear agenda emerged beyond removing Museveni.[3] Besigye and the FDC would announce one day that the elections were rigged and pointless and the next day release poll numbers projecting Besigye's clear victory. In interviews during 2013, opposition leaders insisted that they knew they would lose but were participating so as to build party organization – a position that often sounded like sour grapes. Some claimed that the elections were 'just another opportunity to struggle for change', as MP Ssemuju Nganda phrased it, in particular to prepare for post-election protest, because 'it is easier to mobilize people through elections'.[4]

Whether or not it is true that the opposition participated in the elections strategically as a stepping-stone to popular protest, there certainly was talk of protest before the elections, especially with the unfolding of events in North Africa. When asked about his election strategy, Besigye declared that, instead of depending on courts for 'redressing electoral injustices', he was going to 'use the whole public to come up and demand that there is change' (*Daily Monitor* 2011f). He explained that he would 'support a popular protest against an illegitimate decision of the election', and that the inspector general of police, Major General Kale Kayihura, who had overseen an intensive militarization of the police forces, lacked the 'tools that could prevent a protest like the ones in Tunisia and Egypt' (*Daily Monitor* 2011l). MP Nganda emphasized, however, that, while protests in North Africa had encouraged them, they 'were not copying Egypt. ... This had been planned a long time back.'[5] Commentators meanwhile wondered if this was the calm before the storm, asking 'what plan B' the opposition had up their sleeve (Kalyegira 2011), referring often to the post-election violence in Kenya and to the 2009 Buganda riots.

The January overthrow of Ben Ali and Mubarak catapulted discussions of protest to the centre of public and political attention. Suddenly, Ugandans were asking the question reverberating throughout Africa at that time: Could it happen here? A vigorous debate ensued in the press and on the streets. Some cited similarities between Uganda and the North African countries: a long-standing dictator dependent upon security services for his power; high levels of unemployed youth; and corruption and state apathy making life increasingly difficult for the urban poor. Even Museveni's high poll numbers were taken as a sign of his unpopularity: as one columnist asked, 'how can a ruler tell when 60 or even 80 per cent "support" does not mean approval, but widespread despair?' (Tacca 2011a). As Francis Mwijukye, FDC youth leader and one of Besigye's closest companions, put it, Tahrir Square had shown the 'modern way of removing dictators'.[6]

Others, however, argued that the differences were too great: Uganda's ethnic heterogeneity, as opposed to Egypt's perceived homogeneity; Uganda's lower levels of urbanization and literacy; the weakness of opposition organization in Uganda compared to the strength of organization in Egypt, particularly by the Muslim Brotherhood; and, most ominously, Museveni's firm control over the military and in particular the special forces, which were led by his own son and which, many feared, would not hesitate to slaughter protesters if they posed any real threat to power.

The state reacted predictably to the protest talk. A couple of weeks before the elections, in the middle of the day, a long convoy of dozens of tear-gas vehicles, water cannons, armed personnel carriers, and other military equipment made its way into Kampala, paralysing traffic and making a spectacular show of the force that awaited protesters (*Daily Monitor* 2011q). When asked specifically about the North African protests, Museveni declared that anyone protesting would be jailed and that his own conscience was clear: 'There is not the slightest worry for me because I am a dictator buster. I am the biggest enemy of dictators' (*Daily Monitor* 2011r). A senior army officer explained 'how we shall deal with ringleaders during election violence if there is need to put them out of action. We shall shoot them from close range' (*Daily Monitor* 2011d). On the day of the election, the government went so far as to outlaw SMS messages that included any one of eighteen blacklisted words, including 'Egypt' or 'people power' (Biryaberema 2011).

In the midst of this escalating rhetoric, another factor crept in which would prove to be of great importance in the post-election uprising: inflation. By February 2011, food prices had soared by 20–40 per cent since the end of 2010, and the shilling was depreciating quickly *(Daily Monitor* 2011u). This was compounded by a drought and rising oil prices. The irony is that this inflation, according to reports, was partly an unintended consequence of the NRM's electoral strategy of wholesale bribery. It is hard to calculate just how much money entered the economy through bribes – or 'presidential donations' as they were called – but the 602 billion shillings (about $240 million) making up the supplementary budget passed in early January explicitly included $18 billion (about $7 million) for donations, which was in addition to a massive number of informal donations made during 'poverty tours' around the country over the previous year (*Daily Monitor* 2011e). Post-election reports declared that Museveni had spent a total of 500 billion shillings (about $200 million) on his reelection. External factors were at work as well, with the FAO food price index peaking in December 2010. Inflation would continue to skyrocket after the election, and the government's profligacy, rightly or wrongly, was widely seen as the cause.

Six *From casting ballots to political walking*

Election day, 18 February, saw what Kalinaki (2011a) called 'the most visible deployment of the military since the end of the Bush War [in 1986]'. Voter turnout hit its lowest point in Uganda's post-NRM history and was especially low in opposition areas. Violence, however, remained minimal, especially relative to previous elections. The results were as the NRM had predicted: Museveni won with 68 per cent, and Besigye lost ground from 2006, with only 26 per cent (*Daily Monitor* 2011a).

The NRM seemed to have firmly established the upper hand: the police and military remained in the streets throughout urban areas, and Kampala remained 'under siege' (Tacca 2011b). Donors endorsed Museveni's victory, and, despite reports of irregularities, there was no significant popular response. The opposition was wrong-footed, with uncoordinated messages from different leaders. On 24 February, opposition leaders came together and called on the people to exercise their 'sovereign power' and to demand new elections through peaceful protest (*Daily Monitor* 2011m). Museveni responded with one of the most memorable lines of the election season: when asked about Besigye's threatened protests, he responded, 'I will grab that one like a samosa, I will devour him like a cake' (*Daily Monitor* 2011g). However, only a handful of sporadic and quickly dispersed protests followed, most notably on 9 March in Kampala's Kisekka market and on 11 March in Jinja. People were simply not interested in protesting over the lost elections, and opposition leaders' calls had no traction.

The only hopeful sign for the opposition was the victory by opposition candidate Erias Lukwago in the Kampala mayoral race. On 23 February, the day of the mayoral election, a cache of ballot boxes holding pre-ticked ballots for the NRM candidate were discovered by opposition activists, and a brief flurry of protest forced the Electoral Commission to postpone the elections until mid-March. When the elections did occur, vigilance by Kampala's residents was so intense that the government was unable to rig the election as they had planned. Uganda's urban poor had achieved what swarms of Western 'election observers',

128

despite all their technology and funding, had never managed to accomplish. Lukwago won and immediately became the target of state intimidation and violence, starting with the tear-gassing of his victory convoy on 16 March.

By early April, as the election furore faded into the past, inflation continued to worsen dramatically, hitting double digits in March and continuing to rise in April and May. Fuel prices shot up, and food price inflation hovered around 30–40 per cent. One bunch of *matooke*, the green bananas that are the staple food in the south, increased in price from 9,000 shillings at the end of 2010 to 27,000–30,000 shillings in April 2011 (*Daily Monitor* 2011h). Even the World Bank, which liked to paint the Ugandan economy in rosy hues, admitted that almost a million Ugandans, mostly urban, had been forced back into poverty because of rising food prices (Kalinaki 2011c).

At this point, opposition leaders conceived their one brilliant idea. On 6 April, Besigye announced the formation of a 'pressure group' called Activists for Change, or A4C. Made up of a cross-section of political opposition leaders, A4C called upon 'middle-class' Ugandans to walk to work in order to, in the words of leader Anne Mugisha, 'show solidarity with the increasing number of people who have joined the ranks of hundreds of thousands of poor Ugandans that walk to work every day ... [who] can no longer afford the soaring price of fuel for their cars or the rising taxi and *boda-boda* fares. An increasing number of Ugandans cannot afford even one meal a day.'[7] That was the stroke of genius: to put food prices and increasing poverty at the centre of the agenda, articulated by an ostensibly independent activist group, instead of the tired message of election rigging centred around polarizing opposition politicians. A daily routine engaged in by Kampala's swelling population of poor – walking to work – was appropriated by Activists for Change and turned into a devastating critique of the regime.[8] They would not ask people to take to the streets, but, rather, they would take to the streets themselves in the name of solidarity. Once there they were sure that they would be confronted with the predictable brutal police overreaction, which, ideally, would bring forth large crowds and significant attention.

As expected, police responded in character to the announcement of Walk to Work. Kayihura denounced walking to work as a violation of the constitution. He declared that he had 'reliable intelligence that, rather than a peaceful walk, there are plans of disrupting normal life within Kampala city, creat[ing] chaos and mak[ing] the capital city, and by extension, the country, ungovernable' (*Daily Monitor* 2011o). He accused Besigye and others of 'political walking', illegal without police notification and permission, and of intending to create Uganda's own Tahrir Square (quoted in Mamdani 2011). As political activist Margaret Wokuri asked, 'I am walking, and you arrest me? And you tell me to apply for bail? For what? It was absurd.'[9] Indeed, the NRM did sound somewhat ridiculous in its rhetorical and legal gymnastics in distinguishing regular walking from political walking.

There was no humour to the police response in the streets. From the very first day of the protest on 11 April, the state brought brutal violence down on those who dared to walk to work. Opposition leaders were arrested en masse, and those who came to join the walkers were met with the usual storm of riot police, armed vehicles, tear gas, and bullets. April became a blur of escalating protests and intensifying police and military crackdowns. Walk to Work almost immediately went far beyond anything the opposition had anticipated – as Mwijukye admitted, the FDC 'never called people to the streets'.[10] The reason for the success of Walk to Work was precisely because the protests were not about the political opposition, but about living conditions and then about an expanding list of grievances. This is key to understanding the protests' resonance and also their ultimate decline.

By mid-April, as protests raged throughout the country, it started to appear that a national urban uprising was under way such as Uganda had not seen for decades. Monday and Thursday were established as Walk to Work days. On those days, a few local political figures would begin walking, only to be met by a swarm of police. The radio, heard constantly in the shops and roadsides of urban Uganda, would announce opposition leaders having been arrested. This would bring large numbers of people into the streets, and running battles would erupt, involving stone-throwing, erecting barricades, and physical clashes between police and protesters. *Boda-boda* drivers, atop their ubiquitous motor-cycle taxis, were often at the frontlines of the protests and would ferry information and people from zone to zone. Protesters often managed to get the upper hand for hours, their barricades of burning tyres or vehicles keeping the police at bay. In other cases, state violence was so overwhelming that people had no choice but to run for cover. In many cases, people would take action on their own, blocking roads, rallying workers out of their shops into the streets, and mobilizing through informal networks.

In the face of the protests, Museveni still refused to budge. Even as neighbouring countries reduced fuel prices to avoid protest, the president declared that rising prices were due to international factors and that the solution was for Uganda to build an oil refinery. He proclaimed that higher food prices were a boon for farmers and that subsidies were out of the question. The government made it clear that it wanted a contest of force. It was under no illusion as to the threat it faced: a week into the protests, the military was deployed in and around Kampala. Bystanders became targets: in one shocking episode, the police tear-gassed a primary school and shot live bullets into a second-ary school, justifying their actions by explaining that protesters had used the students as 'human shields' (*Daily Monitor* 2011b). Journalist Gerald Bareebe reports being warned by a military officer that, 'If we accidentally shoot and kill a journalist, it is not our crime' (*Daily Monitor* 2011k).

The death toll mounted in towns throughout the country. The injured flooded the hospitals, and hundreds of others were carted off to prison (HRW 2011). Kampala and other urban areas looked like a war zone. On 15 April, Makerere University students joined in, launching a massive strike against a doubling of tuition fees, which resulted in a military occupation of the campus and over seventy students injured.[11] The brutal crackdown, however, provoked even more opposition: as one informant put it, 'the regime killed people to send a message, to try to kill off the protests. But that plan backfired.'[12] Violence not only brought more people into the streets, but also, in an unprecedented development, wider sections of Ugandan society vocally gave their support to the demands being made by political society.

Unity through tear gas

At the heart of the protests was political society – poor dwellers of Kampala's often informal slum neighbourhoods. Some were employed, while others were unemployed, informally employed, or working in petty trades. Some lived where they worked, while others had to commute long distances every day from the edge of town, all suffering badly under Kampala's neoliberal urbanization and the breakdown in public services, infrastructure, and livelihoods, as well as under the expansion of the highly militarized police force. During a discussion with street-level political activists in a furniture workshop in 2013, they explained that there was broad support and participation within the community for the protests, reaching far beyond Besigye supporters. Even if everyone did not take to the streets themselves, a large majority, they declared, supported the protests directly and indirectly. This was because everyone felt abandoned by the government and everyone was experiencing hunger as a result of rapidly rising prices. Even national hospital workers, the activists said, came down into the streets.[13] Indeed, despite all that been promised by the government during the elections, afterwards things only got worse. In another discussion, a group of drivers sitting in their 'office' – a couple of sheets of corrugated iron on wooden poles on the side of the street – described in similar terms the diversity of motives that brought people to protest and agreed that 'everyone', except those few who were profiting from the high inflation or from NRM connections, was involved in one way or another in the protests.[14]

Uganda's political society, fraught with multiple divisions, was by no means homogeneous. We have discussed ethnicity, in particular the possibility of violent pro-Buganda activism dividing political society from within, but a number of other lines of cleavage also require consideration. For instance, there was an important generational aspect to participation in protest, given the widespread perception that many older Ugandans who remembered the bloody upheavals of the pre-NRM period would rather let Museveni stay in power than risk another descent into fratricidal civil conflict and insecurity – a caution absent from the younger, post-NRM generation. Other ethnic divisions cut through Kampala's political society from within, as did lines of religion, residence, party affiliation, informal versus formal residence status, and employment. Divisions were present between more recent migrants and longer-established residents, between those who had managed to negotiate some benefits with the state through local government and those who were excluded from any privileges, those who had a stake in the vast networks of state corruption and those looking on from the outside. All these require further investigation in order to discern the composition and meaning of today's popular politics in Kampala and in Uganda. In the case of Walk to Work, the movement's novelty resided in the widely heard sentiment that the protests went beyond political party affiliation and that they were immune from the glaring ethnic and racial divisions that had characterized previous bouts of popular protest.

Organizational questions surrounded the protests from the beginning. Participants insisted on their ability to take to the streets without outside direction, but they also recognized the weakness of their mobilization. The drivers, for instance, declared that there was 'no organization in the community', no one planning day-to-day actions, and, in fact, no organization even as the protests continued. This prevented the protesters from succeeding, they thought, as it allowed state violence to be effective. This lack of organization was remarked upon by opposition activists as well. One young activist who had been involved in the very beginning of the organization for Walk to Work explained that those who had pushed for education and organization in the early days of the protests were ignored, which then allowed the protests to degenerate into a contest of force.[15]

These misgivings were the product of hindsight, however; at the time of the protests, excitement and hope reigned in the streets. For many in political society, the protests were their chance finally to bring about change. People threw themselves into what they saw as a revolutionary uprising, their objective being to overthrow Museveni and the NRM. Others may have been content with a lowering of prices, and others still were participating out of more nebulous motivations, a combination of rage and desire to take some concrete action against the state. Many were saying 'enough!' and were committed to an all-or-nothing effort. It seems that ideas about change remained fluid and often undefined, hopes rising and falling with the fortunes of the protests and the government response. The men in the furniture workshop expressed their motivation unequivocally. Their hope, they said, was that the protests would topple the government: 'After what happened in Egypt, and then in Libya, we thought it was possible to do [that] here.'[16] Over and over again, people spoke of their excitement, the giddy hope that the government was finally going to be changed at its highest levels.

Political society had been involved in protests and riots before, but those typically lasted only a matter of hours or days and had been confined to Kampala. Walk to Work managed to overcome the internal divisions within political society for the first time, in particular ethnic and regional divisions. This allowed it to become a truly national movement and continue for several weeks, bringing together a wide array of different social and political forces behind a common set of grievances.

As the police reaction became increasingly brutal and the government's public response more callous, what had started as a popular protest over food and fuel prices became accessible to civil society activists. Civil society – political elites, media, NGOs, religious leaders, academics, and professional associations – got on board and began supporting the protesters' grievances and speaking out against state violence. The media were suddenly full of statements by NGOs and religious groups calling on the government to remedy high food prices and to end its brutality. Anti-corruption campaigns also became more vocal, as the million-dollar presidential swearing-in ceremony and the $740 million fighter jets were held up as powerful symbols of state corruption and impunity.

As civil society's involvement expanded further, so did their demands, coming to include vocal protests against arbitrary arrest, state militarization, corruption, and violations of the rights to free assembly, speech, and association. The Uganda Law Society, for instance, which had roundly condemned the 2009 protests, now came out in protest itself, declaring a three-day strike against government violence and the 'political abuse of the judiciary', calling on the Chief Justice to initiate dialogue on the protests and the cost of living (*Daily Monitor* 2011j). Even the donors came out with statements against the government crackdown. For the first time, a set of demands were laid out that could appeal to Ugandans broadly, that had deep legitimacy, and that entailed an ever-sharper critique of the government, but that did not require open support of the opposition political parties. Museveni's response was to refuse to deviate from his position that the government would not do anything about prices and would deal with protesters without mercy, frequently congratulating Kayihura on the crackdown. His declarations enabled the opposition to focus popular grievances ever more intensely on the regime and on Museveni in particular.

Indeed, Walk to Work marked the first time when Uganda's civil society allied itself, however tentatively, with popular protest. This alliance was only possible because of the apparently non-partisan nature of the grievances and the overwhelming brutality of the security services. Again, the key to this convergence was the fact that the protests' focal point was not the elections. Prominent figures in the opposition were important at the beginning of the campaign, in particular because their physical presence brought people into the streets. However, these individuals were able to spark such a massive response because they did not present themselves as opposition politicians, and because they articulated grievances that those in Uganda's civil society could buy into. In a complex dynamic, what had started among a small section of political party leadership soon became an uprising by political society, which then gained the support of a broader section of civil society.

Civil society's involvement was limited from the beginning, however, by its self-proclaimed 'non-political' character.[17] Civil society activists were always anxious to establish their distance from the realm of politics as a whole. A good example was a march by women banging empty saucepans in protest over food security, unemployment, health, and education. Some prominent women opposition political leaders were involved, but the organizers were careful to declare that it was 'not a politically motivated march' (*Daily Monitor* 2011v).[18] The Kampala City Traders' Association (KACITA) announced a five-day strike over inflation but added that 'we don't want people to politicize our pending strike and that is the reason why we choose not to participate in the walk-to-work protests' (*Daily Monitor* 2011c). The immediate causes for civil society's recoil from politics can be found in the sector's dependence upon donor support and the restrictive NGO laws operative in Uganda. However, as discussed below, it also reflects a deeper weakness at the heart of the Walk to Work movement, as it helped prevent a substantive political vision from being articulated and determined the direction the protests would take.

In short, opposition party involvement was necessary to kick-start the protests – but transcending the parties was also necessary if the protests were going to last. Izama (2013) writes that the protests 'injected a freshly imagined appeal to change or transformation outside elections, and happened in spite of the opposition'. This is true in that the protests lasted as long as they did because they managed to go beyond the opposition. However it misses the point that, without the actions of a handful of opposition leaders, the grievances would not have taken form in massive street protests. The political parties, and a few key politicians in particular, remained the only agents capable of generating popular political mobilization. But that mobilization will have to go beyond the parties if it is ever to effect a substantive transformation.

The Walk to Work convergence provided novel answers to the foundational national questions of Ugandan politics, pointing towards ways to resolve them inclusively. First, by making the government the object of economic grievance, the Asian question did not arise to derail popular political mobilization. Even at its most chaotic, Walk to Work never turned into anti-Asian violence. Despite weeks of intense protesting and rioting, Asians and Asian shops were not targeted as they had been in almost every previous protest. As Mpuuga put it, 'people are now relating economic conditions to governance. ... They see bad governance is keeping them poor'.[19] The focus on state corruption and mismanagement was a step forward towards a national, inclusive opposition political agenda, as it prevented economic grievances from being focused on Asians while absolving the state of responsibility.

The protests also had an unprecedented cross-ethnic character. The Buganda chauvinism of 2009 largely disappeared, while the Buganda leadership stayed remarkably silent during the protests, revealing their own parochial political limitations. Street-level participants in 2011, some of whom had themselves been in the 2009 Buganda riots, insisted that Walk to Work was not a Baganda issue at all, but rather that it involved everyone equally and that the NRM was trying to split the opposition by labelling the protests a Baganda problem.[20] The protests suggest that it is the Baganda elite and NRM establishment who had an interest in projecting the threat of an ethnically exclusivist, potentially violent urban Baganda population. When it came to the Baganda poor themselves, they seemed to have little problem throwing themselves into an inter-ethnic movement.

The protests also had an unprecedented national character. Protests erupted in almost all regions of Uganda and nowhere showed tendencies to ethnic chauvinism. The north in particular was involved in the protests, with Gulu town, the main urban centre, seeing substantial violence. The political grievances that arose out of the NRM's vicious treatment of northern populations since 1986 thus remained and provided a reservoir of resistance ready to be channelled by political opposition. In Teso, protests erupted but were repressed by military officers.[21] The protests revealed the possibility of political alliances between the north and the south, based upon a convergence in the conditions faced by both. Indeed, the military occupation of Kampala and other urban areas made clear the new national political alignments. Whereas in the first two decades of NRM rule, only the north had faced a regime of violent state repression, by 2011, that militarized rule had been expanded to urban areas throughout the country.

The opening and closing of political possibility

The Walk to Work uprising brought together a broad array of forces and individuals with different objectives, from economic reform to revolution, focused around a common critique of the NRM state. People had mixed and fluid motivations, and many surely joined without having explained their involvement entirely even to themselves. This uncertainty means that protests can represent a window of opportunity, a time of political possibility when new ideas can catch fire and old modes of thought can be discarded. Those who take to the streets to protest fuel prices may become revolutionaries. New political leaders, with new visions, may rise to national prominence and steer huge crowds of people, while those who helped spark protest are pushed to the side.

Organization and association can arise through a variety of routes and can steer protest in new directions, sustain it, and give rise to the narratives that people tell themselves to explain their own participation. In short, protest is a realm of contingency, creating new possibilities from the seemingly impossible and rendering the political field briefly, but radically, open. The meaning of protest itself can be created through the process of protest. As Mamdani wrote at the time, Walk to Work 'presents us with a challenge. That challenge is to come up with a new language of politics, a new mode of organization, and a new mode of governance' (2011).

No one, however, stepped up to meet that challenge. The parties remained focused on their own advancement, while no one from outside the parties would engage in politics beyond demands for lower prices and an end to police brutality, along with a critique of corruption. As the protests built up steam, no organization and no prominent individual aside from party leaders was willing to actually take to the streets in the Walk to Work protests. A few small, orderly civil society demonstrations were staged, but always on the margins and always, as noted, within an explicitly 'non-political' framework. Ugandan civil society made clear its lack of political responsibility. At no time in April were NGO leaders, church leaders, or business associations seen walking.

The only people ready to take political responsibility and pay the price, often with their own bodies, were political society and the leaders of the opposition parties. These party leaders can be criticized for bickering and being self-interested and opportunistic, but, during the key month of April, no other potential leaders took to the streets to join the protests. It is also important to note that no new leaders or sustained organization emerged from within political society itself to take the reins or voice a popular political agenda. The result was that individual party leaders remained central to the protests, and so the protests became more and more about those leaders, in particular Besigye himself. As the protests focused on the physical presence of Besigye, he and those around him had no problem becoming the centre of the protests; but once there, they were unable to go beyond their old agendas. The result, as one activist put it, was that 'once the protests were around just one man, they were fated to die out'.[22]

For some sectors of civil society, such as KACITA, their position of supporting the protesters' grievances without walking with them was clearly opportunistic. However, the failure of civil society in general to join the popular protests – not just in failing to take to the admittedly very dangerous streets, but in failing to engage with or help organize the communities that were throwing themselves into the protests to demand their dignity – reflected a more deep-seated political problem on its part. While the political parties were in the streets, all other forces and factions were self-righteously denouncing the parties while proclaiming themselves to be above 'politics', thereby displaying the often anti-democratic character of Uganda's civil society.

The entire responsibility and initiative remained with the handful of opposition leaders, who did nothing to transcend their past political limitations nor to take advantage of the opportunity to organize the communities that were rising up against the government. The protests were far beyond anything the opposition parties had imagined or seen before, so they tried to ride them into power without providing organization, leadership, or programme. Even the most devoted street-level activists were unable to explain what the opposition's agenda was, beyond a vague commitment to getting rid of Museveni and to somehow making life easier for the poor. Throughout the protests, there was never agreement as to what success would actually mean or how the protests could translate into more substantive change.

As a result, nothing was done during those weeks in April when a new vision of politics was desperately needed – a vision based on widespread and legitimate popular grievances, that went beyond multiparty electoral competition, that could present a vision for the entire country, and that could translate popular demands into an agenda beyond anti-corruption and anti-Museveni sentiment. There were no efforts by party activists or civil society activists to go into the communities to help create lasting organization, to hold discussions about the political crisis, to link rural and urban in discourse if not in practice. There was no effort to forge new political ideologies or to build on the possibilities that the protests had revealed in order to develop a new positive national political imagination, one that answered Uganda's deep dilemmas and provided an alternative to the neoliberal, donor-supported military regime of Museveni.

As the protests became focused entirely around the body of one man, they became polarized and polarizing, violent and explosive.

When Besigye was absent, nothing happened; when he showed up, riots broke out. This was what the NRM had been angling for all along, knowing that a national alliance with Besigye at the centre was not sustainable. The regime took this to its logical conclusion when, on 28 April, security agents attacked Besigye, dragged him from his car, doused his face with pepper spray, and threw him into the bed of a police pickup, 'blood dripping from [his] beaten, battered and bruised form' (*Daily Monitor* 2011t). As Besigye was sped away, crowds swarmed the area only to be attacked by police armed personnel carriers. In the words of an editorial in the *Daily Monitor* (2011i), 28 April was the day when Uganda's citizens, 'embodied in the tear-gassed, bruised, and battered Besigye, had gone from being governed to being ruled'.

The next day, with rumours flying that Besigye had been maimed, blinded, or even killed, Uganda's urban population rose up to a new height: there were massive, violent demonstrations in cities around the country. At that point, the true nature of state power was revealed unambiguously: Museveni's son, Lt Col. Kainerugaba Muhoozi, commander of the elite Special Forces Group, led a military operation to seize control of the centre of Kampala. This praetorian guard effectively announced that it would guarantee the president's power against all challenges. In the hail of bullets that followed in markets, streets, and slums throughout Uganda, while the people fought back against the security forces in any way they could, many were killed, hundreds injured, and hundreds more arrested. Meanwhile, all reporting on the uprising was banned, and the British royal wedding was the only thing seen on Ugandan TV.

The end of the road

The outburst on 29 April ended as quickly as it had started, when Besigye was publicly flown to Nairobi for medical treatment. Without a focal point, the protests dissipated, just as the government had foreseen. The unprecedented alliance – across political parties, civil and political society, ethnic groups and regions – unravelled. Without Besigye, the opposition parties were rudderless. One faction called for a new wave of popular participation – in a blood drive. In response, the Ministry of Health announced (untruthfully, as it turned out) that its blood stocks were fine and that the opposition was playing politics with the people's health. Norbert Mao, the Democratic Party presidential candidate, announced differently themed protests for different days, none of which caught on. Mugisha Muntu, another FDC leader, walked to work, but he drew no crowds and was even saluted by soldiers along the way. Olara Otunnu, the Uganda People's Congress presidential candidate, tried one protest in Constitutional Square but ended up doused in pink water from water cannons and another protest in June under the slogan 'Free Uganda Now', which police dogs were sufficient to disperse. A4C declared a car-honking campaign, which made a racket for a few days but then petered out. Besigye and Lukwago, the Kampala mayor, remained the only viable political leaders and would draw huge crowds when they showed up anywhere, which led only to the predicable rain of tear-gas canisters and bullets. As Wokuri put it, selfishness and laziness ensued, as factionalization broke up the opposition and activism was left to Besigye alone.[23]

After April, civil society also broke apart. Some went back to their workshops and donor-supported lifestyles. A few others, such as retired Bishop Zac Niringiye, continued their activism, in particular around corruption, with the NGO-driven 'Black Monday Movement' its most visible example.[24] Far from a 'movement', however, these middle-class activists tended to have a sound moral message but with no popular constituency. The dominant mood among civil society was captured by an editorial titled 'Our interests are above partisanship', which declared that the 'economic wellbeing of citizens ... knows no political stripes', and that Ugandans' 'interests are not defined by political allegiance' (*Daily Monitor* 2011p). Civil society 'politics' was reduced to moral declarations of grievance, focused mainly against corruption, while the work of political organization and action was left to the parties – who, in turn, were condemned as self-interested.

More positively, the Walk to Work protests had illuminated the way in which Uganda's long-standing political questions could be answered, even if they had not been in this case. The Asian question did not arise, while the Buganda question was at least temporarily defused. The Northern question was briefly resolved through a regional alliance around anti-NRM protests in the north and the south. However, without a political programme that articulated the grievances of the north, the protests in north and south, while simultaneous, remained disjointed. Additionally, as the protests became concentrated around Besigye, and thus Kampala, the regional dimensions were undermined. As regional protests focused around local leaders – in Gulu, Norbert Mao – so they broke apart regionally and were more easily dealt with through heavy-handed deployment of security forces. The importance of a national political agenda that integrates northern concerns is particularly resonant today, at a point when a new violent rebellion may become a viable alternative for northern populations.

With protests unable to reach beyond urban areas, the rural–urban question remained unaddressed. Nevertheless, the possibility for a rural–urban alliance may now be increasing. Whereas a few decades ago economic and political conditions faced by urban and rural populations were sufficiently different as to fracture town–country solidarity, today those differences have diminished significantly. The countryside has come to rely on the same markets in food as the urban population and sees disappearing what little access they had to government services. As rural and urban conditions converge, it becomes even more essential for the NRM to keep the political opposition confined to urban areas, which it has done through constant repression of opposition organizers and leaders trying to access the countryside. The 2009 protests managed to achieve a rural–urban link through a mobilization of ethnicity, but urban ethnic violence was the consequence. The 2011 protests went beyond ethnic particularism but were unable to establish an alternative, non-ethnic basis for a rural–urban alliance. Although the conditions seem ripe for such a development, no effort was made – or allowed to be made – to forge such bonds. Indeed, the protests reveal clearly that political activists need to focus on what the foundation for a non-ethnic rural political opposition would be and how non-violent political opposition could bridge rural and urban today.

The structural weaknesses of Walk to Work played into the regime's hands. The real danger to the NRM was not armed rebellion, nor even a purely urban protest movement, but a national political alliance linking north and south, urban and rural, popular and elite, transcending Baganda chauvinism and not devolving into Asian scapegoating. At their height, the protests managed to overcome these divisions perhaps more than any other political movement had, armed or unarmed, in Uganda's post-independence history. Walk to Work thus showed that the promise embodied in Museveni's initial broad-base policy could be fulfilled, a promise that Museveni himself had betrayed by relying on an effective north–south divide for his power. With Walk to Work, this promise seemed to emerge again but only to dissipate at the key moment when no political leadership, from below or above, was able to articulate an agenda that would provide a sustainable basis for a new politics or that would address these national political questions directly and clearly.

The 2011 uprising revealed a final major obstacle that any national protest movement would have to address: state militarization. One opposition leader claimed in an interview that, at the height of the protests, the military had begun to split. However, the presence of Museveni's son and his sizeable special forces at the core of an otherwise often demoralized, ill-equipped, and dispersed military made a meaningful split difficult. The militarization of the police also means that the lines between it and the army are increasingly blurred.

Militarization has an important international dimension. The government could afford to escalate its violence against protesters – as well as against other opponents of the regime – because it knew it would retain donor support, particularly from the United States. In a stark illumination of the true nature of US involvement in Uganda, the US army launched, with much fanfare, its Atlas Drop 2011 joint training exercise with the Ugandan military on

13 April (AFRICOM 2011). On that very day, the Ugandan government was redeploying its army's Field Force Unit, tasked with guarding Uganda's borders, to Kampala to assault protesters. In the midst of the military crackdown, Lt Col. Jeffrey Dickerson, a spokesperson for the US military, declared that it was an 'honor' and 'privilege' to partner with the Ugandan army: 'Our coming together here represents not just the partnership between our militaries but the partnership and the bonds between our nations, our governments, and most importantly, our people' (ibid.) – chilling words for the victims of the NRM regime.

The international support provided to Museveni's regime is not lost on Ugandans. As one opposition spokesman put it, 'as long as their [American] interests are not compromised, Museveni can act as their mercenary, sending our soldiers to Somalia or wherever they want' (*Daily Monitor* 2011n). As explained, the military budget is a key source for discretionary funding used by the regime to consolidate its power. In one political activist's words, 'Obama talks about human rights, but he breeds dictators.'[25] Indeed, the donors quickly returned to their uncompromising support for the regime after the protests, wilfully forgetting its most recent display of violence and impunity. Already by 7 May, donors were instructing the opposition to work for electoral reforms in preparation for 2016, and in June the UK committed 900 billion shillings to development aid. Today, the state's donor-supported militarization continues unhindered.

After walking

If the Ugandan people drew inspiration from the uprisings in Egypt and Tunisia, the Ugandan government may have drawn inspiration from the 2005 crackdown in Ethiopia. However, whereas in Ethiopia the state embarked upon a large-scale effort at co-opting dissent through state developmentalism after the protests ended (see Chapter 7), in Uganda it appears that state corruption, apathy, and unaccountability ran too deep to permit such intensive measures. Indeed, after the 2009 riots, Museveni announced a 15 billion shilling youth jobs initiative, to be managed by his son-in-law. Not a single job was reported to have been created (Kalinaki 2011b). So, even though the 2011/12 budget introduced a 44.5 billion shilling plan to fight unemployment through 'job creation', especially among youth, positive results seem unlikely (ibid.). The best Museveni could provide was the promise at his inauguration that, thanks to oil revenues, Uganda would be a middle-income country by 2016.

Without the carrot, the Ugandan government depends on the stick. In addition to constant arrests of opposition leaders, surveillance and police repression have increased against any suspected opposition in the community – meetings are not allowed, associations are outlawed. The state has focused on Besigye and Lukwago and their circles. Mwijukye, the FDC youth leader, was arrested sixty-seven times in two years. Reviving colonial-era laws that had been designed to repress nationalist activism, the NRM government uses preventive detention and criminalizes association in order to keep opposition leaders in jail, in court, or under house arrest. In fact, the greatest difficulty in interviewing opposition leaders for this book was their regular incarceration by police.

In Kampala itself, the NRM reformed the municipal administration of Kampala so as to undermine Lord Mayor Lukwago's power. The government also divided the authority over Kampala between Lukwago and the Executive Director of Kampala Capital City Authority, appointed in April 2011, Jennifer Musisi. Musisi has undertaken a project of cleaning the city through clearing out traders, filling in potholes, registering *boda-boda* drivers, and trying to beautify some of the public spaces. The comparison with Ethiopia is again telling: whereas in Ethiopia the state undertook a project that tried to incorporate the rebellious political society, in Uganda Musisi has spearheaded a project to try to appeal to Uganda's urban middle class and elite, managing the city in their interest. The result has been significant support for Musisi among this constituency, many of whom see her as their technocratic champion against the rabble-rousing Lukwago. Thus, the gap between civil and political societies in Kampala has increased since 2011, and the bridge that had briefly connected the two will probably collapse amidst any future round of protests, allowing the state to crack down with even more brutal force.

More important, Kampala has been under occupation by the security services – primarily the highly militarized police forces – since the elections. Military vehicles and men in urban combat gear occupy every public space. Long columns of riot police suddenly appear along major roads, and the stench of tear gas is a regular part of Kampala life. 'The government has seen the power of protests,' explained the men in the furniture workshop, 'and it is holding the city prisoner.'

Urban workers and poor were condemned to a pent-up fury at the government. The expansion of the surveillance apparatus had people fearful of speaking out. Organization within political society is extremely difficult. People explained that the regime arrests anyone trying to organize and that 'one out of every five' people is an informant. A Public Order Bill has been passed, among whose draconian provisions is a denial of bail to 'rioters' or 'economic saboteurs'. Most street-level activists said they had little hope for political change, whether through elections or protest, until Museveni himself died. Many people who were involved in the 2011 protests learned a harsh lesson: the government will kill whomever it needs to in order to stay in power and to ensure that it wins in 2016. Some suggested that arms were the only means of forcing Museveni out, but such talk was tempered by recognition of the military's overwhelming power and the lack of popular organization.

Opposition party leaders, however, seem to have taken the opposite lesson from 2011. The protests, according to them, showed Ugandans their own power and revealed that the government could be changed. In Mpuuga's words, the protests were launched in order to 'get people to see that the armed dictator could be confronted', and now 'Ugandans are more willing to stand up against the dictator'. Nganda explained further: 'Now, when tear gas is fired, they are not afraid. They thank the police for proving the importance of their cause!' Some opposition leaders indulge in apocalyptic musings about 2016, reflecting their self-sacrificial attitude during the 2011 protests. As one put it, 'we are preparing the masses for the protest of our lives'. For another, the 2016 strategy was to ensure that 'Museveni doesn't get there' as civil disobedience would bring him down. A commonly expressed sentiment was summed up in the idea that, 'if one million people walk on State House, they can't shoot them all'. Despite these grand plans, the opposition is still unable to get beyond its anti-Museveni agenda. Meanwhile, disappointment with political parties, rather than a new confidence in them, appears prevalent among street-level activists.

However, the opposition leaders do have a point. Since 2011, there has been an upsurge in small-scale protests against the government over degeneration in living standards and the state's apparent apathy towards popular suffering. By May 2011, the first such protests were seen, as a man undressed publicly to protest poor health facilities. In Tabaire's words (2013), 'as walk-to-work has demonstrated, the nature of protest is changing in Uganda'. May 2011 also saw a strike by Kakira sugar plantation workers and a threatened strike among teachers in Bududa over unpaid salaries. In June, there were protests in Nebbi against an unpopular NRM district chairperson, protests throughout the country by government employees over lack of pay, and demonstrations in Moyo over poor health facilities. Some of these protests represent blowback for the government's electoral bribery. Not only had it depleted the budget to the point that the Ministry of Finance announced that the country was bankrupt, but a huge number of pledges of future financial support had been made, bound to produce disappointment after the election. Inflation, too, continued to rise through May and June, feeding further popular resentment. These localized protests continue unabated to the present, fed by a popular perception that protest has new power in the country.

The post-2011 wave of small-scale protests has a significant rural dimension, taking place in villages, on road projects, or on sugar cane plantations, rising up against foreign infrastructure projects, land-grabs, oil drilling, or evictions of squatters. In one typical case, in which rural residents in Busia district threatened to demonstrate over poor roads, one resident declared, 'It's the demonstration language which this government responds to so quickly, so we are adopting it soon' (*Daily Monitor* 2013). Indeed, anti-regime protest seems always on the verge of erupting. As one long-time observer of Ugandan politics explained, almost every public assembly in Uganda, even NRM rallies, tends to turn against the government.[26] Although people are afraid of speaking out when alone, a crowd of any size will give rise to vocal criticism and calls for action against the government. Thus, the NRM typically avoids rallies in urban areas and holds them instead in distant districts where the security apparatus can prevent dissent. This represents an important political legacy of the Walk to Work protests among political society and the rural poor, even if formal organization or national political programmes did not arise among those groups during the protests themselves. A history of urban protest by political society set the stage for Walk to Work, and the protests' repercussions have managed to reach deep into the rural.

This represents one face of today's popular protest – small-scale, particularized demands for improvements in the conditions of specific constituencies, to be attained through informal negotiations with political elites who are pressured by the threat of local upheaval. Indeed, from this perspective, today's small-scale protests are politically limited because they make only local demands from the government for marginal improvements. If such small-scale demands start to be made in a coordinated fashion across the country, however, they could become politically explosive and give rise again to the other face of protest by political society: a general uprising as seen in 2011. As conditions in rural and urban areas converge, perhaps rural protests can provide the basis for a new urban–rural alliance. More fundamentally, while the NRM government can provide small benefits to appease specific constituencies when necessary, it does not appear able to provide basic welfare to the population as a whole. Some in the opposition realize this: Mpuuga explained that 'the challenge of the day is how to consolidate all these protests and energies'.

The bigger question is whether political parties are up to the task or whether new political leadership will emerge from political society or from the rural poor. Political resistance may continue to be restricted to localized flare-ups, armed or unarmed, and easily suppressed by a foreign-funded state security apparatus. However, even as the old dilemmas of Ugandan politics have re-asserted themselves, new possibilities have been revealed beyond multipartyism and beyond the country's long-standing historical divides.

7 | Protest and counter-protest in Ethiopia

'2005 did not happen overnight,' explained the former student activist, sipping strong coffee in the patio of an old downtown hotel, while a man who appeared to be a government informer sat at the next table, trying rather conspicuously to listen. 'The election was just what set everything off; ... the political parties picked up existing grievances and, for the first time, enabled people to see an alternative' to the fourteen-year rule of Meles Zenawi and the Ethiopian People's Revolutionary Democratic Front (EPRDF).[1] With the release of results of the 2005 election declaring the EPRDF the winner, people reacted by taking to the streets in an explosion of popular politics, a mass urban uprising not seen since the 1974 Ethiopian revolution.

Although the protests took place immediately after the elections, it is important to note that, as in Uganda, they were not about the opposition's loss. In fact, the protests represented a critique of the opposition political parties as much as of the state. Although the election outcome ignited the protests, they grew out of a broad set of social, economic, and political transformations that had culminated in 2005. These transformations led a wide array of primarily urban groups – professionals, workers, intellectuals and students, youth in and out of school, and the informal networks spanning political society – to accumulate a set of grievances against the EPRDF regime. The elections simply provided the opportunity for the emergence of dynamic public spheres where those grievances could be aired, discussed, and radicalized, for the activation of a broad mobilization among the population, and for a single issue to provide a focus and a demand around which the many groups could converge.

However, the informer's presence during our 2013 interview made clear that the uprising had not brought about a new regime or even a meaningful reform. Instead, the protests were met with an onslaught of state violence, and then they ushered in an era of intensified, expansive repression and control. The most visible legacy of the protests today is found in the massive developmental works the EPRDF has undertaken in cities across the country, a tremendous, often violent, restructuring of urban Ethiopia. Visitors to Addis or the provincial capitals cannot miss the huge new construction projects, in particular the roads, office buildings, housing, and even a light rail system that has left gaping holes in the middle of Addis's streets. The epitome of the government's urban renovation is an immense donor-supported cobblestone project, which has used environmentally friendly techniques to pave roads in 140 towns, employing 90,000 young people (Broussard and Tsegay 2012). This transition from popular protest to authoritarian development – from nation-wide uprisings to the counter-protest state – is the subject of this chapter.

The rise and the crisis of the EPRDF

The EPRDF, a coalition with the Tigrayan People's Revolutionary Front (TPLF) at its centre, took power in 1991 after almost two decades of rural armed struggle to end the repression of the Derg. The Derg, led by the ruthless Mengistu Haile Mariam, had taken power in the wake of the 1974 protest-led Ethiopian Revolution and consolidated its control through the infamous 'Red Terror', a devastating campaign of violent repression against all possible political opposition. The end point of the 1974 revolution, which had started in an unprecedented popular uprising, was total political demobilization (Bahru 2008). The Derg created an all-consuming one-party socialist state that provided answers to the long-standing questions of Ethiopian politics: the monarchy of Haile Selassie and its institutions had been uprooted; land reform was being carried out; and ethno-regional differences were subsumed under socialism. As Clapham concludes, 'By the early 1980s, the upheavals which had shaken the towns during the early years of the revolution had ceased. The only demonstrations were those organized by the regime' (Clapham 1990: 129). As the possibility for urban-based political movements was eliminated, regionally based, rural movements became the primary way of organizing against the regime, and arms became the only apparent way of challenging it.

Once they had taken power in Addis Ababa, the EPRDF proclaimed a programme of 'revolutionary democracy'. Numerous strategic reorientations have taken place under this banner in the years since (Vaughan 2011), but there also seems to be an overall coherence to ERPDF political practice under Meles, focusing on building a developmental state guided by a dominant party seeking a social consensus (De Waal 2012). The EPRDF's developmentalism has received significant support from donors, whose lionization of the Meles regime continued even after his death in 2013. In the early 2000s, however, the 'developmental coalition' promised by the EPRDF was in short supply, especially in urban areas.

Although the EPRDF formally presides over a multiparty democracy, many argue that in practice it had established effective one-party rule as early as 1995, when, after a campaign of harassment and intimidation of opposition political parties and civic associations, it won over 90 per cent of the vote (Merera 2007: 136). While generally neglecting urban areas, the EPRDF maintained control in rural areas through the top-down structure of the *kebelles* (wards) and through often politicized distribution of services and aid (Lyons 1996: 140). This created significant urban opposition, both in Addis and in provincial cities, among educated professionals and among the poor (Clapham 2005).

The EPRDF gave a concrete answer to Ethiopia's long-standing ethnic fragmentation: federation with the promise of self-determination up to secession. A federation was constitutionalized, but secession became a reality only in the case of Eritrea – and, even in that case, it was not a result of constitutional provisions but of a political deal arrived at by the TPLF and the Eritrean Peoples' Liberation Front in 1975. Eritrean secession, in particular the loss of Ethiopia's only access to the sea, brought significant resentment from many sectors of the population, in particular the Amhara community. These factions often used the language of Ethiopian nationalism to protest the state-led politicization of ethnicity; for minority ethnicities, however, nationalist claims voiced by the Amhara community sounded dangerously close to a programme of Amhara supremacy. Also damaging for the EPRDF's legitimacy was their manipulation of national autonomy, as they created state-aligned regional political parties, repressed independent regional politics, and 'institutionalized ethnicity as the controlling consideration in national politics' (Lyons 1996: 125). Ethnic manipulation was combined with a widespread perception of Tigrayan favouritism by the EPRDF, in particular in business and state and military. Consequently, the EPRDF faced opposition from both Ethiopian nationalists and ethno-nationalists.

The EPRDF coalition had internal tensions as well: the TPLF, the core of the EPRDF, split in the early 2000s, largely over the outcome of the Eritrean war. By 2005, the party could claim only a meagre 760,000 members (Vaughan 2011: 633). In rural areas too, *kabelle* administration left ample room for corruption and mismanagement, producing significant dissatisfaction. The EPRDF tended to compensate for its vulnerability by employing military force, the ultimate foundation of its power (Bahru 2008: 283). The military was used to destroy popular protest on several occasions – including the brutal repression of protesting students in 1993, the crackdown on students protesting against the secession of Eritrea in 2001 when thirty were killed and four hundred injured (Toggia 2008), and the massacre of peaceful demonstrators at Awassa in 2002, when heavy machine guns were used against the crowd and thirty-eight were killed (HRW 2005). Violence was also a constant presence in many rural areas where ethno-nationalist movements were active.

The EPRDF leadership remained oblivious to its falling support in both rural and urban areas. Thinking itself impervious, it submitted to internal and international pressures and opened political space in the run-up to the 2005 elections, allowing opposition parties to hold rallies for the first time as well as allowing public debates to be held and broadcast between the opposition and the EPRDF. The ruling party paid little attention to the rapid support built by the opposition party coalitions. The most important of these was the Coalition for Unity and Democracy (CUD), or Kinijit, a loose coalition of mostly nationalist political parties with divergent ideas on basic questions – land reform, economic policy, the national question – but united in their determination to unseat Meles and the EPRDF. The most vocal leadership evinced a neoliberal bent, with entrepreneurship and state withdrawal cast as the solution to Ethiopia's poverty – an orientation that did not sit well with many leftist political activists. The other principal coalition was Hibret, largely made up of ethno-nationalist parties. The EPRDF's response to the coalitions, once it realized the threat they posed, was to accuse Kinijit in particular of Amhara chauvinism couched in the guise of Ethiopian nationalism.[2]

The opposition coalitions quickly managed to gain widespread support by combining a widely popular message of change at the top – unseating the EPRDF – with a diverse set of appeals, some of them contradictory, to different constituencies. In Addis, as well as other urban centres across the country, the opposition found support across political society: among students, among unemployed, underemployed and poor urban youth, among the taxi drivers and assistants, market sellers, and civil servants, and among professionals, business people, and the intelligentsia. It was this diverse assembly that came together in the protests and determined their outcome. Three groups in particular deserve attention for their involvement in the protests: professionals, students, and intellectuals; urban youth; and political society more broadly, especially taxi drivers and conductors.

The parties to protest

For the first group, politically active intellectuals, students, and professionals, grievances against the regime had developed in part around concerns over democracy and political participation, the closing of political space, and the intolerance of dissent. For this mostly urban group, there were also grumblings around the relative neglect that urban areas had suffered under the EPRDF, with its explicit strategy of building support in and focusing its efforts on rural areas. Although some specific national political issues appealed to members of this constituency – for example, the EPRDF's political instrumentalization of ethnicity through ethnic federalism, the loss of the port of Assab to Eritrea, diminished employment opportunities for graduates – it seems to have been a basic desire for change and freedom that had the most resonance.[3]

This was an opportunity into which the opposition political parties stepped and took full advantage. The political opposition of 2005, for the first time, seemed to offer a credible alternative to the EPRDF. A set of candidates for the opposition – Bertukan Midekesa, Berhanu Nega, Lidetu Ayalew – educated, eloquent, and credible, took advantage of public forums and televised debates to humiliate the EPRDF leadership and to show that Meles' people could be replaced by a more competent and responsive leadership. These educated political leaders provided an alternative to Meles, who was seen as the intellectual of the EPRDF, as well as an alternative to lower-level EPRDF officials, who were seen as less educated and being from military backgrounds.

As some of the activists involved in the protests explained, they felt that the run-up to the 2005 elections was their first opportunity to reflect on the EPRDF government and to ask key questions about the decisions it had made. The space for debate was suddenly open in a way it had not been for decades. Numerous new public spheres emerged in which positions were articulated, opinions formed and, often, radicalized. Feeding into this was a new flourishing of private newspapers, widely available in the urban markets, which, often taking extreme and polarizing positions, further stirred up expectations and resentment. Many political activists and intellectuals became involved in the newspapers, where they saw their role as being to fight authoritarianism and unseat the government; therefore, the more extreme the position articulated, the better.

The result was, in the words of a group of students and

intellectuals who had been active in the 2005 protests, a 'sudden opening of new possibilities' and a 'collective euphoria' that emerged towards the end of 2004.[4] For the first time, people were asking how things could have been different without the EPRDF and how things might be different in the future without it. Such was the popularity of opposition leaders that supporting them became almost a 'fashion',[5] and the participation of artists, writers, and intellectuals gave the opposition additional cachet. Teddy Afro's music echoed through the streets of Addis (Orgeret 2008), his opposition anthems representing an Ethiopian version of the Kenyan 'Unbwogable'. There was a feeling that change, any change, was needed. One popular song by Teddy Afro described the period since the 1974 revolution as one of continual decline, expressing even a nostalgia for imperial times. These newly politicized actors, however, had little political experience and came to harbour what some in retrospect saw as untenable or irresponsible political positions.

Activating informal networks

While these professional, student, and intellectual activists provided the most prominent voices of the opposition, it was a broader section of youth who were at the heart of the protests. Indeed, although students were very important to the 2005 protests and were expected to take a central role given their history of activism, it seems that in fact it was the 'half employed and half unemployed' youth, including both school drop-outs and graduates, who were the real motive force behind the protests (Di Nunzio 2012: 435). Several factors came together in 2005 to create the conditions for this large-scale youth revolt.

One major factor was simply the accumulation in Addis Ababa of youth with few prospects, a situation that arose from many sources. First, the end of the war against Eritrea had released large numbers of young men from the army, many of whom returned to Addis and settled in the poorest neighbourhoods. Also key were changes in the education system: part of neoliberal restructuring had been a new emphasis on vocational schools, the introduction of cost-sharing, and a reduction in the number of years most students spent in school. The result was that many high-school students quit rather than join technical schools, many students were graduating without adequate qualifications, and even those who did go through technical education often found little chance for formal employment. The ranks of the young and unemployed swelled considerably, and there was a common sentiment that responsibility for their low status lay with the government. Poverty, lack of services, and the disjuncture between development rhetoric and the lived reality in the street, driven by the indignities of structural adjustment, all contributed to creating a readiness among youth to participate in protest.

Urban youth involvement in protest derived from interwoven economic, political, and cultural factors, as explored by anthropologists Di Nunzio and Mains, who emphasize the ethnic, class, and religious diversity of this group. They explain that urban youth is characterized partly by the uncertainty of employment and a focus on survival but also by desires and expectations of social advancement (ibid.). Even for those with secondary education, higher education is no panacea: in fact, it corresponds to higher levels of unemployment (Broussard and Tsegay 2012: 21). As a result, as Mains puts it, this group has 'little to lose and everything to gain from participating in political movements' (Mains 2012: 3). This participation in 2005 was enabled by the informal ties in the community and on the street, the 'passive networks' described by Bayat, that hold people together without formal organization and can be activated quickly to bring people out to collective political action (Di Munzio 2012: 437). The *chat* chewing-houses were also a key site of discussion and deliberation among members of this group, and some even called the 2005 protests the '*chat* revolution'.[6] Others emphasized the lesser importance of *chat* houses, however, relative to newspapers and the informal discussions that took place in and around collective taxis.

Rage, disillusionment, frustration, material deprivation, a desperate desire for change – all of these pushed the urban youth to see the opposition as embodying a possibility for radical change.

It is important, however, to keep in mind that the opposition electoral strategy was in fact oriented more towards schools and much less towards the broader swathe of urban youth. As the former vice-chairperson of the CUD youth league explained, the opposition took advantage of government neglect to organize intensely in universities, colleges, and high schools, to 'build awareness and politicize'.[7] The vast body of urban youth out of schools were of 'secondary concern' to the opposition strategy, since these young people were so much harder to organize than students, who had significant organization to begin with.[8] The passionate involvement of this broader sector of youth in the opposition support base, therefore, was more a reaction against the EPRDF, which emerged out of long-standing grievances, than a product of the appeal of opposition parties.

Youth activism was also catalysed by the EPRDF's own missteps: in the run-up to the elections, the ruling party vocally denounced urban youth as *'adegegna bozene'*, or dangerous hoodlums. As a man living in Arat Kilo, one of the places where the protests and government reaction were most concentrated, explained, the government's labelling of all urban youth as *bozene* played a major role in mobilizing those youth against the government – 'they were organized by being named *bozene* by the EPRDF!'[9] The government passed a harsh new anti-*bozene* bill, which effectively criminalized urban youth, affirming once again youth's firm entrenchment in political society. The opposition seized on this and countered by explaining that young people were not criminals but unemployed and that their unemployment was the fault of the government. It was not party organization, therefore, but rather the existing grievances of youth, given shape within a specific opposition discourse and circulated through social networks, that led them to support the opposition in its programme to take the government back from the EPRDF.

Significant participation by political society more broadly was also seen at the time. The most intense participation was in the popular, dense neighbourhoods such as the poor areas of Arat Kilo or Faransi, where there was a history of popular resistance, or Merkato, where particular histories of grievance among groups such as Gurage shopkeepers, who had been victims of violence in 1993, gave rise to protest.[10] What gave popular participation its edge were the acute price hikes in food and oil occurring at that time, injuring further already badly off urban households and giving the urban poor an immediate, physical reminder of their plight and the need for change.

The lead-up to the elections and the protests were, again, a time when new public spheres emerged and existing informal networks were politically activated. Collective taxi drivers, conductors, and the numerous assistants took a central role, as they had in 1974. The collective taxis were one place where large numbers of unemployed young people converged to seek employment, work odd jobs, or just hang out, and so the taxis became a centre of opposition to the government. The taxis themselves were mobile and temporary public spheres for political society. The centrality of the taxis to Addis's economy also meant that stopping transportation was a key step to ensuring the success of a general strike.

Finally, protests arose from those locations in cities hosting high numbers of rural migrants, where life was cheap enough for them to survive. Urban areas outside of Addis often have a strongly rural presence, and protest arose out of areas such as these, with strong linkages between urban and rural areas. There is a significant geographical aspect, a spatial politics in Addis and other urban areas, that fed into the opposition support, the protests, and the government response (Arriola 2013).

In the telling words of a journalist in exile in Kampala, 'during that time, everything was politics'.[11] Accumulated grievances, changes in urban society, and the structure of power suddenly became the substance of discussion and critique. The idea that change was actually possible was activated through the emergence of multiple public spheres, and people came to see the most foundational aspects of life as open to transformation, the old order as no longer necessary. The organization and mobilization around the elections focused energies on a single demand –

that the regime must go – which radicalized and polarized the population. This was a consummate political moment in which new possibilities opened and what was previously unthinkable now appeared ready to be born. Of course, the hopes running rampant at these radical political moments can often end up running head-first into hard political realities.

Elections and protest

The belief that change was not only possible but at hand was cemented by the massive opposition rally on 8 May 2005, in Addis Ababa's Meskel Square. On witnessing the unprecedented spectacle of over one million people in the streets, many of those involved believed that the opposition could not possibly lose the election – indeed, if they did lose, it would be because of election fraud. In that heady atmosphere, the parties did nothing to calm expectations, and the media fanned popular excitement and anger.[12]

The election was held on 15 May and was followed by a confusing series of official announcements, opposition announcements, official retractions, opposition accusations, and official delays, all amid mounting popular frustration and fear that the election was being stolen. From the beginning, the EPRDF admitted that it had lost all seats in Addis and a significant number of seats elsewhere around the country, particularly in urban areas but also in rural constituencies. Indeed, the victory of the opposition, primarily the CUD, cut right across Addis Ababa, where opposition parties received 80 per cent of the vote, and through rural areas. In both, opposition support primarily followed lines of economic deprivation, not ethnicity (Arriola 2007; Clapham 2005). Arriola (2007) notes that the CUD received most support from the unemployed, those who saw themselves as having a declining standard of living, and the more educated. This seems to demonstrate that the opposition had managed to create, however ephemerally, an inter-ethnic coalition – but whether that would have survived the transition from opposition to government can be subject only to speculation. What was never in doubt, according to the government's declarations, however, was that the EPRDF had retained a significant majority in the parliament.

To many in the opposition, and in particular among opposition supporters, an EPRDF majority was simply impossible. As one former student activist explained, 'we thought that if we had won Addis, we should have won everywhere ... [it was] naïve on the part of the people. No one questioned the claims by the opposition that "we won".'[13] He continued: 'It was taken for granted that there would be a total change of government,' and therefore when that change was denied – and especially when it seemed to be denied through manipulation of the vote counting – people refused to accept the outcome. 'Look at Ethiopia's political history,' another explained; 'there has only been radical, total change up until now. So that is what people expected.'[14] Many of those who had supported the opposition parties did not see the elections as part of a democratic process, as part of the give-and-take negotiation of politics. Rather, they were seen only as a tool for bringing about total change, and when that did not happen, change had to be sought through other means. The protests were not about the opposition, and in fact the opposition very quickly lost the support it had enjoyed during the elections. Indeed, the opposition was unable to capitalize on the outpouring of public antipathy against the regime by putting forth a new national political vision or even by retaining its electoral support, thus revealing its significant limitations.

Where exactly the protests started is subject to multiple accounts. Some see the students, perhaps because of their long-standing reputation, as having started the protests, while others see the protests as starting among the broader urban youth and the students joining later. Whatever the case, the students were soon out in the streets to protest the delay in the vote count. When the student protests were met with a violent response from police, something happened which had not happened since the mid-1970s: other social groups came out on to the streets as well. Many of the protesting students were aligned with opposition political parties and brought on to the streets their particular demands – for example, the issue of the port of Assab appealed to many in the nationalist camp. As the protests spread, however, any correspondence to parties disappeared, and the protests became the direct expression of the popular revolt that had taken electoral form a couple of weeks earlier. Opposition party elites argued that the protests were against the election outcome and amounted to a demand for a recount and electoral reform. It is more accurate, however, to understand the protests as far beyond the political parties. The parties were just a convenient vehicle for getting rid of the EPRDF, and they became irrelevant once the elections were over.

At that point, talk of Ukraine's 2004 Orange Revolution was suddenly resonant, and intense memories of the popular upsurge of 1974 returned. But, as one former student activist explained, these were selective memories: people had forgotten, for instance, that 1974 ended with the Derg's Red Terror, or that Ethiopia remained a militarized state, won by the EPRDF through blood, and would not be handed over without a fight. For those few hopeful days, however, before the state brought down the full weight of its military machine, change seemed imminent, with more and more joining in a popular revolution.

Huge numbers of people took to the streets of Addis Ababa, concentrated in the poorest but also most densely populated neighbourhoods. In Arat Kilo, explained a man who lived there in 2005, after the students came not only the unemployed youth, but also collective taxi drivers and assistants, civil servants, and petty traders from the market. Those who didn't take directly to the streets provided refuge for those who did when they were pursued by police or military.[15] The 'passive networks' already in existence among youth and poor urban dwellers were activated to bring people to the protests and to hide those fleeing police pursuit. While text messages played an important part among students and professionals, there is little evidence that such technologies were needed for the mass of the protesters. Whatever the means, students, workers, and the many constituencies of political society were out in force together.

Protest in Ethiopia

As the security crackdown intensified, so did the popular violence, with barricades of burning tyres, petrol bombs, and destruction of government property. Running battles were fought between protesters and security services, and entire parts of Addis were out of state control. Similar protests erupted in provincial capitals around the country. This violence is not evidence of the protests becoming an expression of undirected rage – rather, it was part of the politics of political society protest. Once again, as Fanon helps make clear, violence was not about demanding that the state respect electoral laws, as the opposition parties seemed to believe. Now, the objective of protest, in the eyes of many, was to bring down the regime through the power of people without accepting any compromise. The protest was based in the often invisible networks that tightly held together the dense popular neighbourhoods. Thus, protest derived its meaning from the popular political imagination from which it erupted, not from liberal notions of what a proper protest should look like. Violence was a performance of political agency, a direct attempt to uproot state power, within the 'moral economy' of the street and by those criminalized as 'dangerous hoodlums'.

Once the state retook the initiative on Meles' order to restore control 'at any cost', the destruction was massive. With police balking at firing on civilians, the EPRDF brought in the military, at whose core were the special forces, the *agazi*, mostly Tigrayan and Gambellan troops, many of whom reportedly did not speak Amharic and so could not communicate with the protesters. Tanks came into the streets, machine guns fired into the crowds. At least thirty-six civilians ended up dead, hundreds injured, and thousands arrested in Addis, while dozens were killed and hundreds more arrested in cities around Ethiopia (Abbink 2006; HRW 2005; Lyons 2006).

The political parties, finding the protests spinning out of their control, sought to distance themselves – 'the opposition has never called a protest', explained the sole current opposition member of parliament.[16] The youth mobilizer agreed, blaming government provocateurs for instigating the violence and the unemployed youth for serving as government agents, clearly displaying the traditional distrust of political society's mobilization. The state spread a narrative in which the opposition political parties, egged on and supported by Western diplomats, were responsible for the violence and for provoking counter-violence from the police and military.[17] Importantly, the state's longer-term response to the protests – massive developmental interventions in urban centres – demonstrated that, in fact, it correctly understood protests not as the product of elite manipulation but as arising from widespread popular grievances.

Between June and November 2005, once the first bout of protest had been put down, the EPRDF raised the stakes, reforming laws to undermine opposition victories in parliament and in the Addis Ababa municipal government. The opposition faced the choice of taking their seats in parliament or refusing to accept the highly compromised victory. The CUD opted for the latter course and soon found its leadership under arrest for treason. In hindsight, many opposition and social activists argue that the CUD should have joined parliament so as to de-escalate tensions and begin a parliamentary struggle.[18] However, the opposition's lack of preparation led them to resort to public consultations to discern a way forward, and there the most militant voices triumphed. Protest was left as the only option for the population, even as the CUD publicly tried to stave off demonstrations (Melakou 2008). The CUD had, in fact, planned a protest for 2 October, but called it off for fear of police violence, following up with a call for at-home strikes and boycotts that had little effect (Abbink 2006: 190).

November saw another upsurge in popular protest, but this time with little organization and with state security services bolstered by thousands more officers (Arriola 2013: 12). On 31 October, taxi drivers staged a car-honking protest to which police responded by beating motorists, which, in turn, provoked more protests. On 2 November, the government moved to violently suppress the escalating upheaval, killing dozens. It also adopted a new strategy to deal with the dispersion of the protesters, rooting them out before they took to the streets (ibid.: 14). Thirty to forty thousand people were arrested in Addis's poor areas and sent to prison camps. Mass arrests of nearly all prominent political and civil opposition leaders followed, and civil society and political society were both crushed by state repression. The crackdown was so effective that the November protests ended in a few days, with only sporadic demonstrations afterwards, particularly in the south. The government crackdown marked the brutal end to the 2005 uprising, with a tally of at least two hundred killed, tens of thousands in prison, and an entire generation of political and intellectual leadership in jail, exile, or effectively silenced.

Aftermath: the counter-protest state

'The people taught us,' Meles is reported to have declared after the end of the 2005 popular upheaval. Indeed, the protests brought about perhaps the most significant reorientation of EPRDF power since 1991, as the regime proceeded to roll out 'a deliberate plan in order to prevent any future large-scale protest against their grip on power' (Aalen and Tronvoll 2009: 203). The EPRDF constructed a counter-protest state that combined a single ideological project – developmentalism – with an intensive effort at social control through a greatly expanded party.[19]

One way of preventing future protest was through the legal system, as the government instituted a series of highly restrictive laws against media, NGOs, and political parties. 'Civil society has been reduced to service delivery,' an exiled journalist declared, as independent media were shut down and journalists driven into exile or thrown in jail (Amnesty International 2011). Draconian anti-terrorism laws helped silence any form of dissent against the state (Hagmann 2012). Opposition politicians were regularly denounced as extremist, anti-peace, or anti-development (Merera 2011: 674) and charged with treason or terrorism.

In the years since, Ethiopia has become a model of 'electoral authoritarianism', in which 'manipulated multiparty elections are a means to sustain power' (Aalen and Tronvoll 2009: 203). In the 2010 parliamentary elections, for example, the EPRDF won

99.4 per cent of the seats. Elections thus 'give the appearance of multiparty democracy for international donors' consumption' but keep 'competing parties from bringing about any significant alternatives to the ruling party's policies' (Tafesse and Aklilu 2007: 104). The opposition did itself no favours either, remaining largely without a social base and fragmenting into competing factions.

The manipulation of multiparty elections is relatively trivial compared to the massive social project that the EPRDF undertook, as huge numbers of Ethiopians came to be involved in 'one or another governmental, political, economic, or developmental association, structure or bureaucracy which can in some sense be regarded as a part of EPRDF's "coalition with the people"' (Vaughan 2011: 634). By 2010, party membership had expanded to include over five million Ethiopians. The 'one-to-five' system was established throughout society, in which one 'model' student, worker, or farmer would be given responsibility for guiding and disciplining five others. In rural areas, the EPRDF used donor funding to regain their vote base through reinvigorated, politicized aid delivery and anti-corruption efforts that enabled the development of an expansive security and surveillance regime (Aalen and Tronvoll 2009: 198; Lefort 2007; Tafesse and Aklilu 2007: 109).

The ideological component of this 'coalition with the people' was development, which became a saturating, bombarding language – developmental movies, developmental research, developmental sports and songs. In theory, the EPRDF sought the 'hegemony of developmental discourse' as 'an internalized set of assumptions, not an imposed order' (De Waal 2012: 6), but in practice, popular adherence seems more often for survival or personal advancement.[20] It was a 'coalition' based largely upon fear and desperation, one that has been characterized by some critics as totalitarian.

The expansion of repressive party structures was particularly intense among those groups involved in the protests – students, civil servants, workers, and political society, in particular youth. Addis Ababa University was rapidly depoliticized as the state created and controlled student associations, and public assemblies or even discussions were banned if they lacked state approval. Fear and wariness came to permeate the campus – even a simple outdoor conversation was likely to be under surveillance. To prevent urban opposition from spanning university and city, students from rural areas were recruited into the social sciences, while an ethnicization of student politics was promoted to fracture student groups along regional lines.[21] Academic freedom was strangled, as all research had to be approved by the party as 'developmental' and the EPRDF itself selected students for graduate study (Abbink 2009). A slew of new provincial campuses were built in an attempt to dilute activism through massification. In the words of an exiled journalist, 'Addis Ababa University is dead now.'

Urban 'empowerment'

The urban poor, youth in particular, were the primary targets of the EPRDF strategy, as it initiated a multitude of new development projects for their 'empowerment'. State organization was to replace the youth's informal power, undoing the passive networks that undergirded the uprising, in a kind of state 'empowerment' through autonomous disempowerment.

Urban youth from all backgrounds were given employment so as to mitigate their grievances and to use their labour to transform the city in order to prevent future protest. A massive state works programme was begun, providing employment to thousands of youth associations (Di Nunzio 2012: 439). Jobs were generally labour-intensive and low-skilled, such as those held by 'parking guys, garbage collectors, carpenters, metal workers, rock workers'. Also targeted for state intervention were 'small-scale enterprises, cooperatives and small trade businesses' (ibid.: 443). Even minibus touts were, after 2005, 'politically mobilized by the ruling party and, hence, officially recognized as – in the words of a local official – "groups of private investors"' (ibid.: 440). No longer *agegegna bozene*, urban youth were now 'stakeholders' and 'entrepreneurs'. Particularly active individuals were promoted as leaders of associations and given the chance for social advancement through state patronage.[22] The construction sector alone had created 176,000 jobs by 2010 (Broussard and Tsegay 2012: 33) and facilitated the massive transformation of urban Ethiopia in the years since 2005.

The new urban infrastructure is often heralded by EPRDF supporters as demonstrating concrete development gains. However, as many of those subject to that development point out, it also has many 'victims'. As Mesfin Woldemariam, a long-standing opposition activist, put it, 'there is big development here, yes, but at what cost? For each kilometre of road built, there are thousands of people displaced into the streets.'[23] One man who had been forcefully evicted from Arat Kilo explained the process: 'Infrastructural development is happening, but without human development,' he said, and, in fact, 'infrastructural development is making life much harder'. The government specifically targeted for demobilization the dense, poor neighbourhoods where protests started and protesters could hide. In some cases, like the neighbourhood Kabelle 12, the state punished perceived opposition strongholds. As one evicted resident explained, his own house had been demolished and his only compensation was a thirty-month rental in a distant building without electricity or water. Many others were even worse off, he said, living in iron shacks, while the poorest, who had previously paid only a few cents per day in rent, were now homeless. Whereas before, in Arat Kilo, 'people would help each other … now, development has torn people apart', with entire communities forcibly displaced into 'big apartment blocks without taking into account how they lived, their habits and their daily lives'. Anyone, whether from the neighbourhood or from NGOs, protesting against the evictions was arrested. The state sought to destroy the passive networks that had brought people into the streets, the foundations for political society's politics.

Donor funding, which was frozen after the crackdown, soon returned to its previous levels and has been key to this developmental project and its concomitant 're-ideologization campaign' (Tronvoll 2010: 124). According to Lyons, in 2005 Ethiopia received $1.9 billion in aid each year, of which $800 million was US assistance (2006). Western donors have been subject to withering criticism for their role in supporting Ethiopia's authoritarian regime, to which they typically respond with 'feigned indignation'; in one scholar's words, Ethiopians' 'democratic aspirations and promises are systematically frustrated with the support of those international countries claiming to be champions of freedom and development' (Brigaldino 2011: 328–32; HRW 2010). Opposition leader Berhanu Nega condemns donors for cynically invoking outdated modernization theory to justify funding development without democracy (2010: 190). The Norwegian government, for instance, justified its support of the EPRDF's dictatorship by praising a 'different standard of human rights' that is supposedly operative in Ethiopia, a claim that gave rise to the pathetic spectacle of a European social democracy invoking respect for African difference to justify its funding a military dictatorship. Many donors try to defend themselves by proclaiming their impotence: one EU diplomat is quoted as declaring that, in dealing with the EPRDF, 'we have no space at all to manoeuvre' (Tronvoll 2010: 135). Donors will almost certainly continue to be a key pillar of EPRDF power, as US funding remains tied to the war on terror while Europeans need a 'success story' to meet the poverty reduction targets tied to their aid to Africa.

Politics today

The EPRDF's grand investment in ensuring its grip on power has not been entirely successful, however. The politicized distribution of benefits excludes many; even those included in party patronage must make contributions to the party themselves, increasingly difficult given the rising cost of living in urban areas. The EPRDF in fact lost 40 per cent of the vote in Addis in 2010 elections despite its massive party apparatus (ibid.). The narratives of resistance in those areas could be one key site where possibilities for popular political change may be discerned.[24]

Despair at the possibility of peaceful political change, however, is probably the most widely heard sentiment in Ethiopia today. Peaceful protest appears impossible since demonstrations without government approval are banned, a fact opposition party activists invoke to explain their incapacity to mobilize support. In Merera's words, 'it is useless to stage any demonstrations – it will only kill us ... The civil opposition is back to zero! We will just try to survive the best we can' (quoted in ibid.: 131). The memories of the massive violence of the 'bad days' of 2005 remain strong. Many speak of a recent popular turn to religion, combined with political apathy and a focus on personal survival, in today's increasingly tough times.

One result has been that armed struggle is invoked more frequently as the only route to political change. While this is heard most often from exiles outside Ethiopia, an awareness of the possibility of future violence is certainly widespread. In Berhanu Nega's words, there has been a 'shift in the thinking of the mainstream political opposition and the public at large toward support for armed resistance against tyranny' (2010: 192). While this might be the wishful thinking of an exile, it does reflect a widespread anxiety among activists and academics that, as Mesfin put it, 'all the avenues of peaceful change are being closed'.

Mesfin, however, also warned that if armed struggle does come to Ethiopia, its toll will be terrible. For that reason, even those most despondent about the possibility for peaceful change seem unwilling to even countenance a future where violent struggle is the only option. As the pessimism of the intellect declares non-violent struggle to be impossible, the optimism of the will declares that armed struggle must be kept in abeyance and that the hope of peaceful change must be kept alive. It is in this optimistic spirit that people seize on any stirring of social movements, revitalized popular parties, or small examples of protest. Indeed, student protests do continue (Abbink 2006: 195), lengthy protests by the Muslim community were staged prominently in Addis Ababa, and Ethiopia has seen the advent of 'political running' (perhaps a companion to Uganda's 'political walking') in which runners competing in Haile Gebreselassie's yearly race carry placards with political messages. Political running as a mode of protest has spilled over from Haile's run: in March 2014, a group of women belonging to the Semayawi political party took advantage of a race on International Women's Day to chant 'We can't take it any more! We are hungry! We need freedom! We need freedom! Free political prisoners!' Seven were arrested and put on trial for terrorism, accused of having shouted that they were 'Daughters of Taitu', a nineteenth-century empress (Alemayehu 2014). Perhaps most significantly, in 2013 several political parties were able to carry out marches with government permission, attracting crowds of thousands or tens of thousands. The pessimism of the intellect says that the state allowing protests is just another political machination by the EPRDF, but the possibility of genuine political openings cannot be dismissed.

The Arab Spring had significant resonance for many Ethiopians, especially those with access to international media, leading to significant activity on Facebook around that time. Two Ethiopians – a teacher and a policeman – even set themselves on fire in protest, but to little effect upon the country's political life. Prominent journalist Eskinder Nega, before his imprisonment, sketched in a series of articles how the Arab Spring might come to Ethiopia. Neither Egypt nor Tunisia provided a model, he felt, because the Ethiopian military would not refrain from massacring protesters. Instead, Libya offered the more pertinent example by demonstrating that even the most powerful security services cannot contain simultaneous protests in many cities, which is what 'already happened in November 2005 when half a dozen cities exploded at almost the same time. The EPRDF was almost, but not quite, stretched to the limit' (Eskinder 2011). The Arab Spring helped 'broaden the possibilities at home', he declared, and today, if Ethiopia's people all took to the streets at once, the government would be unable to contain the protests.

The EPRDF's counter-protest strategy is not without its contradictions. Infrastructure development has brought intense inflation to urban areas, and poverty is still very bad, possibly worse than during the 2005 protests. Even the new jobs provided by the state may not have their intended pacifying effect, given their social meaning: it was not the absence of dead-end, unskilled, low-paying work that drove youth to protest; rather, it was frustrated expectations and the 'cutting of hope' (Mains 2012). The new jobs do not offer the possibility of advancement but only cement young people's positions at 'the bottom of urban society' (Di Nunzio 2012: 445). Despite the co-optation of potential community leaders and the destruction of passive networks, the same conditions that gave rise to protest in 2005 remain today, and state associations may become sites of ready-made organization for political opposition.

The cobblestones themselves, their perfect repeating arcs covering what had been muddy, impassable streets and alleys, may someday become the paradigmatic symbol not of the success of the EPRDF's development project, but of its ultimate failure. In a possible future round of urban rebellion, those stones may be prised back up by the same youth who laid them down and turned into so many weapons to be hurled against the state in a rejection of popular pacification.

8 | 'We are fed up!' Sudan's unfinished uprisings

'The people want to bring down the regime!' In late 2013, crowds of protesters marched through Omdurman shouting anti-government slogans, smashing vehicles and attacking petrol stations. The anger erupting out of poorer neighbourhoods within the vast Khartoum metropolitan region surprised committed student activists, who had spent much of the prior four years working, with little success, to incite a popular uprising on the scale of neighbouring Egypt. But the government's response was as brutal as it was predictable. Moving swiftly into the streets, police used live ammunition, batons, and tear gas to disperse the crowds (Kushkush 2013).

Sudan may not appear, at first glance, a useful archetype for understanding events unfolding across Africa. Awkwardly straddling the so-called Arab north and African south, the country in many ways seems anomalous. The brutal grasp of its military rulers is seen as an anachronism, a throwback to an earlier period of African history. The regime's willingness to unleash horrific violence against its own people renders the country, in the views of many, among the least likely to witness a broad popular movement.

Yet Africa's third largest country has often been at the forefront of political transformations that eventually spread across the continent. In 1885, the country was host to the continent's first successful anti-colonial revolt, as a nativist insurrection overthrew the British supported Turco-Egyptian rulers. Despite the widespread belief that Ghana in 1957 was the first country south of the Sahara to gain its independence, a united Sudan, with its vast southern region situated below the great desert, had in fact won independence one year earlier. It remains one of only two African countries to experience a successful secessionist insurgency. Even the current military leader, Omar al-Bashir, holds the notorious distinction of being the first head of state charged by the International Criminal Court. Most relevantly, in 1964 the country was the site of the first popular movement to overthrow a military regime, an extraordinary feat repeated again in 1985.

In this chapter, we examine Sudan's history of popular uprisings in order to grasp the challenges facing today's ongoing movements. Beginning with the October Revolution of 1964, Sudanese have frequently taken to the streets to challenge the authority of their often venal and ineffective rulers.[1] In the 1980s, Sudanese protesters were again in the vanguard of the wave of anti-austerity and pro-democracy protests that swept the continent. As the success of these earlier movements portends, Sudanese rulers are right to remain fearful of a broad-based, truly popular movement, and so they work feverishly to fend off the latest round of would-be revolutionaries.

Three central challenges have determined the success or failure of every popular movement in Sudan. First is the problem of nationalities: the difficulty of coordinating a popular uprising within a country comprised of hundreds of different peoples representing the vast range of Africa's diversity. Sudan's urban popular movements have always intersected, often contentiously, with violent identity-related movements occurring in the rural periphery. Most prominently, relations between Khartoum and the country's southern region have long been defined by the inability of the country's narrow political elite to forge an inclusive national identity. Yet urban popular movements have fared little better, largely failing to win the support of Sudan's massive peripheral regions. The degree to which organizers are able to forge connections between rural struggles and urban conditions of life remains a recurring challenge.

Second is the division between the country's civil and political society, which presents a major challenge to efforts at aligning Sudan's urban constituencies into a unified force. Sudan's restive civil society, comprised primarily of a professionalized middle class, unionized labour, and students and faculty at the country's numerous institutions of higher education, has often been at the forefront of popular movements. Yet, civil society has struggled to forge a connection between its activism and the concerns of political society. Sudan's political society – comprised of poorly educated youth from the rural peripheries (and beyond), who arrive in the rapidly expanding Khartoum metropolitan area seeking relief from often brutal conditions – strive to carve out a tenuous existence within the city's expansive informal economy. Between the two are the Islamists, who vacillate between supporting the ruling party and mounting the most prominent opposition to the regime. The Islamists exist in convoluted relationships with both students and unemployed urban youth, often undermining efforts to forge an alliance between civil and political society.

The role of the military is the final challenge. Sudan's armed forces have not always been a regressive force; indeed, progressive elements have been at the forefront of major political transformations in the country. In those cases when Sudanese popular movements have managed to divide the military, they have successfully overthrown regimes. When they failed, they have been met with brutal crackdowns. Historically, the opposition's ability to navigate each of these three challenges has determined whether a movement will succeed or whether it will splinter and collapse. It is no different today as a new generation of Sudanese takes to the street.

The rise of people power: Sudan's October Revolution of 1964

In 1955, even as Britain sought to turn power over to Sudan's narrow nationalist movement, southern soldiers mutinied, marking the inception of the first civil war. Southerners had grown increasingly agitated by the dismissive attitudes of the country's emerging political elite, including the nationalist leader, Ismail al-Azhari, who denigrated southern discontent as 'childish complaints'. Fed up with their exclusion from negotiations between the colonial authorities and the small Arab elite who comprised the country's exclusivist 'nationalist' movement, soldiers in Torit took up arms against the British authorities on 18 August.[2] Five months later, on 1 January 1956, Sudan became an independent nation with the National United Party (NUP) in power and al-Azhari ensconced as prime minister. Al-Azhari had initially sought to delay Sudan's independence in favour of an aborted attempt at forging a political union with Egypt that would unite the Nile Valley. However, faced with popular outrage that was fuelled by his rivals in the Islamist Umma party, he recanted. But the Umma party was not satisfied and, in connivance with the splinter People's Democratic Party (PDP), forced al-Azhari's dismissal in July 1956.

The Umma–PDP alliance was no better suited to govern Sudan. Lacking a permanent constitution and faced with corruption and internal factionalism, the country entered a period of economic and political crisis that the unresolved southern war only deepened. Popular outrage spread widely, and the coalition flailed as it attempted to resolve the multiple challenges it faced. On 17 November 1958, the Sudanese military, under Ibrahim Abboud, launched a coup that placed him as the head of the newly empowered Supreme Council of the Armed Forces. Though initially embraced by wide sections of Sudanese society, Abboud's regime quickly proved incapable of resolving the country's deep problems.

By 1959, the Khartoum University Student Union (KUSU) began calling for a return to democratic rule, prompting the first of many government crackdowns on student activism. Students had begun to organize in the early 1940s as part of the country's nationalist movement. By the 1950s, student activism had splintered into two separate tendencies that continue to define urban popular politics today. This bifurcation of student activism into a secular left and an Islamist faction paralleled a similar division at the national level in which the Sudan Communist Party vied for influence against various Islamist parties. However, whereas national politics reflected a winner-takes-all mind-set in which political actors had to align with one or the other of the tendencies, KUSU leaders sought to bridge their internal divide. By embracing proportional representation, the union hoped to ensure minority voices would be heard (Hamid 2009: 9–10).

Initially, Abboud sought advice from faculty and students at the university regarding the regime's failed policy towards the south. Such outreach efforts, however, were combined with attempts to assert greater control over student activism. The regime tried and failed to dissolve KUSU in 1961. It had more success reigning in student activism by placing the university under the control of the Ministry of Education (ibid.: 10). By this point, the military junta began to face challenges from a cross-section of Sudanese society, including the initially cautious opposition parties, with the Communist Party and its allies in the trade unions emerging as a particular foil.[3]

Following the death of Ahmed al-Quresh, a student activist killed by police on 21 October 1964, discontent morphed quickly into protests calling for an immediate end to the government's southern policy as well as challenging its policies on education and the economy (El-Affendi 2012). Abboud's attempts to suppress the southern revolt, including his heavy-handed initiative to Arabize Sudan's so-called African tribes, meant that the southern insurgency, which had persisted with sporadic eruptions, had evolved into the far more potent Anya Nya rebellion, placing even more pressure on the regime. The University of Khartoum had become the cradle of the country's first post-independence uprising, what is now celebrated as the October Revolution.

The United National Front (UNF) quickly emerged as the co-ordinating body and brought together the National Front for the Professionals (comprised of academics, lawyers, media personnel and trade unions) with the more conservative National Front of Political Parties (comprised of Sudan's major opposition parties, most led by traditional leaders). The regime's attempt to smother the protests only strengthened the movement's hand, even turning some younger elements of the military against the government. Army officers had made several attempts since 1959 to overthrow the Abboud regime and establish instead a 'popular government' but with no success. Now with the protests gathering steam, the UNF reached out to dissident army officers for support.

On the same day as al-Quresh's funeral, the UNF supported a

general strike that quickly spread throughout the country. Organizers, drawn solely from within civil society, took advantage of widespread anger within political society at the inability of the military regime to deal with the prolonged economic crisis. Particularly resented was Abboud's failure to halt the long-standing slide in the global price of cotton, Sudan's primary export at the time. In particular, 1963 had produced an especially poor cotton crop. Combined with the rising costs of fighting the southern rebellion, there was little the regime could do to ameliorate the economic impact on Sudan's working poor (Hasan 1967: 492).

Responding to the UNF's call, tens of thousands of civilians from across the urban spectrum took to the streets to confront the military through mostly non-violent action but also through bouts of rioting. By 26 October, the strike had succeeded in bringing the country to a halt. Abboud went on the radio to announce the dissolution of the military but a day later seemed to draw back from that promise. On 28 October, the regime opened fire on protesters marching on the presidential palace, killing at least twenty and wounding many others. The attack on protesters fuelled public anger and deepened the split in the military between middle-ranking officers and the top command. According to one participant, an 80-year-old retired lawyer and ex-Communist Party member, the military divide reflected the lack of popular support for the regime: 'We did not fear a crackdown because the leaders of the military regime were not backed by any societal organizations.'[4] On 29 October, with few remaining options for staying in power, Abboud dissolved the Supreme Military Council and turned power over to a civilian-led transitional government.

The October Revolution stands as the first time in African history in which a popular revolution overthrew a military dictatorship (El-Tigani 2003). It established a blueprint for how Sudanese civil society actors can draw on the latent power of political society in order to overthrow a military dictatorship and thus remains a touchstone for contemporary activists.[5] In the words of one Sudanese scholar, 'the October Revolution of 1964 became the inspiration for all subsequent action in Sudanese politics. Every political group or regime ever since sought to derive legitimacy from that event, which ranks higher than Independence in popular esteem' (El-Affendi 2012: 1).

Yet, despite its considerable success, the October Revolution could not resolve the national question. Under the new civilian government, the Round Table conference brought together eighteen representatives of northern political parties with twenty-seven southern leaders in March of 1965. While the conference was successful in addressing several key issues including the repatriation of southern refugees and the question of religious freedom, it failed to implement the key constitutional reforms demanded by the south to resolve Sudan's urban–rural divide. For seven more years, the southern war raged on unabated.

The 'Popular Uprisings' and the rise of the Islamists

The 1964 protests cleared the way for an elected civilian government – a weak coalition of the Umma and NUP parties – that mismanaged the country until 1969. Agreeing on little more than suppressing the Communist Party, and riven by a power struggle between the two party leaders, the civilian government failed to provide the stability that many desired. Meanwhile, the war in the south descended into further brutality. Citing the inability of the government to make decisions and its failure to resolve the country's deepening economic and political woes, a group of young officers, the Free Officers Movement (an explicit reference to the 1952 Egyptian coup), seized power. Under the leadership of Colonel Jaafar Nimeiri, the movement established a ten-member Revolutionary Command Council to run the country.

Positioning the Council as the true inheritor of the October Revolution, Nimeiri promised a new direction for Sudan. In a sequence of events resonating with today's turmoil in Egypt, the coup was welcomed by wide swathes of the population who had been involved with the 1964 protests. Support for Nimeiri, however, was not uncontested. Some members of the Communist Party were wary of the Council's ideological position, thus effectively dividing the party between those who supported the regime and those who did not. This division played out within the ruling Council as well. Council members who supported an overtly socialist path for the new government clashed with others who remained wary of the Communists' influence. Following a failed coup attempt by Communist sympathizers in July 1971, Nimeiri purged the Council of its progressive voices.

The fighting within the Council also spilled over to university campuses, allowing the Islamists to move to the forefront of student unions (Hamid 2009: 13). Seeking to reduce the organizational prowess of the Communists at the societal level, Nimeiri placed trade unions under government control and banned the existence of Communist-affiliated student, women's, and professional associations. In response to his crackdown on the country's progressive forces, Nimeiri was met with recurring protests and strikes by leftist students. Without a social base and facing challenges from across the political spectrum, Nimeiri turned to Islamist leaders for support, famously embracing them in a public display in 1977. In order to curry favour with his new allies, Nimeiri sought to Islamize the constitution, leading to renewed tension with southern leaders.

Building on recommendations that came out of the Round Table conference, Nimeiri had negotiated an end to the war through the 1972 Addis Ababa Agreement, which provided greater autonomy to the southern region. By 1978, already wary of the government's creeping Islamization, southerners once again began to mobilize out of fear that the government intended to claim the substantial oil deposits located in their region. First found in the town of Bentiu in 1978, oil deposits were discovered all over the south in the next few years. During the same period, Sudan's external debt rose precipitously to over $5 billion, forcing the regime to make sharp cuts to social spending. In order to ensure his own political survival, Nimeiri began scheming for ways to abrogate the Addis Ababa Agreement and appropriate southern oil. In 1983, while attempting to outbid the Islamist parties, Nimeiri declared sharia as the basis for the Sudanese legal system, in the process unilaterally abrogating the Addis

Ababa Agreement. Tensions with the south again morphed into a full-fledged war.

In 1984, under pressure from multiple sides, Nimeiri declared a state of emergency. Among his many critics was Mahmoud Mohammed Taha, a noted Muslim reformer, who questioned Nimeiri's imposition of Islamic law (An-Na'im 1996; Mamdani 2011). Taha, who critiqued Islamist politics from a Muslim perspective, was arrested in early January 1985 for distributing a pamphlet critical of sharia. Within two weeks he was convicted in a trial he refused to legitimate with his participation and was hanged in public.

Despite the small number of adherents officially aligned with Taha's Republican Brothers, thousands of protesters took to the street in disgust (Massoud 2013; Packer 2006). Rather than demonstrating the ability of the regime to suppress dissent, Taha's death opened the floodgates of suppressed rage. The date of Taha's execution marked the foundation of *al- Tajammu' al-Niqabi*, or the Trade Union Gathering, which secretly brought together activists representing thirteen professional associations, including doctors, engineers, lawyers, and academic staff (El-Affendi 2012: 4). By this point, Nimeiri had also broken with the Muslim Brotherhood, the last major social force that supported the regime, and arrested its leader, Hassan al-Turabi. Although resistance against Nimeiri had been building for some time, it now emerged from the shadows into the centre of political life in the country.

On 26 March 1985, students at Omdurman Islamic University took to the streets to protest Nimeiri's imposition of austerity measures at the behest of the International Monetary Fund. The cuts led to a doubling in the price of fuel and other essential goods like bread and sugar. Prices on many basic goods had already skyrocketed the year before, so the latest increases were viewed as excessively onerous. The next day, students at the University of Khartoum marched to the city centre where they were joined by large numbers of the *shammasha* – a term referring to unemployed youth and street vendors – representing a novel convergence between civil and political society (ibid.: 5).

In early April, a strike by medical doctors protesting the treatment of student activists snowballed into a public strike by the powerful professional trade unions. Despite a brutal crackdown by the regime, the 'Popular Uprisings', as they became known, brought together a broad assortment of Sudanese civil society, including doctors, lawyers, bankers, and students, with political society. Protesters took to the streets of central Khartoum by the tens of thousands, reflecting the organizational depth of activists (De Waal 2013). Riot police were brought in to suppress the protests, and mass arrests of activists, together with summary judgments in Emergency Courts, became central to the regime's survival strategy. In an attempt to fracture the civil society–political society alliance, thousands of unemployed youth, especially those from western Sudan, were rounded up and deported (El-Affendi 2012).

The Trade Union Gathering quickly sought to position itself at the centre of the nascent movement. It began negotiations with the leading opposition parties, producing a plan for the transitional period. The National Alliance for the Salvation of the Homeland (NANS), which brought together political parties, trade unions, and professional organizations, was established to oversee the transition. NANS took extensive measures to ensure the depth and strength of the movement. It established shadow committees in each town ready to take over organizing responsibilities if the original organizers were arrested. Organizers also established an impressive counter-surveillance capacity to intercept police and army radio communications (De Waal 2013). But, given how little impetus people needed to flood the streets, events soon outpaced organization. Driven by anger within political society, protests escalated in an uncoordinated manner. By 4 April, the country was shut down with demonstrations in every major city on a scale exceeding the October Revolution (El-Affendi 2012: 6).

On 6 April, NANS announced a march on the presidential palace, triggering a debate within the regime on how to handle the expected crowd of tens of thousands. Several army field commanders, fearful of losing control of the protests, argued against a violent crackdown. If police opened fire on the crowd, these commanders made it clear that they would be forced to intervene *against* the regime. Then, on the morning of 6 April, before the march could commence, a group of army officers went on the radio to pre-emptively announce that they had 'decided to side with the people' and depose the president. Nimeiri, in the midst of an American sojourn to call on his primary backer, President Ronald Reagan, was thrown out of office by his own generals, who were increasingly wary of the angry crowds. Hastily, he attempted to return to Khartoum. A NANS supporter inside air traffic control, however, shut down Sudanese airspace, forcing his flight to stop in Egypt, where President Hosni Mubarak welcomed him (De Waal 2013). Nimeiri remained in Cairo as an exile for the next fourteen years (El-Affendi 2012: 6–7).

The generals announced an interim government and called for elections later that year. Yet, once again, no stable civilian government emerged. Contributing to the impasse was the intransigence of the leader of the Sudan People's Liberation Movement/Army (SPLM/A), John Garang, a charismatic ex-military officer who led the second southern revolt from its inception in 1983. Garang felt that events in Khartoum were outpacing his own initiative to position the southern rebels as the only democratic force in the country. He refused to participate in the transition process, illustrating the recurring difficulty of squaring the concerns of the rural periphery with urban political realities and those of a violent armed struggle with an unarmed protest movement (De Waal 2013).

Without the participation of the southern insurgents, a coalition of parties, including the National Islamic Front, run by the powerful Muslim cleric and Taha rival Hassan al-Turabi, and several smaller southern parties came to power. Sadiq al-Mahdi, an Oxford-educated descendant of the leader of the Mahdist movement and a former prime minister, was again selected to lead the country out from military rule. Riven by corruption and nepotism, however, al-Mahdi's regime did little to ameliorate the demands of the popular movement. As a result, protesters continued to challenge what they viewed as the usurpation of their revolution by the country's political elite. In December 1988 and June 1989, protests and riots broke out in Khartoum and Omdurman against austerity-induced price increases and food shortages (Nkinyangi 1991: 162).

In 1989, Omar al-Bashir, an Egyptian-educated army colonel, came to the forefront of Sudanese politics. Bashir had joined the Sudanese army in 1960 and risen quickly through the ranks, even fighting alongside the Egyptian army in the Yom Kippur War of 1973. A popular figure within the military, Bashir lived through both previous Sudanese popular uprisings and played a central role in the denouement of the 1985 protests. Encouraged by al-Turabi, the key Islamist leader, Bashir overthrew the al-Mahdi government in June in a bloodless coup. Building on his popularity within the army, Bashir turned towards the Islamists as the key legitimizing force for his coup.

The democratic opposition, which had benefited from the divided military four years earlier, could do little to challenge Bashir's rise. Having achieved victory prior to forging a durable national coalition, it was ill-prepared to challenge the repressive turn that Bashir's coup commenced. Bashir quickly set about crushing opposition forces. He closed trade unions, repressed student activism, sacked faculty, and chased many other professionals, including doctors and lawyers, out of the country. Torture, disappearances, and targeted killings became a regular feature of Sudanese urban life, while endless counter-insurgency campaigns came to define the rural peripheries. Bashir's ascendance signalled the end of most forms of unarmed oppositional politics in Sudan for the next two decades. Yet, the memory of the 1964 and 1985 popular uprisings lingered, ready to be invoked in future rounds of protest.

Civil society in protest: Girifna and the 2010 elections

On 11 April 2010, Sudanese voters went to the polls to participate in the country's first multiparty elections in almost a quarter century. Six months earlier, just before the start of the voter registration process, a group of young activists in Khartoum had formed 'Girifna' ('We are fed up'). Conceived as an 'open, non-hierarchical, street protest group of young men and women' (Hale and Kadoda 2013: 71), Girifna was founded as a grassroots movement with the aspiration of using the ballot box to overthrow Bashir's National Congress Party (NCP). Populated primarily by middle-class students, it initially had the narrow focus of ensuring that all Sudanese were encouraged – and allowed – to cast their votes.

The election took place at a fraught moment in Sudanese national history, with the regime facing a number of crises resulting from the signing of a comprehensive peace agreement (CPA) with the rebels of the SPLA. The southern war had raged since 1983, with millions dead and little progress towards a resolution. The events of 11 September 2001 shifted the dynamic, increasing international pressure on Bashir. Faced with threats of military action from the emboldened presidency of George W. Bush, Bashir was forced into granting concessions to the southern rebels. This initiated a three-year peace process that culminated in the CPA in 2005. Ultimately, the resolution of Sudan's southern question, problematic though it was, had come not from internal political processes but rather from the threat of war by the remaining global hegemon.

The CPA was predicated on the holding of national elections, allowing SPLA leaders to participate as candidates. It also made Garang, who was expected to contest for the presidency, a vice-president of the country. His triumphant visit to Khartoum on 8 July 2005 drew over a million people into the streets in an extraordinary display of support. At a public address, Garang proclaimed his commitment to Sudanese unity: 'I am among my people. I didn't return to Sudan, I was always in Sudan,' he declared, drawing wild cheers from the crowd, including large numbers of Southern Sudanese who lived in Khartoum (*Gurtong* 2005).

Just three weeks later, Garang was dead, killed in a helicopter accident as he returned to Sudan from neighbouring Uganda. Under his command, the SPLA had sought to position itself as a movement for national reform, establishing branches across the country. Garang's advocacy for a multi-ethnic, democratic and united Sudan represented the first significant attempt to bring together urban civil and political societies within a political agenda, articulated by forces based in the country's rural periphery. The fact that much of Khartoum's political society had roots in the peripheral areas – by some accounts rural migrants constitute over 60 per cent of the total Khartoum population – meant that Garang was uniquely positioned to bridge the long-standing divides.[6] The crowds that turned out for his arrival that day in July were testimony to the appeal of his vision among the country's diverse constituencies. Indeed, memories of Garang still permeate the consciousness of many within political society. As a taxi driver in Khartoum put it, 'The regime killed John Garang, and it has killed us.'[7]

Garang's death triggered a power struggle within the SPLA command, and those who preferred secession eventually moved to the fore. Ultimately the abandonment of Garang's agenda for a 'New Sudan' by his successors inhibits an assessment of whether he had truly found a solution to the country's major challenges. Yet, his ideas continue to have appeal today and are invoked by activists as representing the only approach yet that had the ability to unite civil and political society.[8] Even as the new leadership began to lay the groundwork for dividing the country, the party continued to contest the national elections, hoping to garner legitimacy from its participation.

While Bashir's NCP and the SPLM began mobilizing their supporters ahead of the election, the Umma Party and other opposition parties demonstrated little interest. With the SPLM moving towards secession and the remaining opposition parties ill-prepared to challenge the NCP juggernaut, student activists were compelled to act. Recognizing that no groups were actively involved in voter education and that most voters had little information about how to register, Girifna was founded to fill the void and spur non-SPLM opposition parties to take seriously their role in the election. Why did Girifna activists believe that voter registration efforts would be sufficient to challenge an entrenched regime?

This strategy was, in their view, a pragmatic response to political realities. As Amjed Farid, a 27-year-old activist put it, 'We cannot *not* go to the elections' (Fick 2010). Girifna developed a sophisticated campaign combining both social media and on-the-ground outreach efforts to spread their message, although their reach remained limited. The campaign did receive considerable support from Sudanese living in the diaspora: in addition to financial donations, many others offered expertise, including building the movement's English and Arabic website.[9] Organizers chose orange for their colour, a theme that runs through the website, punctuated by the V-for-victory sign that serves as the movement's logo.

Shortly before the nomination deadline, Salva Kiir, Garang's replacement as SPLA leader, refused to contest the presidency, a move interpreted to signal his preference for secession. A northern ex-Communist Party member, Yasir Arman, was selected as the SPLA's presidential candidate instead. Alongside a number of other parties and candidates, Arman eventually withdrew from the competition in the face of widespread harassment by the NCP and against the instructions of his own party. Confused about where to stand, Girifna supported the opposition boycott in what turned out to be a strategic mistake. Despite withdrawing, Arman's candidacy went on to win over 20 per cent of the presidential vote, evoking for the first time in a generation a sense of hope among Sudanese youth and revealing cracks in a regime long viewed as undefeatable. After two decades of Bashir's autocratic rule, it was ultimately a movement that originated in the periphery that forced a reckoning for the country's ruling elite. SPLM success in national elections demonstrated the interlinked nature of the country's urban and rural struggles but also the hard to reconcile gap between the democratic aspirations of the country's urban centres and the strong desire within some of its rural areas to break away completely.

This division between urban and rural also affected efforts by Girifna and other student groups to position themselves as a national movement for reform. Girifna's platform reflected positions espoused by the SPLM during its abandoned campaign for the presidency, including demands for democracy and representative government. But Girifna was not merely a product of the SPLM, as many of the concerns articulated by the ex-rebels have long animated opposition movements in Sudan. Instead, it demonstrates the ways in which Sudan's rural-based struggles have long understood the national context of their marginalization. It also demonstrates the salience of their message for urban activists, many of whom struggle to make the same connections.

Had the election unfolded fairly and had Girifna been allowed to conduct voter information campaigns, organizers may have wrapped up their efforts after the 2010 election. Instead, the regime declared the movement illegal (ibid.). A month before the election, on 4 March, three Girifna members were arrested at a peaceful election campaign and charged with 'causing "public noisiness"' under Article 77 of the Criminal Act of 1991.[10] After the election, the NCP cracked down further. Press outlets, given limited freedom prior to the election, were censored, and journalists and activists faced a marked increase in repression (HRW 2010).

In response to the crackdown, many youth activists fled the country (Hale and Kadoda 2013). Nagi Musa, a co-founder of Girifna, took a position at York University in England after being beaten and arrested during a protest.[11] In an interview, he explained how he worked with approximately 5,000 volunteers to ensure their safety during voter education and election monitoring campaigns. If a volunteer was arrested or abducted, text messages or social media raised the alarm. As with many other Girifna exiles, Musa continued his activism once abroad. But with their leaders exiled, or in hiding, student activism in Sudan entered a low period. Never very large in terms of numbers, the nascent movement faced an existential crisis as international monitors validated the results of the election (Hamilton 2010). Some pushed forward, carrying on their activities, albeit in diminished form.[12]

The limits of student activism

The student movement found new life and, importantly, new allies in January 2011 as protests spread through Tunisia and

Egypt. Several thousand protesters took to the streets in diverse locations throughout Sudan in late January and early February. Although inspired by events unfolding to their north, protesters were equally concerned with the ongoing turmoil in the southern part of the country. From 9 to 16 January, southern Sudanese flocked to the polls to participate in a referendum on whether the immense region would remain a part of a unified Sudan or go its separate way. Many young people, inspired by the SPLM's success, were nevertheless disappointed by its decision to support secession. In interviews, many professed hope that the secession vote might topple the Bashir regime but also worried about the future of democracy once the south split away.[13]

Bashir calculated that although he could survive the loss of the south, protests in Khartoum and violent challengers in the remaining provinces had to be deterred at all costs. A savvy political operator who has managed to outlast multiple threats to his regime, Bashir understood that international pressure from the US, the International Criminal Court, and human rights activists, which had appeared to threaten his control in the early 2000s, had dwindled. Ever the pragmatist, Bashir decided to take a stand.

Student demonstrators from Girifna, along with other groups including 'Change Now', 'The Spark' and 'Youth for Change', took to the streets throughout January 2011. On 30 January, coinciding with protests in Tunisia and Egypt, several thousand demonstrators, mobilized by social media, gathered at four different locations in Khartoum and Omdurman. Yet, despite the tens of thousands who participated in various online forums, organizers could never muster crowds of more than a few thousand, not nearly enough to threaten the regime. Security forces beat and arrested protesters and used tear gas to disperse the crowds. The regime also shut down activist websites, claiming that the protesters had not secured the required permits. Organizers reported that at least fifty people were arrested. Protests continued through February, but were never able to bring more than a few hundred people to the streets.

In December 2011, student organizers once again attempted to trigger a popular movement – again, with little success. Demanding an end to police violence and the overthrow of the regime, some 16,000 students participated in a sit-in the University of Khartoum (*Al Arabiya* 2011). Smaller actions were reported at other campuses. The protests were quickly broken up by the government, which sent police on to campuses to use tear gas and batons to disperse protesters.

The 2011 protests were crushed easily by the regime, but student energies were not quieted. As the economic crisis dragged on, the regime took actions that provided additional opportunities for activists. Unlike Egypt and Tunisia, where economic crises were driven by a global slowdown, in Sudan, economic difficulties stemmed from austerity measures that were a response to internal pressures. The independence of South Sudan in July 2011 had perilously affected the regime's finances. In January 2012, the new government of South Sudan levelled another blow at the regime by shutting down oil production over a border dispute. Oil revenues are estimated to account for around 20 per cent of Khartoum's total budget expenditures, so the impact was substantial (Tadros 2012). In addition, fighting with South Sudan around the contested Heglig oil field reduced oil revenues by a further 20 per cent (Al Jazeera 2012).[14] Additional austerity measures were introduced. The government floated the Sudanese pound and removed subsidies on transportation, food, and, most dramatically, fuel, causing a 60 per cent price increase. It also raised taxes on consumer goods, banks, and imports, all with the hope of plugging the $2.4 billion deficit caused by the loss of oil revenues. For the majority of the population, the cost of living skyrocketed in response to the government's measures. The cost of basic goods, unemployment, and inflation all doubled (Tadros 2012).

The economic crisis provided a new opportunity for student activists to reach out to political society. In June 2012, four female students at the University of Khartoum decided to protest the rising cost of accommodation. Police overreaction triggered daily protests calling for the fall of the regime. Security forces responded harshly but with little success, using detentions, interrogations, and intimidation to stop the protests – even going as far as firing tear gas and rubber bullets. In response, the protests picked up pace. Smaller protests were reported in the cities of Sennar, North Kordofan, and El Gezira states (Gallo 2012). Although organizers were better able to draw support from political society by focusing on the economic crisis, the protests struggled to achieve a mass scale. Organizers adapted by pursuing a longer-term strategy. Following the initial outburst, smaller weekly protests against the regime – 'Revolutionary-themed Fridays', as they were dubbed by Sudanese bloggers – quickly became part of the Khartoum landscape. Activists gave the weekly protests different names chosen to resonate widely within Sudanese society, such as *Kandaka* to honour the centrality of Sudanese women in democratic movements and to demonstrate the protesters' commitment to advancing women's rights.[15] 'Licking Elbows' was another, drawn from Bashir's frequent rejoinder to critics that they should go 'lick their elbows' (Tadros 2012).

Organizers spread their message to the international media via the #SudanRevolts hashtag on Twitter, generating a degree of international coverage.[16] Yet, many of the most active users of social media were based abroad and did not reflect the actual depth of the protest movement in Khartoum. Twitter and Facebook have tiny audiences even in the Sudanese capital, where most people have irregular, if any, access to the Internet – it is estimated that only 10 per cent of Sudanese have the ability to go online. In addition, many youth became suspicious of social media after the government identified protesters by monitoring their participation on pro-democracy Facebook pages.[17] Instead, mobile phone technologies like text messages moved to the fore. In addition to the relative anonymity SMS technology provides, such messages were far more likely to reach political society given the broader distribution of cell phones.[18] Despite working to build a broad front, the weekly protests came to an end eight weeks later due to a lack of interest, the difficulty of continuing the protests during Ramadan, and repression by the regime (El Sanosi 2012).

In December 2012, four students from Darfur studying at Gezira University, south of Khartoum, were killed after participating in a peaceful sit-in that was disrupted by a pro-government student union. According to a 2006 peace deal between the government and the main Darfuri rebel faction, Darfurians were eligible to receive a five-year fee waiver at national universities (Al-Saleh 2012). However, the terms of eligibility for the waiver had remained opaque, leading to disagreements over whether the agency established to administer the peace deal or the individual institutions would determine eligibility (Ali 2012). Students from Darfur gathered to protest the denial of the fee waiver, only to be attacked by members of the *rabata*, pro-regime militiamen armed with machetes and iron bars. Protesters ran in different directions, chased by the *rabata*. Four students' bodies were later found in a shallow canal and showed signs of having been tortured before being dumped. Initially, the regime claimed they had drowned, despite the fact that the water in the canal was only three feet deep (Gallo 2012). Word of the killings spread fast, and protests in solidarity with the Gezira students were organized at several campuses, including Khartoum, Nilien, and Omdurman Islamic universities. Hundreds protested and tens were detained, but the protests could not match the energy of the earlier outbreaks.

What accounts for the recurring struggles of the student movement? Throughout 2011 and 2012, student organizers demonstrated their potency by organizing protests in Khartoum and beyond that garnered the participation of thousands. Yet, in interviews, student organizers acknowledged that they failed to overcome the boundaries that separated them from both the urban poor and rural populations, hindering their ability to pose a significant threat to the regime. A central challenge was how to reach out to political society, especially the *shammasha*, the unemployed youth who had played a central role in the prior two successful Sudanese revolts.[19] As one informant, a migrant from Khordofan, explained, 'There is a very big gap between the [student] activists and the poor. The way they speak is down to the poor people.'[20]

Or, in the words of a former trade unionist who had participated in the Popular Uprisings:

> [Student activists] are very elitist and not inclusive in engaging youth in the slums around the city. ... Civil society is not related to people from marginalized areas. The problem is the social divide between the activists and the marginalized.[21]

Students from the periphery have also criticized Girifna's reformist agenda and non-violent approach and have formed their own organizations such as *Ambibi*, Darfur Student Association, and Nuba Mountain Student Union to represent their perspectives. They accused Girifna and Change Now members of failing to comprehend the brutality meted out in rural areas – violence, they suggested, that the majority of student activists had never experienced and hence could not understand. In addition, these students called attention to the racial dynamics of state repression, another issue missing from Girifna and other student groups' analysis.[22]

Student organizers were also unable to fully mobilize civil society in support of their efforts. During both the 1964 and 1985 uprising, students, professional associations, and trade unions worked together. Often reacting to fast-moving events on the ground, they were able to quickly forge viable coalitions to give often disconnected protests a clear sense of purpose. More importantly, the protests were timed to capitalize on existing anger within political society which was driven largely by declining economic conditions and whose participation gave the uprisings their mass character. Tensions existed among the formal opposition political parties, most of which had strong ties to traditional Sudanese elites as well as to the more radical professional associations, trade unions, and student organizations, which tended to regard political parties as corrupt and regressive. Yet the movements that emerged had been genuinely popular and included a broad coalition of actors (El-Affendi 2012: 8; Hasan 1967).

During the recent rounds of student-led protest, however, opposition parties have largely remained on the sidelines.[23] Recognizing that the students' chances for success were slim, they instead cut deals with the regime and clamped down on their members who spoke out in support of the protesters (El Sanosi 2012). In addition, Bashir has avoided targeting the Islamist parties even as his relationships with some key leaders, most notably al-Turabi, have deteriorated. In contrast, all of the North African regimes that fell in 2011 were openly hostile to the Islamist parties (El-Affendi 2012: 13). Even where specific opposition leaders have fallen out with the regime, they have not supported the students. Al-Turabi has remained sceptical of popular movements and stoked anxiety over post-revolutionary Sudan, remarking in an interview, 'Look at what happened in Egypt ... We don't want that to happen here, nobody knows who is in charge in Egypt' (Tadros 2012).

In both earlier revolts, military interference played an essential role in allowing the protesters to realize their agendas. Though the military did not hesitate to crack down during the early stages, over time, officers and rank-and-file soldiers alike developed reservations about the use of violence against civilians and pushed for an alternate course. This accounts for the rapid success of both revolutions, what El-Affendi has referred to as their 'blitzkrieg character' (2012: 9). In contrast, the military's fealty to the Bashir regime accounts for the reticence of many soldiers to break ranks. Although cracks have appeared recently, Bashir has continued to successfully cultivate loyalty within the military and security services even as his popularity among the general public continues to slide. In addition, the prior failures of popular movements to develop a viable post-revolutionary democratic order means that many prefer stability over the unknown outcome of a post-Bashir Sudan. The uneven progress in neighbouring Egypt, which has oscillated between a popular uprising, a democratic election, an army coup, counter-demonstrations, and violent repression, furthers the military's hesitation to join the revolt.

Universities are no longer the centre of political activism, and student activists have thus far lacked the capacity to bring large numbers on to the street (Hamid 2009). According to Mohammed El-Tom, a former professor of mathematics who was expelled in 1992, Bashir has successfully depoliticized the universities by directly appointing pro-regime administrators and encouraging pro-NCP students who have taken over the student unions (Martelli 2012). A similar strategy has rendered the trade unions even less of a threat to the regime. Yet, despite the serious challenges facing student activism, recent events demonstrate that Sudan's ongoing uprising still has life.

Political society retakes the stage

If Bashir thought undermining student activists would signal his final triumph over the anti-government protests, he miscalculated the complex nature of the social forces arrayed against him. Although student activism failed to catalyse a broader popular movement, political society was being primed for action. In July and August 2013, heavy rains overwhelmed Sudan's poor infrastructure and much of the country was affected by extensive flooding. The government's response, however, was minimal: 'There is no government here,' in the words of one market woman, 'nobody provides services.'[24] Relief supplies donated by the country's wealthier neighbours were found for sale in local markets, a product of the regime's corruption and indifference to suffering. Student activists working through an 'apolitical' initiative known as Nafeer did provide some relief, efforts that were notable for bringing middle- and upper-class 'Arab' youth in contact for the first time with the harsh living conditions faced by Khartoum's primarily 'African' political society.[25]

Compounding the misery, in early September the government announced that it would soon lift subsidies on oil in order to deal with the relentless economic crisis (*Al Arabiya* 2013). Coming soon after the bungled official response to the flooding, residents of the city's slums had little patience for a further downturn in their already meagre standard of living. Officials were unprepared for political society's response. On 22 September, the day the increase took effect and quickly doubled fuel prices, the *shammasha* took to the streets. Around Khartoum and especially across the White Nile in Omdurman, poorer neighbourhoods went into open revolt.

The spatial distribution of the protests, located as they were in the poor and working-class neighbourhoods that surround Khartoum and teem with populations from the country's marginalized regions, initially befuddled the government. Metropolitan Khartoum is divided by the two Niles into three distinct spaces that are connected by a series of bridges designed to keep protests from spilling across regions. But the localized nature of the protests meant that the disparate groups of protesters had little interest in coming together to form a unified front. Public property, including police stations, buses, and petrol stations, was burned down. The widespread destruction led many media outlets to dismiss the protests as riots. Others, however, saw the targeting of petrol stations as a statement against government profiteering on oil rents, as government insiders were known to own several of the stations attacked.[26] Witnesses also testified that protesters chanted anti-government slogans as they engaged in bouts of targeted destruction (Kushkush 2013).

The regime had sought to pre-empt the protests by arresting student activists and opposition leaders, some of whom were detained on 18 September, four days before the subsidies were lifted (HRW 2013). Yet, because the protests did not originate within civil society, government efforts at repression proved futile. Government agencies even shut down the internet on the second day in a misguided attempt to undercut organizers presumed to be using social media to coordinate the protests (Kushkush 2013). Officials sought to dismiss the importance of political society protests by racializing them, claiming they were riots organized by 'nigger gangs'. By deploying an English slur to criminalize the protesters, the regime sought to link them to stereotypes of a supposed US 'ghetto' culture (*New Sudan Vision* 2009).

Having failed to stop the outbreak, the government reverted to a more hardline approach, using brutally repressive measures that it had never deployed against student activists.[27] Authorities responded with an 'iron fist', turning to live ammunition and tear gas to break up the scattered protests. The Caroor Market in Umbedda at the edge of Omdurman was transformed into a killing zone as government snipers opened fire on the raucous crowds, killing at least twenty.[28] According to informants, some members of the security forces were reluctant to crack down on protesters, as they had been during the October Revolution and the Popular Uprisings. Rumours spread that Bashir was relying on members from the dreaded Janjaweed to stymie the protests.[29] Sudanese rights groups claimed that two hundred died by the end of the protests five days later, overwhelming the numbers killed during the earlier student protests and underlining the greater threat that political society protest posed to the regime.

The scale of the protests and their social composition posed a considerable challenge to students and other civil society organizers.[30] Student activists acknowledge that they had little to do with triggering or coordinating the 2013 protests but were anxious to capitalize on the energies of political society.[31] The question they face is how to unite the undeniable energy of political society with the organizing acumen of the formal pro-democracy movement. As the Sudanese columnist Abdel-Latif el-Bouni remarked, 'Anger is not enough for change.' Yet, he continued, 'if geared into political momentum, it has the potential to become a revolution' (Kushkush 2013).

While some student organizers lamented the lack of organization and the fact that political society protests never converged with civil society action, others recognized that this was the opportunity they had been waiting for. Earlier protests led by students had failed to spark a movement, and an overreliance on social media had provided an entry point for government infiltration. A movement that lacked a hierarchical structure and embraced a decentralized approach, however, would not be crushed as easily. Considering the government's counter-protest strategy, the lack of a hierarchical structure among protesters could prevent infiltration of the movement's ranks as each neighbourhood could keep its actions coordinated within a tight circle of individuals. Instead of co-opting political society protest, some student organizers sought to advance an alternate model. Building on lessons learned from Nafeer and the 2013 protests, student organizers are actively reaching out to leaders of the neighbourhood protests to educate them about their significance for a general anti-government uprising. By allowing the agency and initiative of the protests to remain at the local level, organizers hope to reassure political society leaders that civil society activists are not usurping their activism. As one long-time activist engaged with both political and civil society explained, referring to political society activism, 'They don't want to be followers. They must lead themselves.'[32]

Sudan today stands at a crossroads. While the 2013 protests demonstrated political society's potency, it is unclear whether civil society activists can find a viable strategy for merging the formal and informal sides of the movement. What is undeniable is that the political imagination of younger Sudanese, most of whom have known only life under the Bashir regime, has been awakened in new ways.[33] Although the military has thus far proven unwilling to decisively break with Bashir, the emergence of a truly popular movement able to weave together the country's diverse ethnicities and cross class lines has the potential to split the military and overthrow the regime. For the first time in decades, many are daring to imagine a post-Bashir Sudan. For them, the question is not whether the Bashir regime will fall, but when, and, once it does, how to learn from Sudan's two previous popular revolts and prevent revolutionary fervour from turning into post-revolutionary malaise.

Conclusion: Africa in a world of protest

Across the world today, we are witnessing an eruption of urban uprisings. Despite different histories, governments, and divisions of class and race, the uprisings bear a strong family resemblance. In city after city, people are taking to the streets, often without significant formal organization, designated leaders, or concrete political programmes, but with the same demand for total change: Ash-sha'b yurīd isqāt an-niẓām! Y'en a marre! Que se vayan todos! Vy nas dazhe ne predstavliaete! We are the 99 per cent! Ya Basta! The protests everywhere appear to signal a crisis of political representation, a dramatic disjuncture between the people and the governing institutions that control their daily lives. Everywhere, too, difficult questions arise for those heralding the protests as opening new political possibilities: Why do the protests appear to have ushered in so little concrete change? Why have their explosive energies mostly failed to translate into sustained political movements?

Africa has been largely left out of the debate over global protest, as we discussed earlier. Except for North Africa, which has been divorced from the continent and made part of an 'Arab Spring', African protests have typically been dismissed as riots or ignored altogether. Considering the vast sweep of protests unfolding across the continent today, this exclusion is unjustifiable. In this conclusion, we draw on Africa's history of protest, and in particular its ongoing third wave, to qualify and expand the debate around the global protest upsurge. We begin by considering the two most prominent narratives of the global protest wave – the first focusing on the centrality of the middle class, and the second on the centrality of newly precarious workers – and show that neither of these can encompass African protest. We argue that the crucial importance of political society to protest in Africa reveals the inadequacies of these dominant narratives, inadequacies that undermine their relevance to many parts of the world as well as their claims to universal validity.

We then go beyond these existing narratives and suggest that the African experience of protest can help illuminate today's world-wide protest upsurge in novel ways. As political society protest appears to be becoming more widespread and politically germane throughout the world, it is the African experience, where such protest has deep roots and a vast reach, that is becoming ever more resonant globally. Indeed, given its increasing importance, political society protest is in pressing need of deepened theorization, a theorization that, we believe, can draw essential lessons from the long history of political society protest in Africa. Thus, as we show in this chapter, engagement with African political society protest can be a starting point for rethinking the ongoing global wave of protest and helping to clarify its dilemmas and possibilities, as well as its future.

Middle-class revolt?

The most prominent narrative of today's global protest declares that the world is seeing a succession of protests by a rising middle class that constitutes a 'cosmopolitan civil society' (Youngs 2013). Fukuyama provides a succinct sketch of this position, arguing that a global 'middle-class revolution' is taking place: 'in Turkey and Brazil, as in Tunisia and Egypt before them, political protest has been led not by the poor but by young people with higher-than-average levels of education and income' (Fukuyama 2013). These middle-class activists 'are technology-savvy and use social media' to organize. They are globally empowered, oriented, and connected. Fukuyama declares this rising global middle class to be taking to the streets against corruption and mismanagement, against 'ineffective and unresponsive government' by entrenched national elites who refuse the middle class political power equal to its new economic status. These new middle classes are the bearers of inherent democratic tendencies, he explains, spurred into action by 'the gap' between their reality and their aspirations. This liberal narrative is a story of global neoliberal capitalism and its rising classes triumphing over national 'crony capitalism'. It is up to Western donors and international institutions to engage with these middle-class activists and work to foster a spirit of 'democratic cosmopolitanism' among them so as to advance global liberal progress (Youngs 2013). This universal narrative resonates with the Africa Rising story, which champions the professional, globalized middle class as leading Africa's transition towards deepened democracy.

The middle-class narrative has little resonance with the African popular protests considered in this book, however. The four cases discussed were characterized by the widespread presence in the streets of the poorest urban inhabitants and by the tensions and conflicts between these underclasses and the middle class and elites, which led protest to unpredictable outcomes. The presence of significant numbers of largely poor, non-middle-class protesters can, in fact, be found in the more nuanced accounts of even those protest movements that have been held up as exemplars of middle-class revolt around the world. For instance, the middle-class 'Facebook' narrative of Arab Spring protests has been disputed by those who place lower-class and provincial youth at their centre (Abul-Magd 2012; Beinin 2014). In this sense, North Africa's 2011 protests can be brought back into the continental African protest wave rather than divorced from it. Brazil's 2013 protests and Russia's 2011–12 protests likewise saw a diversity of classes taking to the streets, according to many accounts.[1] The African experience of protest thus affirms that the occurrence and outcomes of urban uprisings worldwide cannot be predicted from a universal model of liberal progress driven on by a middle class, but are contingent upon complex political dynamics between a diversity of classes in the streets.

The protest politics of Africa's middle classes do not necessarily fit into the global liberal narrative either. This is despite the fact that Africa's middle classes can be seen rallying around anti-corruption agendas, like middle classes elsewhere. The small size and tenuous status of Africa's middle classes, however, along with their widespread reliance on donor funding or international organizations, means that anti-corruption is often a slogan used to seek intervention by Western donors against African states. In India or Brazil, by contrast, large-scale middle-class anti-corruption protests have been used by powerful right-wing forces for nationalist or neoliberal agendas.[2] Anti-corruption can be a guise for very different political programmes, many of which may not be democratic or even liberal (Therborn 2014). This undermines the liberal narrative's basic assumption that a global middle class with a shared a set of democratic values even exists (Kurlantzick 2014; Montlake 2014). The experience of regions with more substantial middle classes is at the same time a warning to Africa that it cannot count on its incipient middle class to pursue democratic reform, despite the assurances of the Africa Rising narrative.

The African experience of protest makes clear that the narrative of a global middle-class revolt can hide the very real participation of poorer and more marginalized classes throughout today's global protest wave and can hide the often undemocratic politics of middle-class protest. African protest also reveals how the middle-class narrative legitimates popular exclusion from political participation. The counter-narrative considered next takes more seriously the participation of these popular classes in protest but cannot effectively comprehend protest in Africa either.

Precariat revolution?

The second prominent narrative of today's global protest wave declares protest to be arising among those suffering the depredations of global capitalism, not those benefiting from it. According to this left narrative, capitalism is everywhere creating intensely exploited, precarious working classes comprising those who are unemployed, underemployed, and indebted – a 'precariat', 'new proletariat', or 'multitude' – who often have increased expectations and education but falling prospects. As these precarious workers rise up, new political possibilities open (Badiou 2012). In this story of universal progress, the many revolts against neoliberalism are thus ultimately about the same thing: in Harvey's words, there is a 'militant opposition emerging all around the world, from London to Durban, Buenos Aires, Shenzhen, and Mumbai', that is causing 'the brutal dominions of big capital and sheer money power everywhere [to be] on the defensive' (2012). Optimism prevails that a global movement will arise: Hardt and Negri propose that the protesters themselves 'have a clearer vision than those outside the struggle, and they can hold together without contradiction their singular conditions and local battles with the common global struggle' (2012: 7).

Although this narrative is more inclusive than the middle-class story of global protest, it is equally unable to do justice to Africa's protest wave. First, the intensity of the material hardship and devastating insecurity experienced by the African urban population is such that their grievances, needs, and objectives may have little in common with those of the precariat in North America, Europe, or the rising economies of Asia and South America. The daily struggle for survival of precarious urban populations in Africa – where extreme poverty grips almost half the population – is not equivalent to, for instance, the plight of precarious workers in the West who must take on multiple jobs and go into debt to fund an attenuated consumer lifestyle. Categories like the precariat, the multitude, or the new proletariat can therefore obscure significant differences among the poor in different regions or even within the same country. The African experience of protest calls attention to the importance of looking beyond such homogenizing categories in analysing today's global protest wave and of determining whether the poorest urban inhabitants are included in protest everywhere.

Second, precariousness in urban Africa is not a recent development under neoliberal capitalism but, rather, has determined the status of most of the urban population since the colonial period and has only intensified since the inception of structural adjustment. Protest is just one part of long histories of popular efforts to survive in Africa's cities. In fact, all domains of life have long been precarious for Africa's urban poor, and protest responds to that long-standing reality. Protest arises from the experience of precarious life in all its aspects – not just from economic insecurity, but from an entire political and social condition that we have labelled political society.

Our argument that protest by Africa's urban poor cannot be understood outside of the broader condition of political society suggests that the understanding of uprisings by precarious classes everywhere should be historicized within long-existing forms of political action by those populations instead of being submerged under universal narratives. Throughout the global south, political society can be found to have long histories of protest and struggle from which today's global wave emerges, histories that the dominant narratives miss. And, in places where precarious urban life is truly a more recent development, using Africa's experience as a lens can illuminate emerging political trends and identify political possibilities there as well.

Global political society

Political society is thus the concept that resonates most strongly with today's protest wave. Class categories, while important, have proven to be inadequate to grasp the political importance of protests in Africa today – just as Fanon made clear regarding the first wave of protest. By developing the concept of political society in this book, alongside and in contrast to civil society, we seek to emphasize the importance of protesters' political identities and visions for political change. As Mbembe puts it, 'the imaginary infrastructure of the political has deeply determined the nature and the forms and shapes of social struggle' (Mbembe and Nuttall 2012). In widening our scope from Africa's ongoing protest wave to the global wave, we find both civil society visions and political society visions present among protesters. The contrast between civil society and political society can thus, we argue, play an important role in grasping the possibilities and limitations of protest everywhere today.

Civil society political visions are basically reformist, oriented towards securing political freedoms, civil rights, and economic and social guarantees for citizens from the state. Protesters conforming to a civil society vision may seek an expansion or entrenchment of civil society from democratic or authoritarian states or seek to prevent states from taking away the citizenship guarantees that people already have.

This vision is found today among anti-austerity protesters who refuse to stand by while the social and political content of their citizenship is hollowed out. Middle classes under pressure seek to protect their entitlements to social and political rights, as in Brazil's protests or in many of the US-based Occupy protests. Alternatively, such protests are concerned with protecting 'the commons', as in the projects to preserve public space in Turkey (Eken 2014). In some contexts, civil society protest is an effort to avoid the dangerous possibility of being cast from civil society into political society, having one's formal relations with the state and guarantees of citizenship severed, and being relegated to a realm in which the direct use of force predominates in state–society relations. A civil society vision of politics can inform protests by those currently in political society, such as those 'without papers' who seek entry into the formalized guarantees of civil society, the kind of demand that was seen in the massive May Day protests in the US in 2006.

Africa's second wave of protest saw a civil society-oriented political imagination well represented, as elites, professionals, and workers who had enjoyed formal relations with the developmental state found neoliberal austerity dismantling those guarantees. Today, however, across the continent, this imagination is less germane. African states, captured by elites and dependent on violence, often do not appear to be even a potential terrain for struggle. Moreover, in Africa, multiparty democracy was born at the same time as neoliberal capitalist economies, and so there has been little opportunity for the kind of disillusionment experienced by those in the West who are only now discovering that liberal democracy may be devoid of meaning when confronted by a newly rampant neoliberal capitalism. Activists in the West who today rise up against austerity measures in their own countries are, in many ways, following paths that were first walked by African activists who have faced choiceless democracies and austerity for decades (Gabay 2012).[3]

Political society protest, long prevalent in the African context, is coming into its own globally. As we explored in our account of African popular protest, a political society vision understands seeking state reform to be pointless because civil society, the liberal state, and the law have been stripped of political relevance or never had any in the first place. Protest informed by political society politics is not about creating or expanding civil society against the state. Neither is it about trying to maintain civil society and the state as a meaningful terrain of citizenship against the onslaught of global capitalism and austerity. Rather, an engagement with African political society protest has shown that it is largely about thinking and acting outside the state–civil society dichotomy entirely.

Political society protest arises from a crisis of representation on the part of existing political institutions and finds voice in demands for total, immediate change. It can be an effort to do politics directly within society in an attempt to change one's conditions of life, or it may represent the direct use of force against the state in an attempt to impel concessions by changing the facts on the ground. In many African cities, the state's legacy of predation and apathy towards the urban population has led protest to seek not an expansion of civil society but, rather, a contraction of the state through attempts to push it back physically by subverting its power, destroying its symbols, or creating alternative orders beyond its reach. And when such protests reach the level of general uprisings, they may seek to overthrow the entire social and political system.

The history of African political society provides a framework that helps us understand protest around the world today, as people everywhere are finding civil society to be an empty promise. Political society may help illuminate many protests in Latin America where, Reyes argues, the dramatic limitations on even leftist governments to effect change have been made manifest. Social movements, no longer blinded by faith that the state can be used to end the inequities of capitalism, seek more radical transformation beyond state reform (Reyes 2012: 19). In the US, the protests in Ferguson, Missouri have shown that many communities of colour find themselves deep in political society, criminalized, and without the guarantees of civil or political rights or even of the basic human right to life. The massive response by militarized riot police, who faced off with unarmed protesters, their hands raised, made obvious to what extent many of the urban poor throughout the US tread the tightrope between state neglect and direct state violence, the same situation confronted by political society today in Dhaka or Rio.

As security states expand, with their reliance on ubiquitous technological surveillance and militarized police forces, and as state violence is placed above the law and citizens outside of it – all ostensibly for our own protection – political society may displace modern citizenship globally as the dominant political experience. In this context, political society protest may become the primary mode of political resistance and the African experience the key site to look to illuminate developments globally. At the same time, the example of African protest reveals the extent to which political society protests have long characterized popular politics in many parts of the global South, where these long-standing forms of political action have traditionally been dismissed as riots, looting, or the violence of shapeless crowds.

Dilemmas of protest

It must be kept in mind, however, that political society is not a homogeneous category, whether in Africa or elsewhere, and so we should take account of the way in which the politics, possibilities, and limitations of popular protest are differently structured in different contexts. In Africa, protest takes place amidst the political divisions and exclusions of colonial and post-colonial power, a form of power that determines all aspects of urban dwellers' lives and that is institutionalized in the economy, law, geography, and identity. These overlapping forms of power mean that protest that successfully challenges some forms of inequality or oppression can end up entrenching other forms. An important lesson of Africa's political society protest is, therefore, that protest anywhere will face political dilemmas that are not easily solved, many deriving from the colonial legacy.

For instance, even the most popular urban protest needs to take into account the rural–urban divide if it is going to avoid reproducing that political fracture. This principle resonates with recent events in Latin America, where developmental policies adopted by leftist governments as a response to popular protests have often favoured urban areas and had negative consequences for indigenous peoples and rural dwellers. The declaration of a 'right to the city' as the standard for an inclusive political programme (Harvey 2012) may run the risk of failing to include rural inhabitants, thereby exacerbating rural–urban divides.

Protest that focuses on class or formal citizenship can obscure the ways that power operates differentially through race or ethnicity (Al-Bulushi 2012). The recognition of this fact helped give rise to significant discussion in the US around how the Occupy protests could go beyond their largely white image and address the intersection of race, class, and political identity. In Brazil, too, the noted absence of the poorest, overwhelmingly black, members of urban society raised questions about the protests' potential for addressing racial structures of power and inequality. Similarly, protests in India largely avoided questions of caste or the conditions of rural *adivasis* in favour of foregrounding the needs of an imagined cosmopolitan Indian. How can protest address and not entrench the gendered nature of power, or its generational dimension? These problems are exacerbated by the tendency to dismiss urban uprisings that *do* challenge racialized structures of power, such as in Rio, Paris, Los Angeles, or Ferguson, as mere 'riots' instead of seeing them as genuine forms of political protest and asking how lines of solidarity might be developed between them and other forms of protest. The very definition of 'popular protest' is itself an open question, one subject to political conflict and negotiation, susceptible to different answers in different parts of the world.

Political innovation or political failure?

By using political society protest as a framework, one theorized from the African experience, difficult questions that have been posed of the global protest wave can be rethought in productive ways. Almost everywhere protest breaks out today, activists and analysts alike have remarked upon its horizontal and leaderless organization and its lack of concrete political programmes (Fraser 2013: 121). For those with an eye to Africa's history of protest, this is familiar ground, of course, a reiteration of accusations that have been made against protest in Africa since the days of the Accra 'riots'.

In today's global wave, these accounts continue; when demands are made, they tend to be either so broad and vague – for the 'end of the regime', for 'change' – as to be open to multiple and even contradictory political agendas. Or, they tend to be so dispersed and fragmented as to be unable to gather sustained force behind them. While there is general agreement on the left that a crisis of political representation has led to widespread popular disillusionment with existing politics, there is disagreement over whether the resulting lack of leadership, formal organization, and programmes on the part of protesters represents a political failure to be overcome or a harbinger of a new politics. We argue that a consideration of the African protest experience can help correct the dominant debate's tendency either, first, to downplay or, second, to romanticize the political relevance of leaderless protest and its lack of formal organization and can thus shine new light on this key aspect of the global wave.

Those taking the first position argue that protests without programmes can dissipate without results or be hijacked by more shrewd operators. Ali is firm about the need for protesters to come up with a programme, for 'members of a crowd become a revolution only when they have, in their majority, a clear set of social and political aims. If they do not, they will always be outflanked by those who do, or by the state that will recapture lost ground very rapidly' (Ali 2013b). Others point out how an emphasis on anti-statism and autonomy can be easily co-opted by neoliberal programmes (Harvey 2012).

These dangers are illustrated by Brazil's 2013 mass mobilizations, which signalled the crisis of the PT government, other political parties, and even social movements (Mische 2013) – so much so that 'the demonstrations were, generally, against politics *as a whole*' (Saad-Filho and Morais 2013: 241). However, without leadership, organization, or alternative programmes, the protests became easy prey for more well-organized right-wing movements (Singer 2014). In North Africa, Beinin argues that the 'lack of a political organization or program, indeed the distrust of what passed for "politics" in the Mubarak era by most Egyptians, meant that when Mubarak fell, they had no effective levers to shape the transition to the new regime' (2014: 403), eventually leading to the military's complete takeover. The Occupy protests loomed large but then disappeared without having introduced substantive political change.

From this viewpoint, today's wave of African protest could also be accused of political irresponsibility. African protest has long been said to lack leadership or political demands and, consequently, has had its political relevance dismissed. It is true that the African experience reveals the dangers of political society protest without strong supporting organization, leadership, or programmes. From the channelling of popular protest into nationalist politics in the colonial era and the subsequent popular demobilization, to the consolidation of multipartyism and neoliberalism in the 1990s on the back of a vast protest upsurge, to the brief outbursts of today that seem to dissipate under state violence or that are steered by elites into ethnic, racial, or nationalist violence, all resonate with different aspects of the problems being noted around the world.

However, an engagement with the African experience of political society protest makes clear that this lack of leadership, organization, and programmes must be contextualized within the political conditions from which protest arises. As Fanon so clearly explained, what may appear to be a failure on the part of political society protesters can be better understood as a collective political response to contexts in which organization, leadership, or formal programmes and demands make little sense. What look like unorganized, destructive protests may arise out of expansive informal popular organization seeking autonomy or an end to state repression. Demands for change may be so clear to everyone marching in the streets – and to the state they are opposing – that there is no need to draw up formal programmes, which the state will ignore anyway. Protests may not be about proposing formal political alternatives but about creating informal alternatives. African protest encourages us to see that, in many cases of protest around the world, the lack of leadership, programmes, and formal organization can represent a positive political response to difficult conditions; in other cases, it also can reflect the limitations imposed upon protest by state violence and by destructive external interference.

The second position in this debate, which romanticizes the lack of hierarchical leadership and formal political programmes as a strength that makes possible original and creative political experiments, should also be qualified in light of Africa's history of political society protest. Those taking this second position argue that, by refusing to put forth demands or programmes, protests refuse to provide a handle with which the state, political parties, or self-interested leaders can manipulate or co-opt them, thus protecting their spontaneity and autonomy. This position celebrates the horizontal arrangements for welfare, decision-making, and education that have been seen to arise in Zuccotti Park, Tahrir Square, and Taksim Square, in Moscow and Madrid, which are understood to provide a window on to novel political possibilities that go beyond struggles over representation (Hardt and Negri 2012; Sitrin 2014). Part of a new 'politics of movement' (Badiou 2012), these developments are said to signal novel forms of politics that would not only 'reject the capitalist status quo' but would themselves put into practice 'the slogan "Another world is possible" ... [and] develop prefigurative forms of post-capitalist organization, activity, and life' (Gunn and Wilding 2014: 339). Anarchist anthropologist David Graeber similarly praises the protesters' leaderless tactics as 'acting as if one is already free' (2011).

By placing its focus on these very visible political developments taking place among protesters in squares and streets, this position may also dismiss the importance of Africa's political society protests, which have rarely witnessed sustained alternative forms of social and political organization emerging among protesters in public spaces. By romanticizing the supposedly spontaneous emergence of horizontal and experimental structures among protesters, according to which protesters instinctively incorporate themselves into a global upsurge with similar non-hierarchical, inclusive, and communal values, this position misses other forms of popular politics that do not take place in full view in streets and squares. This may help account for the left's lack of attention to political society protests in Africa today.

African popular protest makes clear that looking only to the streets and squares where protesters congregate in order to discern evidence of extra-state politics and social alternatives is to look in too limited a place. Instead, African protest signals that the creation of alternatives to formal state arrangements is going on all the time within political society, throughout the world – indeed, such creativity is its very condition for survival and protest is just one aspect. These alternatives – as opposed to, say, the clean-up committees in Zuccotti Park – are occurring in less visible and less media-friendly ways, and sometimes in ways that may offend the politics of the left. Indeed, some of the most stark alternative projects involve social cleansing, which can represent efforts to build and strengthen the ties within political society but can also involve violence against nationally, ethnically, or racially defined groups. Taking political society protest seriously makes clear that the romantic desire to see protest beyond the state as prefiguring an emancipatory politics yet-to-come needs to be tempered

Conclusion

by a recognition that, in many places, these political and social arrangements have been the stuff of everyday life for a long time and have a much more complex and ambiguous politics than the left might wish for. Nevertheless, the African urban experience is full of less obvious and less apparent experiments in social and political order undertaken constantly by political society, experiments that have deep resonance with protests among political society elsewhere.

Futures of protest

At its height in 2011, the global protest wave was celebrated by many as an exceptional, epochal event. Viewing the protests in context of the years before and after, however, reveals them to be both less and more significant than they were sometimes made out to be. They are less significant not so much because of the disappointments suffered in the years since but rather because of the long histories of protest within which the 2011 global wave must be understood. These multiple regional histories show 2011 not to be an exception but rather a notable moment in long-term popular struggles and political conflicts.

The events of 2011 are also more significant because, as Claude Ake explained, protests should not be judged on their immediate impact but rather on the way they have transformed political imaginations and ideas about what is possible. For Arundhati Roy (2011), recent popular protests have 'reawakened our imagination. Somewhere along the way, capitalism reduced the idea of justice to mean just "human rights", and the idea of dreaming of equality became blasphemous.' In Ali's words, 'Sometimes people say: "But nothing much has changed". This is true. But one thing that's changed is that the people, the masses, have realized that in order to bring about change they have to move and become active. And that is a big lesson from these uprisings' (Ali 2012).

These transformations are not unqualified, however. States throughout the world quickly recognized the importance of struggle on the terrain of the political imagination and turned to violence to crush new possibilities emerging from the protests.

214

The expansion of security states, counter-terror regimes, 'humanitarian' intervention, and regional militarization are all part of this material and ideological counter-protest project. In Libya, a militarized interventionist imagination was asserted, in which civil protest was rendered meaningless through NATO bombing and arming militias. Ethiopia introduced its own counter-protest state with the assistance of donors, expanding surveillance and state repression widely. The crushing of protest in Uganda left people unwilling to take to the streets, knowing how steep the price would be. The securitization and militarization of public space throughout the world as part of a neoliberal military urbanism (Graham 2011), the expansion of a totalizing surveillance structure, the reorientation of urbanism towards protecting capital and controlling slums – all of these seek to hinder us from imagining, let alone creating, new political possibilities in response to the global protest wave.

In this context, violence may insinuate itself back into the popular political imagination as it comes to be seen as the only tool left to contest the power of the state and capital. This is, of course, exactly what state security regimes desire, for then they can expand their powers and reach with citizens' support by stoking fears of insecurity and terrorism. Africa is deeply familiar with devastating cycles of violence and counter-violence. Given the choice between political engagement that ends in widespread destruction and political disengagement, many will choose to just survive as best they can in the face of increasingly desperate circumstances because the cost of challenging their deprivation is simply too high.

Any transformative politics today thus faces a dilemma. Should it seek to organize popular pressure to challenge the state and its violence even though the state will certainly arm further in response? Or should it seek to build alternatives outside the state even though doing so absolves the state of political and social accountability and may leave broader structures of exploitation and violence still unaddressed? Either way, protest today must seek strategies to render the state's arms irrelevant. The African experience provides important lessons for this task: despite state violence relentlessly shutting down democratic political possibilities ever since the colonial era, dramatic popular efforts to forge those possibilities in thought and in practice have continued equally relentlessly. As intellectuals and activists in political society and civil society experiment with solutions to these and other dilemmas, African protest may become the locus from which powerful new political imaginations emerge, ready to be taken up by popular struggles not only on the continent but also around the globe.

Notes

1 Protests and possibilities

1 See the breakdown of the ongoing wave of global protests detailed in Ortiz et al. (2013).

2 See Harsch (2012) and Dwyer and Zeilig (2012).

3 For example, in 2013 the Modern Language Association proposed dividing African literatures into three categories, 'Arab', 'Sub-Saharan Africa', and 'Southern Africa.'

4 Joschka Philipps, 'New Debate – Old Concepts: Revisiting the Study of Social Movements in Africa', unpublished manuscript, 2014, discusses these cases.

5 Efforts to derive theory based upon empirical studies of African political reality that provide guidance for this project include, on social movements, Mamdani and Wamba-dia-Wamba (1995), and on urbanism, Myers (2011) and Simone (2004).

6 See Tilly and Tarrow (2006) for a definitive analysis of the dominant model of protest. Also Schock (2003).

7 For critical accounts of the dominant model's failure to fit non-Western contexts, see McAdam et al. (2005); Boudreau (1996). For critiques of the applicability of the dominant social movement model, see Ellis and

Van Kessel (2009); Mamdani and Wamba-dia-Wamba (1995).

8 Chilembwe's revolt resonates into the current era and his countenance continues to grace all of Malawi's currency (Dionne et al. 2013).

2 Mobs or mobilizers?

1 See the debate in Worsely (1972), Cohen and Michael (1973), Waterman (1975), and Wallerstein (1979).

2 As Myers points out, there is a new generation of studies striving to take seriously the lives and urbanisms of the majorities of African cities, who 'find themselves entangled within power dynamics that position them at the city's margins, literally and figuratively, working to make places they can live with in the face of injustice, inequality, violence, or underdevelopment' (2011: 13). As this literature grows, it can provide a new foundation for thinking about the politics of this urban majority as well.

3 Chatterjee is best known as a key figure within Subaltern Studies, an intellectual approach originating in South Asia that sought to centre the actions and beliefs of non-elites in analyses of historical

events. His discussion of 'political society' is a departure from the subaltern school, but is equally concerned with the politics of the masses. Chatterjee's approach is also distinct from Gramscian or liberal understandings of the concept, in which it refers to the sphere of formal political organizations and parties (see Cohen and Arato 1992). In our usage, we diverge somewhat from Chatterjee, who explicitly links political society to 'governmental' forms of power in a Foucauldian framework. 'Uncivil society', a concept introduced by the South African scholar Michael Neocosmos and that builds on Chatterjee's political society, is perhaps the closest to our usage (2011).

4 Marx coined 'lumpenproletariat' from the German term for miscreant to refer to the underclass who could not achieve a revolutionary consciousness, contrasting it to the positive attributes he ascribed to the proper working class.

5 This does not prevent analysts from insisting on a difference between economic and political protest in Africa; see Mueller (2013). See Abdelrahman (2012) for a critique.

6 For a similar account of the political imagination in youth protest, see Bathily et al. (1995).

7 Quoted in Sutherland and Meyer (2000: 41). Sutherland attended the conference as a guest of Nkrumah, and his book provides a personal account of the

debate between the two legendary Pan-Africanists.

3 A democratic transition?

1 This last figure extends the numbers provided in Bratton and Van de Walle (1997: 8); see also the balance sheet in Wiseman (1996: 20–31).

2 For our account of postcolonial politics, we draw primarily on Ake (1995); Mamdani (1996); Nugent (2004); and Young (2012).

3 The debate over civil society in Africa is extensive. See Ekeh (1975); Bayart (1986); Hutchful (1995/6); Monga 1996; Comaroff and Comaroff (1999); Lewis (2002).

4 The third wave

1 For the most economically rigorous independent assessment of twenty years of structural adjustment in Africa, see Mkandawire and Soludo (1999).

2 See in particular Lumumba-Kasongo (2005).

3 See Roy (2011) for a critique of this 'subaltern urbanism'.

4 Gacheke Gachihi, personal communication, 23 July 2014.

5 See Žižek (2013) for a discussion of this tendency elsewhere.

6 See the debate between Tariq Ali (2013a) and Asef Bayat (2013) in the *New Left Review* for an exploration of this question in the context of the Arab Spring.

5 Occupy Nigeria

1 Among others, Farooq Kperogi, an Atlanta-based

Nigerian academic blogger, offered the most substantive calls for an 'Occupy' style protest movement that appeared on the influential Sahara Reporters website, various Nigerian newspapers, and his own blog. See for example, Kperogi (2011a, 2011b).

2 Interviews, Ogaga Ifowodo, via email, 16 June 2013; Omolade Adunbi, via email, 24 January 2013; Shettima 1993: 83.

3 Interview, Omolade Adunbi, via email, 24 January 2013.

4 Campaign for Democracy, 'Be Ready for More Action as from Monday July 5, 1993'. Cited in Ihonvbere (1996: 202).

5 Abiola remained in prison until his death in 1998 during the country's post-Abacha transition period. Many expected him to compete and win the 1999 presidential election. He died under mysterious circumstances while meeting with a delegation from the United States that included Thomas Pickering and Susan Rice, the current National Security Advisor.

6 Among others, Abiola's daughter Hafsat launched the Kudirat Initiative for Democracy, named in honour of her slain mother, and Wole Soyinka developed the National Liberation Council of Nigeria.

7 Interview, Gbenga Komolafe, via email, 2 June 2013.

8 Interview, Olúwáfirópò Ewénlá, via email, 5 June 2013.

9 Interview, Chido Onumah, via email, 2 June 2013.

10 Interview, Rotimi Babatunde, via email, 30 May 2013.

11 Interview, Ayodele Olofintuade, via email, 3 June 2013.

12 Interview, Olúwáfirópò Ewénlá, via email, 5 June 2013.

13 For the full list, see the welcome address delivered by Tunde Bakare at the International Conference Centre, Abuja, on Monday 31 May 2010.

14 Interview, Gbenga Komolafe, via email, 2 June 2013.

15 During the second Obasanjo regime, the pro-democracy and human rights groups (commonly referred to as civil society in Nigeria) joined together with labour to challenge a fuel price hike leading to a sustained engagement between the two.

16 Interview, Chido Onumah, via email, 2 June 2013.

17 Interview, Gbenga Komolafe, via email, 2 June 2013.

18 Interview, Ayodele Olofintuade, via email, 3 June 2013.

19 Interview, Denja Yaqub, via email, 28 May 2013.

20 Interview, Abiodun Aremu, via email, 25 May 2013. Aremu's response contained several spelling and grammatical errors that have been cleaned up by the authors without changing the meaning. The original text is in our possession and available upon request.

21 Interview, Ogaga Ifowodo, via email, 16 June 2013.

22 Among other responses, on 28 January, the Centre for

Contemporary Art in Lagos held an exhibition of photography, videos and performance art that featured leading Nigerian artists, including many who participated in the protests, and sought to 'discursively engage the nation's current state of affairs, the mechanisms underpinning Occupy Nigeria as well as the movement's immediate impact and potential long-term effects' (Centre for Contemporary Art 2012; Alakam 2012).

23 Interview, Chido Onumah, via email, 2 June 2013.

24 Interview, Ayodele Olofintuade, via email, 3 June 2013.

25 Interview, Olúwáfirópò Ewénlá, via email, 5 June 2013.

6 Political walking in Uganda

1 www.usaid.gov/locations/sub-saharan_africa/countries/uganda

2 This account relies on Brisset-Foucault (2014); however, Joschka Philipps informed us that, according to a police officer he interviewed, about thirty per cent of those arrested were non-Baganda (personal communication, March 2014). This would imply that the 'Buganda' riots may have also involved a wider turn to direct action by Kampala's political society, thus being a harbinger of 2011.

3 Although in an interview, MP Mpuuga insisted on the existence of such an agenda (Kampala, 5 July 2013).

4 Interview, Ssemuju Nganda, Kampala, 11 July 2013.

5 Ibid.

6 Interview, Francis Mwijukye, Kampala, 6 April 2013.

7 See http://activists4change.blogspot.com/2011/04/walk-to-work-day-one.html

8 Thanks to Joseph Kasule for making the importance of this clear.

9 Interview, Margaret Wokuri, Kampala, 17 July 2011.

10 Interview, Francis Mwijukye, Kampala, 6 April 2013.

11 At Makerere Instutute of Social Research, we remember that day as when we had to flee our exposed meeting room and continue a seminar deep inside our bunker-like library.

12 Interview, Mathias Mpuuga, Kampala, 5 July 2013.

13 Confidential interview, Kampala, July 2013.

14 Confidential interview, Kampala, July 2013.

15 Interview, political activist, Kampala, 3 July 2013.

16 Confidential interview, Kampala, July 2013.

17 Interview, Margaret Wokuri, Kampala, 17 July 2013.

18 Ibid.

19 Interview, Mathias Mpuuga, Kampala, 5 July 2013.

20 Confidential interview, Kampala, July 2013.

21 Sandrine Perrot, personal communication, December 2013.

22 Interview, political activist, Kampala, 3 July 2013.

23 Interview, Margaret Wokuri, Kampala, 17 July 2013.

24 Ibid.

Notes

25 Interview, political activist, Kampala, 3 July 2013.

26 Personal communication, July 2013.

7 Protest in Ethiopia

1 Confidential interview, Addis Ababa, May 2013.

2 See Samatar (2005) for accusations that the opposition were ethnic chauvinists intent on re-imposing a Christian, Amhara identity.

3 See Balsvik (2007) for a discussion of student politics.

4 Group discussion, Addis Ababa, 9 May 2013.

5 Group discussion, Addis Ababa, 9 May 2013; confidential interview, Kampala, 22 June 2013.

6 Interview, Marco Di Nunzio, Addis Ababa, 7 May 2013.

7 Interview, Solomon, Addis Ababa, 8 May 2013.

8 Ibid.

9 Confidential interview, Addis Ababa, May 2013.

10 Interview, Solomon, Addis Ababa, 8 May 2013.

11 Confidential interview, Kampala, 22 June 2013.

12 Group discussion, Addis Ababa, 9 May 2013.

13 Ibid.

14 Ibid.

15 Confidential interview, Addis Ababa, May 2013.

16 Interview, Girma Seifu Maru, Addis Ababa, 8 May 2013.

17 See the narrative by the head of the EPRDF's public relations, Bereket Simon, in his Amharic-language *A Tale of Two*

Elections: A National Journey that Averted Calamity (Mega Enterprises, Addis Ababa, 2011) for an account of this position.

18 Personal communication, former MP, Addis Ababa, May 2013.

19 Interview, Mesfin Woldemariam, Addis Ababa, 9 May 2013.

20 Confidential interview, Addis Ababa, May 2011.

21 Interview, Marco Di Nunzio, Addis Ababa, 7 May 2013.

22 Confidential interview, Addis Ababa, May 2011.

23 Interview, Mesfin Woldemariam, Addis Ababa, 9 May 2013.

24 Interview, Marco Di Nunzio, Addis Ababa, 7 May 2013.

8 Sudan's unfinished uprisings

1 The 1964 and 1985 protests were not the only mass protests in the country, though they stand as the most successful. In 1961, 1973, and 1982 sustained campaigns including country-wide student protests and large union strikes organized by the opposition failed to topple the regime. In these cases, repressive tactics taken by the government were able to crush the movements.

2 South Sudan now commemorates 18 August as Heroes Day.

3 Interview, Mohieldin Awouda, Khartoum, 15 August 2014.

4 Ibid.

5 Interview, Dalia Haj Omar, via email, 9 July 2013.

6 The official population figures for Khartoum are widely assumed to undercount the

teeming population of the city's informal settlements. Members of political society in particular are often undercounted due to the their informal status.

7 Interview, 'Abdul', Omdurman, 13 August 2014.

8 Interviews, 'Wided', Khartoum, 13 August 2014; Nisrin El-Amin, via email, 2 February 2014.

9 Hamilton (2010); Interview, Bashir Hamid, New York, 11 October 2013; Interview, Nisrin El-Amin, via email, 2 February 2014.

10 Girifna members were also prevented from serving as election monitors, though some members circumvented this prohibition by applying to the National Elections Commission through established organizations (HRW 2010; Fick 2010).

11 Interview, Nagi Musa, via email, 29 May 2013; Hamilton (2010).

12 In July 2010, three members were arrested while distributing a pamphlet with the organization's mission statement in a suburb north of Khartoum.

13 Interviews, 'Wided', Khartoum, 13 August 2014

14 Bashir portrayed the fuel hikes as a nationalist reaction to the government of South Sudan's provocations, furthering the divide within the opposition and providing the regime with a convenient scapegoat for its actions.

15 Interview, Ahmad Mahmoud, via email, 13 June 2013. *Kandake* is a term used to refer to the warrior queens of ancient

Kush, which encompassed parts of modern Sudan and Ethiopia. Sudanese women have long played a central role in popular movements, including in the October Revolution of 1964 and the 1985 Popular Uprisings.

16 Interview, Dalia Haj Omar, via email, 14 June 2013.

17 Interview, Hafiz Mohamed, Omdurman, 11 August 2014.

18 Interview, Ahmed Kagoom, Omdurman, 13 August 2014.

19 Interview, Nuha, Khartoum, 14 August 2014.

20 Interview, Hamid Bakheet, Khartoum, 10 August 2014.

21 Interview, Hafiz Mohamed, Omdurman, 11 August 2014.

22 Group conversation with students from Darfur and Nuba Mountains, Omdurman, 14 August 2014. Interview, Nisrin El-Amin, via email, 2 February 2014.

23 Though opposition parties remained on the sidelines during the 2011–12 protests, they have shown some willingness to engage since. The most overt expression was the founding of a loose coalition of opposition parties, armed groups, and women's and youth groups pushing forward a 'New Dawn Charter'. Signed in Kampala, Uganda, on 6 January 2013, the charter calls on signatories to work together to topple the Sudanese regime and establish a 'democratic federal system' through 'democratic, civil, peaceful means' alongside 'revolutionary armed struggle'. Signatories included members of

the Sudan Revolutionary Front coalition, which numbers among its members armed groups such as the SPLM, the Sudan Liberation Movement, and the Justice and Equality Movement; representatives of the National Consensus Force, comprising over ten opposition parties; representatives of the trade unions; and women's and youth groups, including Girifna and Change Now. The regime took a harsh line with the signatories, arresting at least six opposition party members and activists upon their return to Khartoum and labelling them 'traitors' (IRIN 2013). Vice President Al-Haj Adam Yousif threatened to ban any opposition party that refused to denounce the charter. Many signatories complied.

24 Interview, 'Aisha', Omdurman, 13 August 2014.

25 Interview, Rehab Hamed, Khartoum, 12 August 2014.

26 Anonymous interviews, Khartoum, 12 August 2014; Nisrin El-Amin, via email, 2 February 2014.

27 Interview, Hafiz Mohamed, Omdurman, 11 August 2014.

28 Anonymous interviews, Caroor Market, Omdurman, 13 August 2014.

29 Interview, Ahmed Adam, New York, 30 July 2014. Others discounted this, pointing to the lack of familiarity of Janjaweed fighters with the Khartoum area.

30 Group conversation with students from Darfur and Nuba Mountains, Omdurman, 14 August 2014. Interviews, Nuha, Khartoum, 14 August 2014; Dalia Haj Omar, via email, 9 July 2013.

31 Interviews, Rehab Hamed, Khartoum, 12 August 2014; Bashir Hamid, New York, 11 October 2013.

32 Interview, Hafiz Mohamed, Omdurman, 11 August 2014.

33 Interview, Nagi Musa, via email, 29 May 2013.

Conclusion

1 In Brazil, the expanding urban precariat took to the streets along with with middle classes who felt under threat from the Partido dos Trabalhadores (PT) government, all in a context where class categories themselves were taking new meanings (Braga 2013; Saad-Filho and Morais 2013; Singer 2014). The dominant Western liberal narrative of Russia's 2011–12 protests has similarly been qualified by accounts that note the importance of 'extremely informalized, unprotected, and precaritized labour' to the uprising (Penzin 2014: 164; Chehonadskih 2014).

2 In India, for instance, middle classes were central to the 2011 anti-corruption protests, in which anti-corruption was wielded against the Congress Party-led government in an ostensibly non-political campaign, behind which lurked the Hindu nationalist party and its leader, Narendra Modi. In Brazil, anti-corruption became the

rallying cry for an alliance between middle-class protesters and those capitalist forces that sought to dismantle the social reforms introduced by the PT government.

3 There is some irony, of course, in the fact that overly confident Western governments were the ones who prescribed austerity for Africa, never expecting that they would eventually have the same cure forced upon them.

References

Aalen, L. and K. Tronvoll (2009) 'The end of democracy? Curtailing political and civil rights in Ethiopia', *Review of African Political Economy* 36 (120): 193–207.

Abbink, J. (2006) 'Discomfiture of democracy? The 2005 election crisis in Ethiopia and its aftermath', *African Affairs* 105 (419): 173–99.

— (2009) 'The Ethiopian second republic and the fragile "social contract"', *Africa Spectrum* 44 (2): 3–28.

Abbink, J. and I. van Kessel (2005) *Vanguard or Vandals: Youth, Politics and Conflict in Africa*, Leiden: Brill.

Abdelrahman, M. (2012) 'A hierarchy of struggles? The "economic" and the "political" in Egypt's revolution', *Review of African Political Economy* 39 (134): 614–28.

Abdoul, M. (2002) 'The production of the city and urban informalities: the borough of Thiaroye-sur-Mer in the city of Pikine, Senegal', in O. Enwezor et al. (eds), *Under Siege: Four African Cities: Freetown, Johannesburg, Kinshasa, Lagos*, Documenta 11, Lagos: Platform 4.

Abdullah, I. (2002) 'Space, culture, and agency in contemporary Freetown: the making and remaking of a postcolonial city', in O. Enwezor et al. (eds), *Under Siege: Four African Cities: Freetown, Johannesburg, Kinshasa, Lagos*, Documenta 11, Lagos: Platform 4.

Abrahamsen, R. (1997) 'The victory of popular forces or passive revolution? A neo-Gramscian perspective on democratisation', *Journal of Modern African Studies* 35 (1): 129–52.

Abul-Magd, Z. (2012) 'Occupying Tahrir Square: the myths and the realities of the Egyptian revolution', *South Atlantic Quarterly* 111 (3): 565–72.

Addo-Fening, R. (1972) 'Gandhi and Nkrumah: a study of non-violence and non-cooperation campaigns in India and Ghana as an anti-colonial strategy', *Transactions of the Historical Society of Ghana* 13 (1): 65–85.

Adetula, V. A. O. (2002) 'Welfare Associations and the Dynamics of City Politics in Nigeria', in O. Enwezor et al. (eds), *Under Siege: Four African Cities: Freetown, Johannesburg, Kinshasa, Lagos*, Documenta 11, Lagos: Platform 4.

African Development Bank (2011) *The Middle of the Pyramid: Dynamics of the Middle Class in*

Africa, Market Brief, 20 April, AfDB.

AFRICOM (2011) 'Exercise Atlas Drop begins in Uganda', 15 April. Available at www.africom.mil/Newsroom/Article/8213/exercise-atlas-drop-begins-in-uganda

Ahiuma-Young, V. (2012) 'How the strike was hijacked', *Vanguard* (Lagos), 21 January.

Ahlman, J. (2010) 'The Algerian question in Nkrumah's Ghana, 1958–1960: debating "violence" and "nonviolence" in African decolonization', *Africa Today* 57 (2): 67–84.

Ake, C. (1989) *The Political Economy of Crisis and Underdevelopment in Africa: Selected Works of Claude Ake*, edited by J. Ihonvbere, Lagos: JAD Publishers.

— (1995) *Democracy and Development in Africa*, Washington, DC: Brookings Institution Press.

— (1996) *Is Africa Democratizing?*, Lagos: Malthouse Press for the Centre for Advanced Social Science.

Al Arabiya (2011) 'Sudan's police describe student protests "politically motivated"', 27 December. Available at http://english.alarabiya.net/articles/2011/12/27/184760.html

— (2013) 'Sudan to lift oil subsidies in troubles economy, says ruling party', 9 September. Available at http://english.alarabiya.net/en/business/energy/2013/09/09/Sudan-to-lift-oil-subsidies-in-troubles-economy-says-ruling-party.html

Al-Bulushi, Y. (2012) 'Learning from urban revolt: from Watts to the Banlieues', *City* 16 (1/2): 34–56.

Al Jazeera (2012) 'Sudan says no retreat on cuts despite protest', 26 June. Available at www.aljazeera.com/news/africa/2012/06/201262673155203765.html

Al-Saleh, O. (2012) 'Student protests in Sudan drag on', Al Jazeera. Available at http://blogs.aljazeera.com/blog/africa/student-protests-sudan-drag

Alakam, J. (2012) 'Subsidy matter: how did artists occupy Nigeria?', *Vanguard* (Lagos), 2 February.

Alemayehu G. Mariam (2014) 'Rise of the daughters of Ethiopia!', 17 March. Available at http://ecadforum.com/2014/03/17/rise-of-the-daughters-of-ethiopia/

Ali, A. A. E. (2012) 'Hundreds of Sudanese in protest call for "revolution"', *Agence France-Presse*, 10 December.

Ali, T. (2011) 'Tariq Ali on #Occupy: "The fog of confusion has finally lifted"', *Links: International Journal of Socialist Renewal* 25. Available at http://links.org.au/node/2586

— (2012) 'Julian Assange interviews Noam Chomsky and Tariq Ali'. Available at http://assange.rt.com/chomsky-ali-episode-ten/

— (2013a) 'Between past and

future: reply to Asef Bayat', *New Left Review* (80): 61–74.

— (2013b) 'What is a revolution?', *Counterpunch*, 4 September. Available at www.counterpunch.org/2013/09/04/what-is-a-revolution

Amadiume, I. (1995) 'Gender, political systems and social movements: a West African experience', in M. Mamdani and E. Wamba-dia-Wamba (eds), *African Studies in Social Movements and Democracy*, Dakar: CODESRIA.

Amin, S. (2014) 'Popular movements toward socialism: their unity and diversity', *Monthly Review* 66 (2).

Amnesty International (2011) 'Ethiopia must end crackdown on government critics', 16 September. Available at www.amnesty.org/en/news-and-updates/ethiopia-must-end-crackdown-government-critics-2011-09-16

An-Na'im, A. (1996) *Toward an Islamic Reformation: Civil Liberties, Human Rights and International Law*, Syracuse, NY: Syracuse University Press.

Anderson, P. (2011) 'On the concatenation in the Arab world', *New Left Review* (68): 5–15.

Andrae, G. and B. Beckman (2011) 'Trade unions, tailors, and civil society', *Labour, Capital and Society* 44 (1): 19–42.

Anikulapo-Kuti, S. (2012) 'End of fuel subsidy is treason against Nigerians', *CNN*, 10 January. Available at http://edition.cnn.com/2012/01/10/opinion/seun-kuti-opinion/index.html.

Anofochi, V. (2012) 'Rampaging Ogba youths assuaged', *Daily Times* (Lagos), 11 January.

Anyang' Nyong'o, P. (1987) *Popular Struggles for Democracy in Africa*, London: Zed Books.

Arendt, H. (1970) *On Violence*, Orlando, FL: Harcourt Brace and Company.

— (1990) *On Revolution*, New York: Penguin Books.

Arnaut, K. (2005) 'Re-generating the nation: youth, revolution and the politics of history in Côte d'Ivoire', in J. Abbink and I. van Kessel (eds), *Vanguard or Vandals*, Leiden: Brill.

Arriola, L. (2007) 'The Ethiopian voter: an assessment of economic and ethnic influences with survey data', *International Journal of Ethiopian Studies* 3 (1): 73–90.

— (2013) 'Suppressing protest: the geographic logic of mass arrests', unpublished draft, 24 January.

Badiou, A. (2012) *The Rebirth of History: Times of Riots and Uprisings*, London: Verso.

Bahru Zewde (2008) *Society and State in Ethiopian History*, Addis Ababa: Addis Ababa University Press.

Balsvik, R. R. (2007) *The Quest for Expression: The State and the University in Ethiopia under Three Regimes, 1952–2005*, Addis Ababa: Addis Ababa University Press.

Bathily, A., M. Diouf, and

M. Mbodj (1995) 'The Senegalese student movement from its inception to 1989', in M. Mamdani and E. Wambadia-Wamba (eds), *African Studies in Social Movements and Democracy*, Dakar: CODESRIA.

Bayart, J.-F. (1986) 'Civil society in Africa', in P. Chabal (ed.), *Political Domination in Africa: Reflections on the Limits of Power*, Cambridge: Cambridge University Press.

— (2009) *The State in Africa: The Politics of the Belly*, Cambridge: Polity.

Bayat, A. (2013) 'Revolution in bad times', *New Left Review* (80): 47–60.

Beinin, J. (2014) 'Civil society, NGOs, and Egypt's 2011 popular uprising', *South Atlantic Quarterly* 113 (2): 396–406.

Berhanu Nega (2010) 'Ethiopia is headed for chaos', *Current History* 109 (727): 186–92.

Bibangambah, J. (2001) *Africa's Quest for Economic Development: Uganda's Experience*, Kampala: Fountain Publishers.

Biryaberema, E. (2011) 'Uganda bans SMS texting of key words during poll', *Reuters*, 17 February.

Bond, P. and S. Mottiar (2013) 'Movements, protests and a massacre in South Africa', *Journal of Contemporary African Studies* 31 (2): 283–302.

Boudreau, V. (1996) 'Northern theory, southern protest: opportunity structure analysis in cross-national perspective', *Mobilization: An International Journal* 1 (2): 175–89.

Braga, R. (2013) 'The June days in Brazil', *Global Dialogue* 3 (5): 12–13.

Branch, A. (2011) *Displacing Human Rights: War and Intervention in Northern Uganda*, New York: Oxford University Press.

Bratton, M. and N. van de Walle (1997) *Democratic Experiments in Africa: Regime Transitions in Comparative Perspective*, Cambridge: Cambridge University Press.

Brigaldino, G. (2011) 'Elections in the imperial periphery: Ethiopia hijacked', *Review of African Political Economy* 38 (128): 327–34.

Brisset-Foucault, F. (2014) 'What do people do when they riot? Patterns of past and present street politics in Uganda', unpublished paper presented at ASA 2014 Annual Meeting. Abstract available at http://ssrn.com/abstract=2414765

Broussard, N. and Tsegay Gebrekidan Tekleselassie (2012) *Youth Unemployment: Ethiopia Country Study*, Working Paper 12/0592, London: International Growth Centre.

Brownell, J. (2012) '"Bloody coxcombs, but no bodies": the policy and practice of crowd control in post-war British Africa, 1948–1959', *Journal of Colonialism and Colonial History* 13 (2).

Burton, A. (2005) *African Underclass: Urbanization, Crime*

and Colonial Order in Dar es Salaam, Athens, OH: Ohio University Press.

Busari, S. (2012) 'What is behind Nigeria fuel protests?', *CNN*, 13 January. Available at http://edition.cnn.com/2012/01/06/world/africa/nigeria-fuel-protest-explained/?hpt=wo_t4

Bush, R. (2010) 'Food riots: poverty, power and protest', *Journal of Agarian Change*, 10 (1): 119–29.

Business Day (2011) 'Christine Lagarde's visit to Nigeria', *Business Day* online, 22 December. Available at www.businessdayonline.com/NG/index.php/analysis/editorial/31127-christine-lagardes-visit-to-nigeria

Cabral, A. (1969) *Revolution in Guinea: Selected Texts by Amilcar Cabral,* translated and edited by Richard Handyside, New York: Monthly Review Press.

— (1979) *Unity and Struggle: Speeches and Writings*, New York: Monthly Review Press.

Centre for Contemporary Art (2012) 'Press release on Occupy Nigeria exhibit,' Centre for Contemporary Art, Lagos, Nigeria. Available at www.undo.net/it/mostra/133642

Chatterjee, P. (2011) *The Politics of the Governed: Reflections on Popular Politics in Most of the World*, New York: Columbia University Press.

Chehonadskih, M. (2014) 'The class composition of Russia's anti-Putin movement', *South Atlantic Quarterly* 113 (1): 196–209.

Chikhi, A. (1995) 'The working class, the social nexus and democracy in Algeria', in M. Mamdani and E. Wamba-dia-Wamba (eds), *African Studies in Social Movements and Democracy*, Dakar: CODESRIA.

Clapham, C. (1990) *Transformation and Continuity in Revolutionary Ethiopia*, Cambridge: Cambridge University Press.

— (2005) 'Comments on the Ethiopian crisis', *MediaEthiopia*, 7 November. Available at www.mediaethiopia.com/Election2005/Christopher Clapham_Commentson EthiopianCrisis.htm

Clark, J. and D. Gardinier (1997) *Political Reform in Francophone Africa*, Boulder, CO: Westview Press.

Cohen, J. and A. Arato (1992) *Civil Society and Political Theory*, Cambridge, MA: MIT Press.

Cohen, R. and D. Michael (1973) 'The revolutionary potential of the African Lumpenproletariat: a skeptical view', *Bulletin of the Institute of Development Studies* 5 (2/3): 31–42.

Cole, J. (2014) 'What the Arab youth movements have wrought: don't count them out yet', *Informed Comment*, 30 June. Available at www.juancole.com/2014/06/youth-movements-wrought.html

Comaroff, J. L. and J. Comaroff (1999) *Civil Society and the Political Imagination in Africa*,

Chicago, IL: University of Chicago Press.

Cooper, F. (1983) 'Introduction: urban space, industrial time and wage labour in Africa', in F. Cooper (ed.), *Struggle for the City: Migrant Labour, Capital, and the State in Urban Africa*, Beverly Hills, CA: Sage.

— (1996) *Decolonization and African Society*, Cambridge: Cambridge University Press.

— (2002) *Africa since 1940: The Past of the Present*, Cambridge: Cambridge University Press.

Coquery-Vidrovitch, C. (2005) *The History of African Cities South of the Sahara from the Origins to Colonization*. Princeton, NJ: Markus Weiner.

Dabashi, H. (2012) *The Arab Spring: The End of Post-colonialism*, London: Zed Books.

Daily Monitor (Kampala) (2011a) 'Besigye: I can't rule out war', 28 February.

— (2011b) 'Besigye shot, 45 injured', 15 April.

— (2011c) 'City traders demand tax cuts', 22 April.

— (2011d) 'Commandos ready to deal with violence during polls', 8 February.

— (2011e) 'Generosity or patronage?', 7 January.

— (2011f) 'I can win with 60% – Besigye', 1 February.

— (2011g) '"I will devour protesters like samosa," says Gen Museveni', 26 February.

— (2011h) 'Inflation driving markets to new highs', 2 April.

— (2011i) 'Is Uganda returning to the days of Amin', 29 April.

— (2011j) 'Lawyers petition Chief Justice over judicial abuse', 5 May.

— (2011k) 'Man dies in city protests', 19 April.

— (2011l) '"Museveni will rig," opposition tell US', 6 February.

— (2011m) 'Opposition, chiefs call for protests', 25 February.

— (2011n) 'Opposition dismiss US and UK endorsement of Museveni win', 24 February.

— (2011o) 'Opposition insist on a walk demo', 11 April.

— (2011p) 'Our interests are above partisanship', 13 May.

— (2011q) 'Police arm heavily ahead of elections', 17 January.

— (2011r) '"Protestors will be jailed" – Museveni', 17 February.

— (2011s) 'Tears as police soak Besigye in teargas', 29 April.

— (2011t) 'Ugandans should expect to dig deeper into their pockets for food purchase', 8 February.

— (2011u) 'Women demonstrate as opposition walk to work', 10 May.

— (2013) 'Demo looms over roads', 11 January.

Daily Post (Lagos) (2012) 'Balarabe, others continue protest in Kaduna, Yaba', 17 January.

Danquah, F. K. (1994) 'Rural discontent and decolonization in Ghana, 1945–1951', *Agricultural History* 68 (1): 1–19.

Davis, A. (1990) *Women, Culture and Politics*, New York: Vintage Books.

Davis, M. (2006) *Planet of Slums*, New York: Vintage Books.

De Villers, G. and J. O. Tshonda (2004) 'When Kinois take to the streets', in T. Trefon (ed.), *Reinventing Order in the Congo*, London: Zed Books.

de Waal, A. (2012) 'The theory and practice of Meles Zenawi', *African Affairs* 112 (446): 1–8.

— (2013) 'Making sense of the protests in Khartoum', *African Futures*, 11 October. Available at http://forums.ssrc.org/african-futures/2013/10/11/making-sense-of-the-protests-in-khartoum/

de Waal, A. and R. Ibreck (2013) 'Hybrid social movements in Africa', *Journal of Contemporary African Studies* 31 (2): 303–24.

Demessie, F. (2007) 'Imperial legacies and postcolonial predicaments: an introduction', in F. Demessie (ed.), *Postcolonial African Cities: Imperial Legacies and Postcolonial Predicaments*, New York: Routledge.

Di Nunzio, M. (2012) '"We are good at surviving": street hustling in Addis Ababa's inner city', *Urban Forum* 23 (4): 433–47.

Dionne, K., J. Kadzandira and A. Robinson (2013) 'Risk of political violence and protest participation: evidence from contemporary Malawi', unpublished manuscript.

Diouf, M. (1996) 'Urban youth and Senegalese politics: Dakar 1988–1994', *Public Culture* 8 (2): 225–49.

Dulani, B., R. Mattes, and C. Logan (2013) 'After a decade of growth in Africa, little change in poverty at the grassroots', *Afrobarometer Policy Brief*, No. 1, October.

Dwyer, P. and L. Zeilig (2012) *African Struggles Today: Social Movements since Independence*, Chicago, IL: Haymarket Books.

Ekeh, P. (1975) 'Colonization and the two publics in Africa: a theoretical statement', *Comparative Studies in Society and History* 17 (1): 91–112.

Eken, B. (2014) 'The politics of Gezi Park resistance: against memory and identity', *South Atlantic Quarterly* 113 (2): 427–36.

El-Affendi, A. (2012) 'Revolutionary anatomy: the lessons of the Sudanese revolutions of October 1964 and April 1985', *Contemporary Arab Affairs* 5 (2): 292–06.

El Sanosi, M. (2012) 'A non-violent 24 year old gets Sudanese intelligence mobilising', *openDemocracy*, 20 November. Available at www.opendemocracy.net/maha-elsanosi/non-violent-24-year-old-gets-sudanese-intelligence-mobilising

El-Tigani, M. (2003) 'October 21, 1964? Ways to Return', *Sudan Tribune* (Paris) webpage, 21 October. Available at www.sudantribune.com/spip.php?article646

Elkins, C. (2005) *Imperial Reckoning: The Untold Story of Britain's Gulag in Kenya*, New York: Henry Holt and Company.

Ellis, S. and I. Van Kessel (2009) *Movers and Shakers: Social Movements in Africa*, Leiden: Brill.

Englund, H. (2006) *Prisoners of Freedom: Human Rights and the African Poor*, Berkeley and Los Angeles, CA: University of California Press.

— (2011) *Human Rights and African Airwaves: Mediating Equality on the Chichewa Radio*, Bloomington, IN: Indiana University Press.

Eskinder Nega (2011) 'Libya's Gadhafi and Ethiopia's EPRDF', 25 February. Available at www.abugidainfo.com/index.php/17384

Fanon, F. (1963) *The Wretched of the Earth*, translated by C. Farrington, New York: Grove Press.

Ferguson, J. (2006) *Global Shadows: Africa in the Neoliberal World Order*, Durham, NC: Duke University Press.

Fick, M. (2010) '"Girifna": student activists in Khartoum have had enough', *Enough Project*, 6 April. Available at www.enough project.org/publications/ girifna-student-activists-khartoum-have-had-enough

Ford, J. (2012) 'Democracy and change: what are the prospects for an "African Spring"?', *African Futures*, 14 July. Available at http://forums.ssrc.org/ african-futures/2012/07/14/ democracy-change-prospects-african-spring

Fraser, N. (2013) 'A triple movement? Parsing the politics of crisis after Polanyi', *New Left Review* (81): 119–32.

Freund, B. (2007) *The African City: A History*, Cambridge: Cambridge University Press.

Fukuyama, F. (2013) 'The middle-class revolution', *Wall Street Journal*, 28 June.

Gabay, C. (2012) 'Who's heard of the "African Spring"?', *openDemocracy*, 25 July. Available at www.opendemocracy.net/ clive-gabay/who's-heard-of-'african-spring'

Gallo, C. J. (2012) 'Why Sudanese are protesting in the streets', *UN Dispatch*, 23 June. Available at www.undispatch.com/why-sudanese-are-protesting-in-the-streets

Gelvin, J. (2012) *The Arab Uprisings: What Everyone Needs to Know*, New York: Oxford University Press.

Gervais, M. (1997) 'Niger: regime change, economic crisis, and perpetuation of privilege', in J. Clark and D. Gardinier (eds), *Political Reform in Francophone Africa*, Boulder, CO: Westview Press.

Gingyera-Pinycwa, A. G. G. (1989) 'Is there a "northern question"?' in K. Rupesinghe (ed.), *Conflict Resolution in Uganda*, London: James Currey.

Golooba-Mutebi, F. (2011) 'Settling the Buganda question: a peek into the future', *Transition* (106): 10–25.

Graeber, D. (2011) 'Occupy Wall Street's anarchist roots', *Al Jazeera*, 30 November. Available at www.aljazeera. com/indepth/ opinion/2011/11/20111128728359 04508.html

Graham, S. (2011) *Cities under Siege: The New Military Urbanism*, New York: Verso.

Gunn, R. and A. Wilding (2014) 'Recognition contradicted', *South Atlantic Quarterly* 113 (2): 339–52.

Gurtong (2005) 'Rebel leader returns to Khartoum after 22 years', 9 July. Available at www. gurtong.net/ECM/Editorial/ tabid/124/ctl/Article View/ mid/519/articleId/1819/Rebel-Hamid

Gyimah-Boadi, E. (1996) 'Civil society in Africa', *Journal of Democracy* 7 (2): 118–32.

Hagmann, T. (2006) 'Ethiopian political culture strikes back: a rejoinder to J. Abbink', *African Affairs* 105 (421): 605–12.

— (2012) 'Supporting stability, abetting repression', *New York Times*, 11 July.

Hale, S. and G. Kadoda (2013) 'The changing nature of political activism in Sudan: women and youth "activists" as catalysts in civil society', in E. Grawert (ed.), *Forging Two Nations: Insights on Sudan and South Sudan,* Addis Ababa: OSSREA.

Hamid, M. B. (2009) 'Raising the phoenix: the rise and decline of student political activism in the Sudan', unpublished paper presented at the National Conference on Fostering Political Participation of University Students and Youth in Development, Khartoum, 12–13 December.

Hamilton, R. (2010) 'Activist group Girifna aims to educate voters in Sudan', *Washington Post*, 14 August.

Harbeson, J. W. (1994) 'Civil society and political renaissance in Africa', in J. W. Harbeson, D. Rothchild and N. Chazan (eds), *Civil Society and the State in Africa*, Boulder, CO: Lynne Rienner.

Hardt, M. and A. Negri (2012) *Declaration*. Available at https://antonio negriinenglish.files.wordpress. com/2012/05/93152857-hardt-negri-declaration-2012.pdf

Harrison, G. (2002) *Issues in the Contemporary Politics of Sub-Saharan Africa: The Dynamics of Struggle and Resistance*, New York: Palgrave Macmillan.

Harsch, E. (2012) 'An African spring in the making: protest and voice across a continent', *Whitehead Journal of Diplomacy and International Relations* 13 (1): 45–61.

Harvey, D. (2012) *Rebel Cities: From the Right to the City to the Urban Revolution*, London: Verso.

Hasan, Y. F. (1967) 'The Sudanese Revolution of October 1964', *Journal of Modern African Studies* 5 (4): 491–509.

Holt-Giménez, E. and R. Patel (2009) *Food Rebellions: Crisis and the Hunger for Justice*, Oakland, CA: Food First Books.

Honwana, A. (2013) *Youth and*

Revolution in Tunisia, London: Zed Books.

Honwana, A. and F. De Boeck (eds) (2005) *Makers and Breakers: Children and Youth in Postcolonial Africa*, Oxford: James Currey.

HRW (Human Rights Watch) (2005) 'Ethiopia: crackdown spreads beyond capital', 16 June. Available at www.hrw.org/news/2005/06/14/ethiopia-crackdown-spreads-beyond-capital

— (2010) *Development without Freedom: How Aid Underwrites Repression in Ethiopia,* New York: Human Rights Watch, October.

— (2011) 'Uganda: launch independent inquiry into killings', 8 May. Available at www.hrw.org/news/2011/05/08/uganda-launch-independent-inquiry-killings

— (2012) 'Uganda: 3 Years On, No Justice for Riot Victims', 10 September. Available at www.hrw.org/news/2012/09/10/uganda-3-years-no-justice-riot-victims

— (2013) 'Sudan: dozens killed during protests', 27 September. Available at www.hrw.org/news/2013/09/27/sudan-dozens-killed-during-protests

Hundle, A. K. (2013) 'The politics of (in)security: reconstructing African–Asian relations, citizenship and community in post-expulsion Uganda', unpublished PhD thesis, Ann Arbor, MI: University of Michigan.

Hutchful, E. (1995/6) 'The civil society debate in Africa', *International Journal* 51 (1): 54–77.

Ihonvbere, J. (1996) 'Are things falling apart? The military and the crisis of democratisation in Nigeria', *Journal of Modern African Studies* 34 (2): 193–225.

— (1997) 'Organized labor and the struggle for democracy in Nigeria', *African Studies Review* 40 (3): 77–110.

Ihonvbere J. and J. M. Mbaku (2003) 'Introduction', in J. Ihonvbere and J. M. Mbaku (eds), *Political Liberalization and Democratization in Africa: Lessons from Country Experiences*, Westport, CT: Greenwood.

International Network of Civil Liberties Organizations (2013) *Take Back the Streets: Repression and Criminalization of Protest around the World*, New York: ACLU, October.

IRIN (Integrated Regional Information Networks) (2011) 'Analysis: understanding Nigeria's Boko Haram radicals', *IRIN*, 18 July. Available at www.irinnews.org/report/93250/analysis-understanding-nigeria-s-boko-haram-radicals

— (2013) 'Sudan continues crackdown on opposition groups', *IRIN*, 15 January. Available at www.irinnews.org/printreport.aspx?reportid=97253

Isaacman, A. (1990) 'Peasants and rural social protest in Africa', *African Studies Review* 33 (2): 1–120.

Israel, A. M. (1992) 'Ex-servicemen

at the crossroads: protest and politics in post-war Ghana', *Journal of Modern African Studies* 30 (2): 359–68.

Izama, A. (2013) 'Crisis and change: what next for the opposition in Uganda?', *Daily Monitor* (Kampala), 12 June.

James, C. L. R. (1977) *Nkrumah and the Ghana Revolution*, Brooklyn, NY: Lawrence Hill and Company.

Juma, C. (2011) 'The African Summer', *Foreign Policy*, 28 July. Available at www.foreignpolicy.com/articles/2011/07/28/the_african_summer

Kaci, M. (2011) 'Boko Haram: of the sensible and the insensible', *Nigerians Talk*, 20 September. Available at http://nigerianstalk.org/2011/09/20/boko-haram-of-the-sensible-and-the-insensible

Kagwanja, P. M. (2005) 'Clash of generations? Youth identity, violence and the politics of transition in Kenya, 1997–2002', in J. Abbink and I. van Kessel (eds), *Vanguard or Vandals*, Leiden: Brill.

Kalinaki, D. (2009a) 'Riots give Museveni the biggest test of his career', *Daily Monitor* (Kampala), 11 September.

— (2009b) 'Uganda: Museveni wins battle but war still on', *Daily Monitor* (Kampala), 14 September.

— (2011a) 'What would Museveni of 1980 do after the 2011 polls?', *Daily Monitor* (Kampala), 24 February.

— (2011b) 'Do we need rocket scientists to give us jobs?', *Daily Monitor* (Kampala), 23 June.

— (2011c) 'With more tractors, we won't need teargas trucks', *Daily Monitor* (Kampala), 21 April.

Kalyegira, T. (2009) 'Uganda: surface calm disguises wild currents', *Daily Monitor* (Kampala), 14 September.

— (2011) 'Shall we have a quiet election?', *Daily Monitor* (Uganda), 10 January.

Killingray, D. (1983), 'Soldiers, ex-servicemen, and politics in the Gold Coast, 1939–50', *Journal of Modern African Studies* 21 (3): 523–34.

Konings, P. (2005) 'Anglophone university students and anglophone nationalist struggles in Cameroon', in J. Abbink and I. van Kessel (eds), *Vanguard or Vandals*, Leiden: Brill.

Kperogi, F. A. (2011a) 'Fuel subsidy removal: time to "Occupy" Nigeria!', *Notes from Atlanta*, 22 October. Available at www.farooqkperogi.com/2011/10/fuel-subsidy-removal-time-to-occupy.html

— (2011b) 'Biggest scandal in oil "subsidy removal" fraud', *Sahara Reporters*, 5 November. Available at http://saharareporters.com/article/biggest-scandal-oil-"subsidy-removal"-fraud-farooq-kperogi

Kurlantzick, J. (2014) 'Behind a pattern of global unrest, a middle class in revolt', *Bloomberg Business Week*,

20 February. Available at www.businessweek.com/ articles/2014-02-20/behind-a-pattern-of-global-unrest-a-middle-class-in-revolt

Kushkush, I. (2013) 'Sudan erupts in deadly protests and gas prices rise', *New York Times*, 26 September.

Kwaja, C. (2011) 'Nigeria's pernicious drivers of ethno-religious conflict', *Africa Security Brief* 14, Africa Center for Strategic Studies, Washington, DC, July.

LeBas, A. (2011) *From Protest to Parties: Party-Building and Democratization in Africa*, New York: Oxford University Press.

Lefort, R. (2007) 'Powers – *Mengist* – and peasants in rural Ethiopia: the May 2005 elections', *Journal of Modern African Studies* 45 (2): 253–73.

Lewis, D. (2002) 'Civil society in African contexts: reflections on the usefulness of a concept', *Development and Change* 33 (4): 569–86.

Lewis, P., P. Robinson and P. T. Rubin (1998) *Stabilizing Nigeria: Sanctions, Incentives, and Support for Civil Society*, New York: Council on Foreign Relations.

Lindell, I. (ed.) (2010) *Africa's Informal Workers: Collective Agency, Alliances and Transnational Organizing in Urban Africa*, London and Uppsala: Zed Books and The Nordic Africa Institute.

— (2011) 'Introduction to the special issue: organizing across the formal-informal worker constituencies', *Labour, Capital and Society* 44 (1): 3–16.

Lumumba-Kasongo, T. (ed.) (2005) *Liberal Democracy and Its Critics in Africa: Political Dysfunction and the Struggle for Social Progress*, Dakar: CODESRIA.

Lyons, T. (1996) 'Closing the transition: the May 1995 elections in Ethiopia', *Journal of Modern African Studies* 34 (1): 121–42.

— (2006) 'Ethiopia in 2005: the beginning of a transition?', *CSIS Africa Notes* 25, CSIS, Washington, DC.

Mains, D. (2012) *Hope is Cut: Youth, Unemployment, and the Future in Urban Ethiopia*, Philadelphia, PA: Temple University Press.

Mamdani, M. (1976) *Politics and Class Formation in Uganda*, Kampala: Fountain Publishers.

— (1987) 'Contradictory class perspectives on the question of democracy: the case of Uganda', in P. Anyang' Nyong'o (ed.), *Popular Struggles for Democracy in Africa*, London: Zed Books.

— (1995) 'Introduction', in M. Mamdani and E. Wamba-dia-Wamba (eds), *African Studies in Social Movements and Democracy*, Dakar: CODESRIA.

— (1996) *Citizen and Subject: Contemporary Africa and the Legacy of Late Colonialism*, Princeton, NJ: Princeton University Press.

— (2011) 'An African reflection on Tahrir Square', *Pambazuka News* (529), 12 May.

Mamdani, M. and E. Wamba-dia-

Wamba (eds) (1995) *African Studies in Social Movements and Democracy*, Dakar: CODESRIA.

Mampilly, Z. (2013) 'Accursed by man, not God: the fight for Tanzania's gas lands', *Warscapes*, 20 August. Available at www.warscapes.com/reportage/accursed-man-not-god-fight-tanzanias-gas-lands

Martelli, S. (2012) 'Sudan students at forefront of rising social unrest', *Agence France-Presse*, 23 June.

Massoud, M. F. (2013) *Law's Fragile State: Colonial, Authoritarian and Humanitarian Legacies in Sudan*, New York: Cambridge University Press.

Mbaku, J. M. (2003) 'Transition to democratic governance in Africa: learning from past failures', in J. Ihonvbere and J. M. Mbaku (eds), *Political Liberalization and Democratization in Africa: Lessons from Country Experiences*, Westport, CT: Greenwood.

Mbembe, A. (2001) *On the Postcolony*, Berkeley, CA: University of California Press.

Mbembe, A. and S. Nuttall (2008) 'Introduction: Afropolis', in S. Nuttall and A. Mbembe (eds), *Johannesburg: The Elusive Metropolis*, Durham, NC: Duke University Press.

— (2012) 'Revolts and resistance – a Pan-African perspective', web video, Haus der Kulturen der Welt, Berlin, 27 November. Available at www.youtube.com/watch?v=56w4Jt72Iis

McAdam, D., R. J. Sampson, S. Weffer and H. MacIndoe (2005) '"There will be fighting in the streets": the distorting lens of social movement theory', *Mobilization: An International Journal* 10 (1): 1–18.

Melakou Tegegn (2008) 'Power politics: Kinijit in the 2005 elections', *Journal of Developing Societies* 24 (2): 273–306.

Merera Gudina (2007) 'Party politics and elections in Ethiopia: 1991–2005', in Kassahun Berhanu, Tafesse Olika, Asnake Kefale, and Jalele Erega (eds), *Electoral Politics, Decentralized Governance and Constitutionalism in Ethiopia*, Addis Ababa: Addis Ababa University Press.

— (2011) 'Elections and democratization in Ethiopia, 1991–2010', *Journal of Eastern African Studies* 5 (4): 664–80.

Milne, J. (1999) *Kwame Nkrumah: A Biography*, Bedford: Panaf.

Miner, H. M. (ed.) (1967) *The City in Modern Africa*, New York: Frederick Praeger.

Mische, A. (2013) '"Come to the streets, but without parties": the challenges of the new Brazilian protests', *Mobilizing Ideas*, 4 September. Available at http://mobilizingideas.wordpress.com/2013/09/04/come-to-the-streets-but-without-parties-the-challenges-of-the-new-brazilian-protests

Mitullah, W. (2010) 'Informal workers in Kenya and transnational organizing: networking and leveraging resources', in I. Lindell (ed.), *Africa's Informal Workers*, London and Uppsala: Zed Books and the Nordic Africa Institute.

Mkandawire, T. (1998) 'Crisis management and the making of "choiceless democracies" in Africa', in R. Joseph (ed.), *The State, Conflict, and Democracy in Africa*, Boulder, CO: Lynne Rienner.

— (2002) 'The terrible toll of post-colonial "rebel movements" in Africa: towards an explanation of the violence against the peasantry', *Journal of Modern African Studies* 40 (2): 181–215.

Mkandawire, T. and A. Olukoshi (1995) *Between Liberalisation and Oppression: The Politics of Structural Adjustment in Africa*, Dakar: CODESRIA.

Mkandawire, T. and C. Soludo (1999) *Our Continent, Our Future: African Perspectives on Structural Adjustment*, Dakar: CODESRIA.

Monga, C. (1996) *The Anthropology of Anger: Civil Society and Democracy in Africa*, New York: Lynne Rienner.

Montlake, S. (2014) 'Property rights + middle class = democracy? Not in Thailand', *Christian Science Monitor*, 31 May.

Mueller, L. (2013) 'Democratic revolutionaries or pocketbook protesters? The roots of the 2009–2010 uprisings in Niger', *African Affairs* 112 (448): 398–420.

Mugaju, J. and J. Oloka-Onyango (eds) (2000) *No-Party Democ-racy in Uganda: Myths and Realities*, Kampala: Fountain Publishers.

Mwenda, A. (2007) 'Personalizing power in Uganda', *Journal of Democracy* 18 (3): 23–37.

— (2010) 'Uganda's politics of foreign aid and violent conflict: the political uses of the LRA rebellion', in T. Allen and K. Vlassenroot (eds), *The Lord's Resistance Army: Myth and Reality*, London: Zed Books.

Mwenda, A. and R. Tangri (2005) 'Patronage politics, donor reforms, and regime consolidation in Uganda', *African Affairs* 104 (416): 449–67.

Myers, G. (2011) *African Cities: Alternative Visions of Urban Theory and Practice*, London: Zed Books.

Nabudere, D. (2009) 'Ethnicity and conflict in Uganda', *Daily Monitor* (Kampala), 20 September.

Ndegwa, S. (1996) *The Two Faces of Civil Society: NGOs and Politics in Africa*, West Hartford, CT: Kumarian Press.

Neocosmos, M. (2011) 'Transition, human rights and violence: rethinking a liberal political relationship in the African neo-colony', *Interface: A Journal for and about Social Movements* 3 (2): 359–99.

New Sudan Vision (2009) '"Nigger" gangs controlled – Hamid', *New Sudan Vision*, 4 July. Available at www.newsudanvision. com/sudan/1768-nigger-gangs-controlled-hamid

New Vision (Kampala) (2009)

'Museveni addresses MPs on riots', 15 September.

Nkinyangi, J. (1991) 'Student protests in Sub-Saharan Africa', *Higher Education* 22 (2): 157–73.

Nkrumah, K. (1971) *Ghana: The Autobiography of Kwame Nkrumah*, New York: International Publishers.

— (1973) *Revolutionary Path*, New York: International Publishers.

Nugent, P. (2004) *Africa since Independence: A Comparative History*, New York: Palgrave Macmillan.

Nwajiaku, K. (1994) 'The national conferences in Benin and Togo revisited', *Journal of Modern African Studies* 32 (3): 429–47.

Nzongola-Ntalaja, G. (1984) 'Amílcar Cabral and the theory of the national liberation struggle', *Latin American Perspectives* 11 (2): 43–54.

— (2002) *The Congo from Leopold to Kabila: A People's History*, London: Zed Books.

Odebode, N., J. Alechenu and O. Adetayo (2012) 'Lagos fuel subsidy protests sponsored – Jonathan', *Punch* (Lagos), 19 September.

Ogunseye, T. (2012) 'In Nigeria, nobody wants to die for nothing – Akinnaso', *Punch* (Lagos), 29 January.

Oladesu, E. (2012) 'Soyinka: don't reduce anti-fuel subsidy removal protests to ethnicity', *Nation* (Lagos), 24 January.

Onimode, B. (1992) *A Future for Africa: Beyond the Politics of Adjustment*, London: Earthscan.

Orgeret, K. S. (2008) 'When will the daybreak come? Popular music and political processes in Ethiopia', *Nordicom Review* 29 (2): 231–44.

Ortiz, I., S. Burke, M. Berrada and H. Cortés (2013) *World Protests 2006–2013*, New York: Initiative for Policy Dialogue and Friedrich Ebert Stiftung.

Packer, G. (2006) 'The moderate martyr: a radically peaceful vision of Islam', *The New Yorker*, 11 September.

Peiffer, C. and P. Englebert (2012) 'Extraversion, vulnerability to donors, and political liberalization in Africa', *African Affairs* 111 (444): 355–78.

Penzin, A. (2014) 'Tumult in the land of managed democracy', *South Atlantic Quarterly* 113 (1): 162–8.

Philipps, J. (2013) *Ambivalent Rage: Youth Gangs and Political Protests in Conakry, Guinea*, Paris: Éditions L'Harmattan.

Prashad, V. (2008) *The Darker Nations: A People's History of the Third World*, New York: The New Press.

— (2012) *Arab Spring, Libyan Winter*, Oakland, CA: AK Press.

Rathbone, R. (1999) *Nkrumah and the Chiefs: The Politics of Chieftaincy in Ghana, 1951–1960*, Athens: Ohio University Press.

Reno, W. (2002) 'Uganda's politics of war and debt relief', *Review of International Political Economy* 9 (3): 415–35.

Renton, D., D. Seddon and

L. Zeilig (2007) *The Congo: Plunder and Resistance*, London: Zed Books.

Reyes, A. (2012) 'Revolutions in the revolutions: a post-counterhegemonic moment for Latin America?', *South Atlantic Quarterly* 111 (1): 1–27.

Riley, S. P. and T. W. Parfitt (1994) 'Economic adjustment and democratization in Africa', in Walton, J. and D. Seddon (eds), *Free Markets and Food Riots: The Politics of Global Adjustment*, Oxford: Blackwell.

Robinson, P. (1994) 'The national conference phenomenon in francophone Africa', *Comparative Studies in Society and History* 36 (3): 575–610.

Roy, Ananya (2011) 'Slumdog cities: rethinking subaltern urbanism', *International Journal of Urban and Regional Research* 35 (2): 223–38.

Roy, Arundhati (2011) 'We are all occupiers', *The Guardian*, 17 November.

Saad-Filho, A. and L. Morais (2013) 'Mass protests: Brazilian spring or Brazilian malaise?', *Socialist Register 2014*, New York: Monthly Review Press.

SACSIS (The South African Civil Society Information Service) (2014) '"Protest nation": What's driving the demonstrations on the streets of South Africa?', interview with T. Ngwane, SACSIS, Johannesburg. Available at http://sacsis.org.za/site/article/1930

Sahara Reporters (2012) 'Interview: Wole Soyinka – the next phase of Boko Haram terrorism,' *Sahara Reporters*, 6 February. Available at http://sahara-reporters.com/interview/interview-wole-soyinka-next-phase-boko-haram-terrorism-thenews

Samatar, A. I. (2005) 'The Ethiopian election of 2005: a bombshell and turning point?', *Review of African Political Economy* 32 (104/105): 466–73.

Sampson, O. (2012) 'Occupy Nigeria victory: President to cut fuel prices', *Christian Science Monitor*, 16 January.

Schmitt, E. (2013) 'US Army hones antiterror strategy for Africa, in Kansas', *New York Times*, 18 October.

Schock, K. (2003) 'Nonviolent action and its misconceptions: insights for social scientists', *Political Science and Politics* 36 (4): 705–12.

Scott, J. C. (1985) *Weapons of the Weak: Everyday Forms of Peasant Resistance*, New Haven, CT: Yale University Press.

Sharp, G. (2005) *Waging Nonviolent Struggle: 20th Century Practice and 21st Century Potential*, Boston, MA: Porter Sargent Pub.

Shettima, K. A. (1993) 'Structural adjustment and the student movement in Nigeria', *Review of African Political Economy* 20 (56): 83–91.

Shivji, I. (2007) *Silences in NGO Discourse: The Role and Future of NGOs in Africa*, Oxford: Fahamu.

Shonekan, S. (2009) 'Fela's foundation: examining the revolutionary songs of Funmilayo Ransom-Kuti and the Abeokuta market women's movement in 1940s western Nigeria', *Black Music Research Journal* 2 (1): 127–44.

Simone, A. (2004) *For the City Yet to Come: Changing African Life in Four Cities*, Durham, NC: Duke University Press.

— (2005) 'Urban processes and change', in A. Simone and A. Abouhani (eds), *Urban Africa: Changing Contours of Survival in the City*, Dakar: CODESRIA.

— (2010) *City Life from Jakarta to Dakar: Movements at the Crossroads*, London: Routledge.

Singer, A. (2014) 'Rebellion in Brazil', *New Left Review* (85): 19–37.

Sitrin, M. (2014) 'Goals without demands: the new movements for real democracy', *South Atlantic Quarterly* 113 (2): 245–58.

Sjogren, A. (2013) *Between Militarism and Technocratic Governance*, Kampala: Fountain Publishers.

Southall, A. (1967) 'Kampala-Mengo', in H. E. Miner (ed.), *The City in Modern Africa*, New York: Frederick Praeger.

Sowore, O. (2013) 'Nigerians still waiting for their "African Spring"', CNN, 12 January. Available at www.cnn.com/2013/01/12/world/africa/nigeria-protests-african-spring

Stiglitz, J., J. L. Yifu and E. Patel (eds) (2013) *The Industrial Policy Revolution II: Africa in the Twenty-first Century*, New York: Palgrave.

Stren, R. E. (1989) 'The administration of urban services', in R. E. Stren and R. R. White (eds), *African Cities in Crisis: Managing Rapid Urban Growth*, Boulder, CO: Westview Press.

Sudan Tribune (Paris) (2012) 'Sudan clamps down on the "Kandaka" protest of Friday', 13 July.

Sutherland, B. and M. Meyer (2000) *Guns and Gandhi in Africa: Pan African Insights on Nonviolence, Armed Struggle and Liberation in Africa*, Trenton, NJ: Africa World Press.

Tabaire, B. (2013) 'Inside source: one man's naked act points to the roaring fire next time', *Daily Monitor* (Kampala), 7 May.

Tacca, A. (2011a) 'Museveni's biggest dilemma: to go or not to go', *Daily Monitor* (Kampala), 30 January.

— (2011b) 'Uganda: the mayor, the NRM and the stealing culture', *Daily Monitor* (Kampala), 20 March.

Tadros, S. (2012) 'How Sudan's Bashir survived the Arab Spring', *Al Jazeera*, 26 September. Available at http://www.aljazeera.com/indepth/features/2012/09/201292116 4748873959.html.

Tafesse Olika and Aklilu Abraham (2007) 'Legislation, institutions and the post-1991 elections in Ethiopia', in Kassahun Berhanu, Tafesse Olika, Asnake

Kefale, and Jalele Erega (eds), *Electoral Politics, Decentralized Governance and Constitutionalism in Ethiopia*, Addis Ababa: Addis Ababa University Press.

Therborn, G. (2014) 'New masses? Social bases of resistance', *New Left Review* (85): 7–16.

Tilly, C. and S. Tarrow (2006) *Contentious Politics*, New York: Oxford University Press.

Timberg, C. (2006) 'Bid to allow Nigerian a third term hits snag', *Washington Post*, 13 May.

Toggia, P. (2008) 'The state of emergency: police and carceral regimes in modern Ethiopia', *Journal of Developing Societies* 24 (107): 107–24.

Trefon, T. (2004) 'Introduction: reinventing order', in T. Trefon (ed.), *Reinventing Order in the Congo*, London: Zed Books.

Tripp, A. M. (2004) 'The changing face of authoritarianism in Africa: the case of Uganda', *Africa Today* 50 (3): 3–26.

Tronvoll, K. (2010) 'The Ethiopian 2010 federal and regional elections: re-establishing the one-party state', *African Affairs* 110 (438): 121–36.

Turner, T. (1997) 'Flying high above the toads: Mobutu and stalemated democracy', in J. F. Clark and D. E. Gardinier (eds), *Political Reform in Francophone Africa*, Boulder, CO: Westview.

UN (United Nations) (2014) *The Millennium Development Goals Report 2014*, New York: UN.

UN Habitat (2010) *The State of African Cities 2010: Governance, Inequality and Urban Land Markets*, Nairobi: UN Habitat.

— (2014) *The State of African Cities 2014: Reimagining Sustainable Urban Transitions*, Nairobi: UN Habitat.

Vaughan, S. (2011) 'Revolutionary democratic state-building: party, state and people in the EPRDF's Ethiopia', *Journal of Eastern African Studies* 5 (4): 619–40.

Wallerstein, I. (1979) 'Fanon and the revolutionary class', in *The Capitalist World-System*, New York: Cambridge University Press.

Waterman, P. (1975) 'The "labour aristocracy" in Africa: introduction to a debate', *Development and Change* 6 (3): 57–73.

Wiredu, K. (1986) 'The question of violence in contemporary African political thought', *Praxis International* 6 (3): 373–81.

Wiseman, J. (1986) 'Urban riots in West Africa, 1977–85', *Journal of Modern African Studies* 24 (3): 509–18.

— (1996) *The New Struggle for Democracy in Africa*, Aldershot: Avebury.

World Bank (1981) *Accelerated Development in Sub-Saharan Africa*, Washington, DC: World Bank.

— (1983) *World Development Report 1983*, Washington, DC: World Bank.

— (2013) *Nigeria Economic Report (1)*, Washington, DC: World Bank.

Worsely, P. (1972) 'Fanon and the "lumpenproletariat"', in R. Miliband and J. Savile (eds), *Socialist Register*, London: Merlin Press.

Yörük, E. (2014) 'The long summer of Turkey: the Gezi uprising and its historical roots', *South Atlantic Quarterly* 113 (2): 419–26.

Young, C. (2012) *The Postcolonial State in Africa: Fifty Years of Independence, 1960–2010*, Madison: University of Wisconsin Press.

Young, R. J. C. (2005) 'Fanon and the turn to armed struggle in Africa', *Wasafiri* 20 (44): 33–41.

Youngs, R. (2013) 'Worldwide protests portend the shaking of authority', *Canberra Times*, 27 December.

Zeilig, L. (2012) *Revolt and Protest: Student Politics and Activism in Sub-Saharan Africa,* London: I. B. Tauris.

Žižek, S. (2012) *The Year of Dreaming Dangerously*, London: Verso.

— (2013) 'Trouble in paradise', *London Review of Books* 35 (14): 11–12.

Index

Index